I0800964

IMAGES
of America

WASHINGTON, D.C.'S DEANWOOD

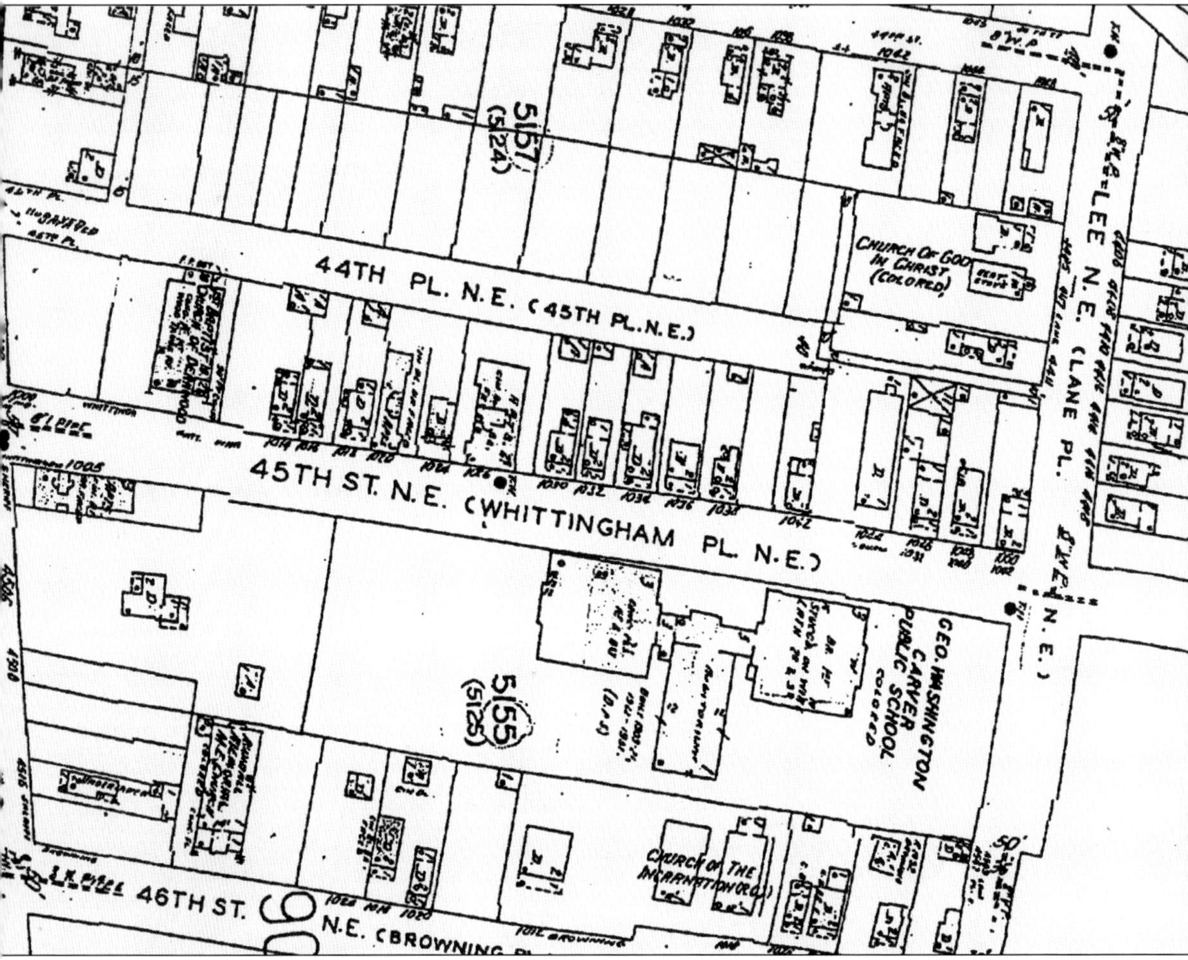

DEANWOOD MAP, C. 1920. This Sanborn insurance map of the 1920s displays the social center of Deanwood formed by the George Washington Carver Public School (formerly the Deanwood School) and the circle of churches of varying denominations: the Randall Memorial United Methodist Church, the First Baptist Church of Deanwood, the Church of God in Christ, and the Church of the Incarnation (Catholic). (D.C. Public Library, Washingtoniana Division.)

ON THE COVER: Civic participation is a hallmark of Deanwood life. Residents don't hesitate to support causes they believe in or protest those they don't. The National Foundation for Infantile Paralysis, established in 1938, fought the disease through the March of Dimes campaign. Around 1943, a group of Deanwood students and their teacher gather in downtown D.C. to give their dimes and dollars toward the effort. (Bettie Staley Littlejohn.)

IMAGES
of America

WASHINGTON, D.C.'S DEANWOOD

The Deanwood History Committee

ARCADIA
PUBLISHING

Copyright © 2008 by The Deanwood History Committee
ISBN 978-0-7385-5350-4

Published by Arcadia Publishing
Charleston, South Carolina

Printed in the United States of America

Library of Congress Catalog Card Number: 2007937799

For all general information contact Arcadia Publishing at:
Telephone 843-853-2070
Fax 843-853-0044
E-mail sales@arcadiapublishing.com
For customer service and orders:
Toll-Free 1-888-313-2665

Visit us on the Internet at www.arcadiapublishing.com

This book is dedicated to Deanwood residents past and present who contributed their time, stories, pictures, criticisms, corrections, but mostly love, to this work. We hope we did you proud.

Contents

ACKNOWLEDGMENTS

The Deanwood History Committee—Elaine King Bowman, Kia Chatmon, Deidre R. Gantt, Alverna M. Miller, and Barbara J. Moore—first convened in 2004 with the purpose of producing an architectural survey leading to historic designation of the Deanwood neighborhood. The committee decided to create a 16-page brochure on the community's history to be used as the foundation of this survey. The community was so forthcoming with information for this brochure that it could not all be contained in a mere 16 pages, so the committee continued to meet and compiled the information into this book on a 90-year period of Deanwood's history.

We want to first thank God and then the dozens of Deanwood residents whose hard work and love of their community helped to make this book possible. We also want to offer special thanks to the following individuals and institutions for their donation of financial and human resources, research assistance, photographs, and meeting space, without which this project could not have been completed:

All churches and schools featured
Attendees of the Deanwood Storytelling Event of July 2006
Courtney Bailey
Rev. Sarah Britt and the First Baptist Church of Deanwood
Dennis Chestnut
Cultural Tourism D.C.
D.C. Office of Planning
D.C. Public Library, Washingtoniana Division
Sr. Michael Kathleen Deane
Deanwood Citizens Association
Deanwood Heritage Trail Committee
Helen Gordon Hasty
Rev. Everett Augustus Hewlett
Historical Society of Washington, D.C.
Patsy Fletcher, D.C. Historic Preservation Office
Marya Annette McQuirter, Ph.D.
IDEA Public Charter School
Principal Rita O. Johnson and the Nannie Helen Burroughs School
Joe Lapp
Philoma Logan
Donna Logan-Sanders
Marshall Heights Community Development Organization
National Trust for Historic Preservation
Ruth Ann Overbeck (deceased)
Laura Shumate
Earl Simpson (deceased)
Sons and Daughters of Deanwood
Charles Sumner School Museum and Archives
Stephen Syphax, National Capital Parks-East, National Park Service
Herbert Turner
Sam Waring
Evie Washington
Geraldine Washington
Howard Ways
Brett Weary
Aressa V. Williams
John Woodson
Woodson Senior High School

Finally, we wish to thank the D.C. Historic Preservation Office and the Humanities Council of Washington, D.C., for their support and funding of this project.

COURTESY LINE LEGEND

DCHPO—District of Columbia Historic Preservation Office
HSWDC—Historical Society of Washington, D.C.
JTWC, HSWDC—John T. Wymer Collection, HSWDC
SMKD—Sr. Michael Kathleen Deane
EKB—Elaine King Bowman
RP—Reggie Parker
WF—Wells family
NCPE, NPS—National Capital Parks-East, National Park Service
DCPL—D.C. Public Library
AM—Alverna Miller
NHBS—Nannie Helen Burroughs School
WD—Washingtoniana Division

INTRODUCTION

Deanwood is one of the oldest consistently African American communities in Washington, D.C., with residents who have called it home for generations. It is a stable neighborhood with a small-town feel located in Ward 7 of the District of Columbia, in the far northeast section of the city. It lies along the Watts Branch, the longest city park and creek in Washington, D.C., which is part of the stream system that feeds into the Anacostia River. It was upon this rich, fertile soil that the early farm families, who were white, first laid the foundation upon which Deanwood's history is built.

Originally this area along the river was populated by the Nacochtanke Indians, also known as the Anacostank, who developed a trading center specializing in beaver pelts. Local landowners, the Sheriffs among others, had vast collections of Native American artifacts from sites along the Anacostia River terraces and floodplain. In fact, this interest in native artifacts and culture led to the establishment of the Anthropological Society of Washington in the 1870s.

The following excerpt from the February 6, 1916, edition of the *Evening Star*'s weekly feature column, "The Rambler," provides a description of the landscape and location of the community:

> From the east angle of the District a wide valley leads west. It is the widest break in the great ridge east of the Anacostia River and within the District. A stream, Watts branch, courses down this valley, passes through the low, flat garden lands northeast of the Benning race track, noses through that marsh called Licking banks and mingles with the Eastern branch [*sic*]. Through this valley run the Chesapeake junction cars of the Washington Railway and Electric Company, the cars of the Washington, Baltimore and Annapolis electric railroad and a little used track of the Chesapeake Beach railroad connecting the Chesapeake junction terminus of that railroad with freight tracks of the Baltimore and Ohio and the Pennsylvania railroads at Deanwood.

The area was first part of the 1703 land grant to Ninian Beall, a white farmer and landowner. In the 1790s, William Benning, another white landowner, purchased 330 acres from Beall after he moved to the Federal City to help establish the Benning Bridge. After his death, his nephew, Anthony, purchased the land and sold it to Levi Sheriff in 1833. Sheriff eventually acquired a total of 524 acres of land on which he raised cattle, hogs, and a variety of crops, which he tended with the help of slave labor. By 1850, Sheriff held 19 enslaved persons. In 1838, another white farmer, James H. Fowler, purchased 83.25 acres between the District's eastern boundary and the Sheriff farm. After Sheriff died in 1853, his land was divided among his three daughters, Margaret E. Lowrie, Emmeline Sheriff, and Mary Dean. According to the same "Rambler" article:

> Soon after the division of the estate the town of Lincoln was laid out on the land of Mary Dean, south of Watts branch . . . on the lands of Margaret E. Lowrie and Mary Dean, north of Sheriff Road and extending north to Piney Run and Indian Springs Branch, the town of Deanwood has grown up . . . [and] on the lands apportioned to Emmeline Sheriff the town of Burrville and several other settlements have grown up.

Today, depending on whom you ask, Deanwood has two different boundaries—a triangular area bounded by Eastern Avenue, Kenilworth Avenue, and East Capitol Street, or a rectangular area bounded by the Baltimore and Ohio Railroad (Sheriff Road), Eastern Avenue, Division Avenue, and Nannie Helen Burroughs Avenue (formerly Deane Avenue). An article in the *Washington Post* in 1910 describes the area served by the Deanwood Civic Association as "the community bounded on the north by Division Avenue, on the west by Minnesota Avenue, on the east by Fiftieth Street Northeast, and on the south by the Chesapeake and Ohio Railroad Tracks."

While Deanwood's borders may not be easily agreed upon, all who are familiar with the community do agree that it is a humble, close-knit, and self-sufficient community with a history worth preserving. Many notable Washingtonians—both African American and not—visited the neighborhood or called Deanwood home. In 1909, Nannie Helen Burroughs established the National Training School for Women and Girls on Deane Avenue, one of Deanwood's main thoroughfares. Burroughs, a clubwoman, activist, and lecturer, was born in Virginia and educated in Washington, D.C. She founded the school on behalf of the National Baptist Convention (now known as the Progressive National Baptist Convention). Howard Dilworth (H. D.) Woodson, a renowned engineer and architect who designed many buildings in the District between the 1920s and the 1950s, not only made Deanwood his home but also helped to establish many of its civic institutions. Today the only D.C. public senior high school in Ward 7 is named for him. Alice Roosevelt, the eldest daughter of Pres. Theodore Roosevelt, was reported to have spent many hours at the Benning Race Track, located in the adjoining neighborhood of Kenilworth on the Anacostia River. The racetrack enjoyed a special relationship with Deanwood, as it employed a number of its residents, many of whom relocated from the South to work in the horse industry.

Deanwood was also home to lesser known craftsmen and businessmen who made quite an impact on the community. For example, two brothers from Deanwood, Jacob and Randolph Dodd, built numerous houses in the neighborhood between 1921 and 1930, and many still exist today. Suburban Gardens, the only permanent amusement park ever operated within Washington, D.C., city limits, opened in Deanwood in 1921.

Like many neighborhoods in Ward 7, Deanwood's infrastructure suffered from a lack of attention and investment of city resources for many years. However, community leaders and institutions have continued to work to improve neighborhood conditions. Today these efforts are paying off, as Deanwood is attracting the city's attention, and new investments are being made. The presence of a Metro station, its location between two major thoroughfares, and its detached homes and sprawling lots are bringing increased attention to the neighborhood. What was once a "sleeper" neighborhood that not many people knew about is now also attracting the attention of developers. The negative side of this is that some are entering the community and tearing down its historical architecture only to replace it with condominiums and modern homes that are out of scale with the neighborhood character.

Before the landscape is completely changed, members of the Deanwood History Committee wanted to do what they could to ensure that the rich history of the neighborhood is preserved. The point of this book is to share pieces of Deanwood's legacy through the stories and images of previous generations of residents who helped to create this community that others now find so desirable.

This is not an all-inclusive history of Deanwood. While members of the committee have made a concerted effort to reach out to residents past and present to collect their stories, pictures, and memories, we realize that there are many more stories to tell. It is our hope that this book not only informs but also inspires others in Deanwood and other communities—in Washington, D.C., and beyond—to explore, preserve, and share their personal and community histories.

One

Building Homes of Our Own

Deanwood began its gradual transition from a rural to a suburban neighborhood with the 1871 arrival of the Baltimore and Potomac (B&P) Railroad along its western boundary. The lands owned by the Sheriff and Deane families were subdivided in the late 1880s. However, development was sluggish, and the community remained rural and underdeveloped. The poor land sales provided an opportunity for black home ownership. By 1893, houses were scattered throughout the community, with black and white residents living as neighbors. This pattern of mixed residency continued in Deanwood until the 1930s, in spite of strict housing segregation in other parts of the city. By the 1920s, Deanwood was predominantly black.

Census records of the early 1900s show a number of the black residents of Deanwood were laborers and craftsmen. These men designed and built homes for themselves and their neighbors. Among the earliest entrepreneurs in the neighborhood were brothers Jacob and Leroy King, who built homes on Forty-fourth and Forty-fifth Streets; James Lacey, who constructed several buildings between 1897 and 1910; Clarence Turner Sr., a master plasterer; and Lewis Logan, who constructed buildings on Browning Place. Craftsmen Randolph Dodd and Jacob Dodd built almost 200 homes in Deanwood between 1921 and 1940. Similarly, residents Howard Dilworth Woodson and Lewis Giles Sr. left their mark on the community and the city. Woodson, an architectural engineer and civic leader, designed buildings on Forty-ninth Place and on Deane Avenue. The architect for hundreds of buildings in the District, Giles also designed the ticket office and dance pavilion for Suburban Gardens, in which Woodson was an investor. Giles and Woodson were responsible for designing a majority of the homes in the neighborhood from the 1920s to the 1940s.

The architectural landscape of Deanwood reflects popular small-town and suburban detached styles. Its early homes are mostly vernacular or folk, modest single-family and semi-detached frame dwellings built between 1895 and the 1920s. Later styles include folk Victorian, neoclassical, Colonial Revival, prairie, and Craftsman. These structures, designed and built both by lay and professionally licensed craftsmen, are a testament to the industriousness of Deanwood's residents.

Building Permits.

The following building permits were issued yesterday:

E. F. Davis, one brick dwelling, at No. 38 N street northwest, at a cost of $3,500; Leon Dessez, three brick stores, at corner of Seventh street and Florida avenue, at a cost of $8,800; J. W. Dean, three frame dwellings, at Deanwood, near Benning's, on Sheriff avenue, at a cost of $4,000; Dennis Byrne, one brick dwelling and store, at No. 12 C street northwest, at a cost of $700; F. R. Freas, one brick dwelling, at No. 11 Ninth street southeast, at a cost of $5,500; J. W. Reed, three brick dwellings, at Nos. 38 to 42 McCullough's alley northwest, at a cost of $1,800; A. Margat, one frame dwelling on Bunker Hill road, at a cost of $8,000; Rev. S. Miller, one frame church on Shepherd's road, at a cost of $8,000; Robert L. Waring, one brick dwelling, at No. 1019 P street northwest, at a cost of $4,500; James M. York & Son, five brick dwellings on Wylie street northeast, at a cost of $6,000; D. P. Morgan, to build a third story in brick and make general repairs on a private stable in alley on Rhode Island avenue, between Fourteenth and Fifteenth streets northwest, at a cost of $3,400.

BUILDING PERMIT, JULY 8, 1890. This public listing of building permits includes several taken by Julian W. Deane, of the original Sheriff landowning family. Deane built about 16 homes along Sheriff Road in the 1880s and 1890s, shortly after the estate was subdivided in 1875. (DCPL, WD.)

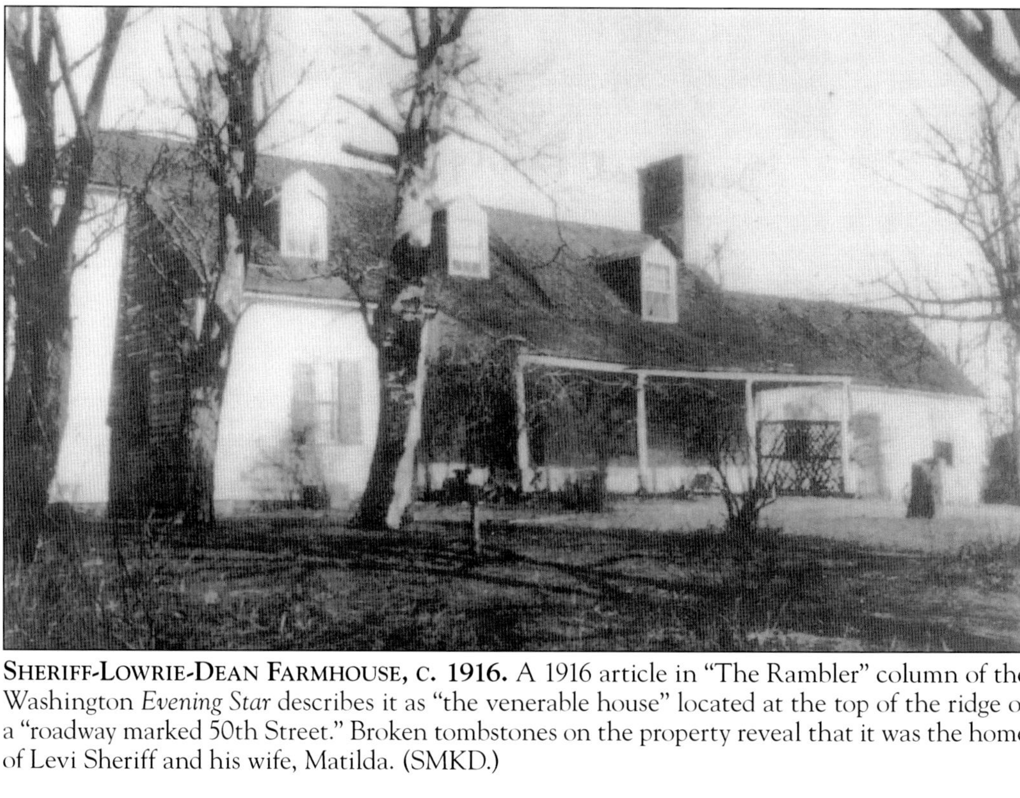

SHERIFF-LOWRIE-DEAN FARMHOUSE, C. 1916. A 1916 article in "The Rambler" column of the Washington *Evening Star* describes it as "the venerable house" located at the top of the ridge of a "roadway marked 50th Street." Broken tombstones on the property reveal that it was the home of Levi Sheriff and his wife, Matilda. (SMKD.)

TOM BOWLES, C. 1916. "The Rambler" came across Tom Bowles as he explored the Sheriff-Lowrie-Dean family house. Bowles acted as the caretaker of the estate after the last family members moved out. Here he stands among the thick overgrowth and fragments of scattered tombstones in the families' cemetery. (HSWDC.)

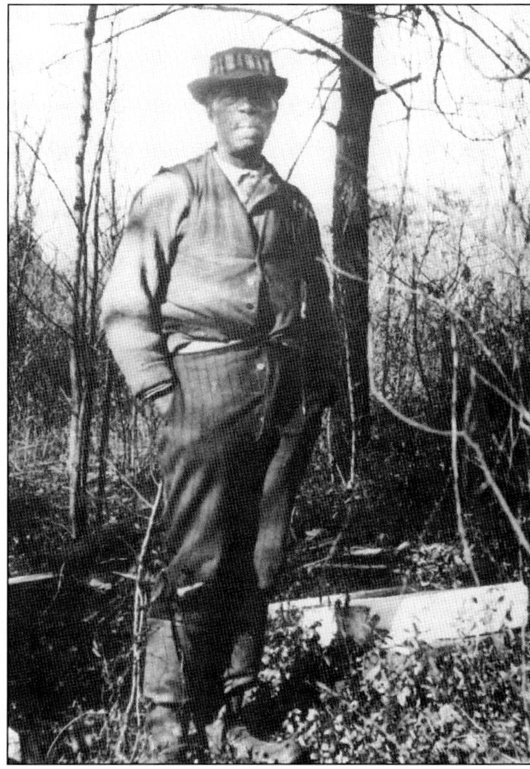

BENNING ROAD BRIDGE, 1920S. The Benning Road Bridge connected Deanwood and other Washington County communities east of the Anacostia River, and Maryland, to Washington City. Entrepreneur James Benning built the bridge as a toll road. It quickly became a landmark for Deanwood residents as they were leaving or returning home. (*Star* Collection, DCPL; @*Washington Post*.)

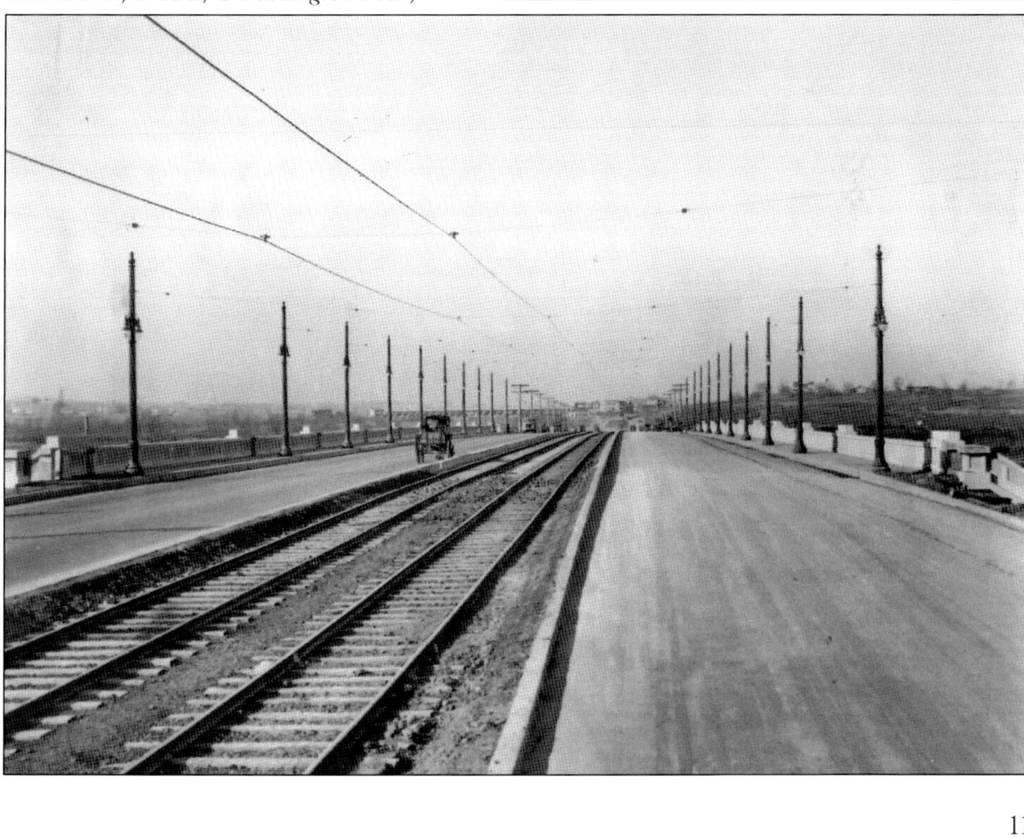

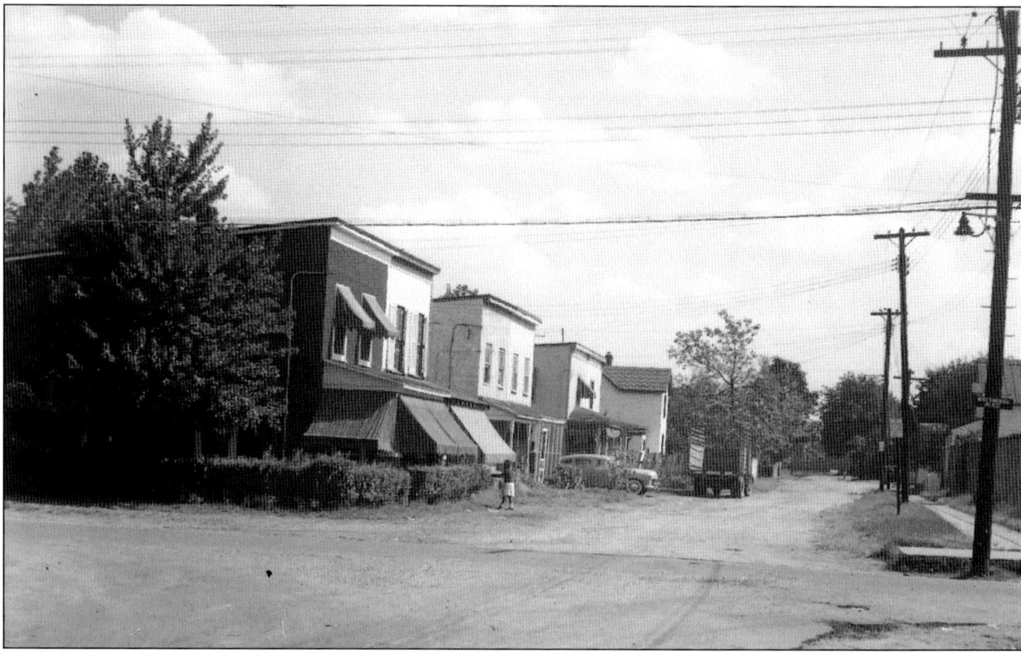

LANE PLACE, SEPTEMBER 25, 1948. Formerly known as Lane Place, Lee Street in 1948 shows the distinctly semi-rural streetscape of Deanwood. The houses constructed in the modified row house style, so characteristic of this and other suburban D.C. neighborhoods east of the Anacostia River, reflect the middle-class aspirations of Deanwood residents. (JTWC, HSWDC.)

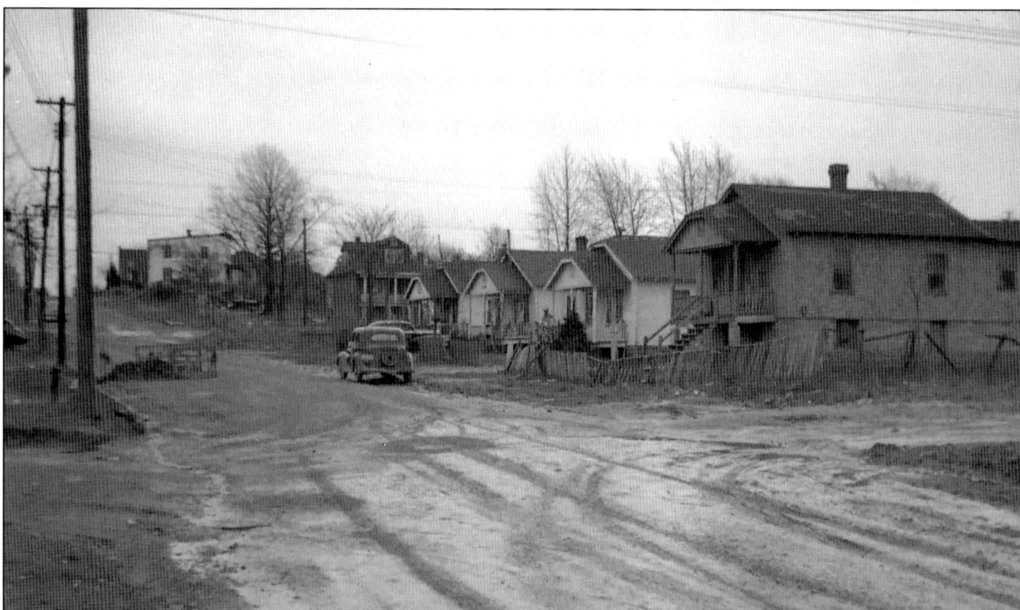

LEE STREET, MARCH 27, 1949. This view of Lee Street shows the 1920s development primarily by white real estate speculator Howard Gott, designed by Lewis Giles Sr., and built by Randolph Dodd. The Craftsman-style housing became a popular design in Deanwood. As they were constructed without plumbing or sewer access, owners later had to pay for improvements or risk having their homes condemned. (JTWC, HSWDC.)

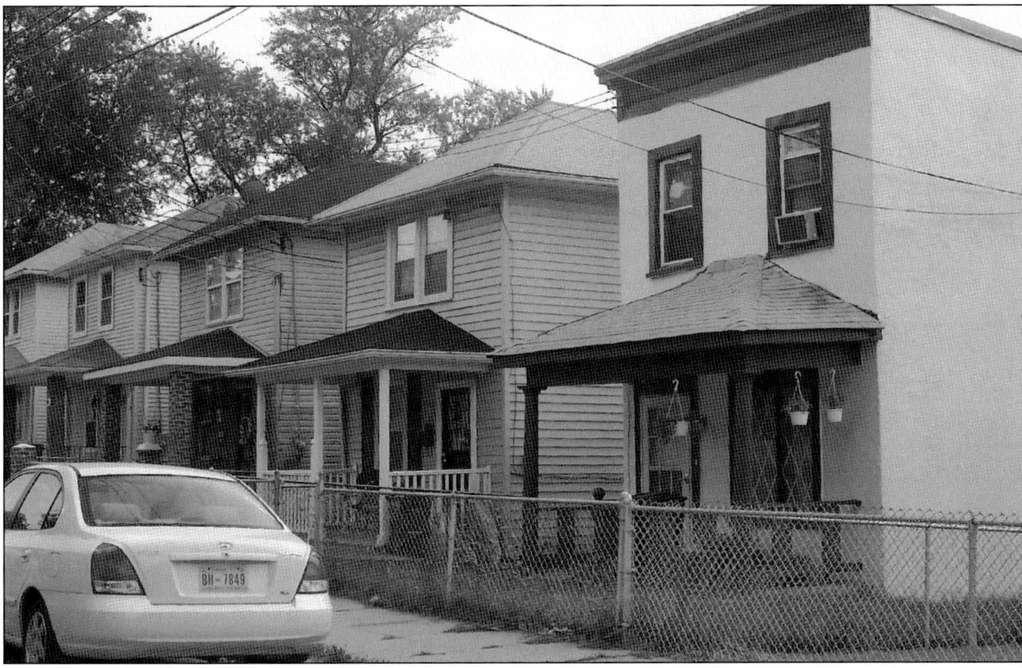

900 BLOCK FORTY-FIFTH PLACE, 2005. In these backyards grew seedless grape vines, red delicious apples, and black cherry trees. Neighbors shared fruit for canning and jelly. The families living in these homes in the 1940s were the Downings, the Broaduses, the Cottons, the Warings, and the Carters. Architect and resident Lewis Giles Sr. designed these homes in the 1920s. (DCHPO.)

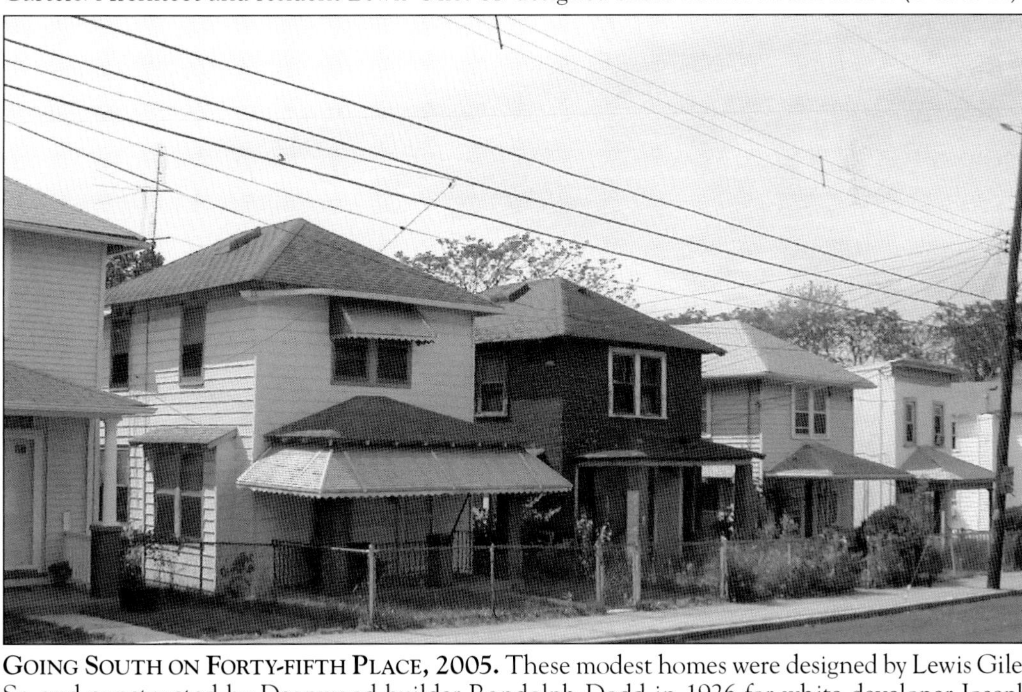

GOING SOUTH ON FORTY-FIFTH PLACE, 2005. These modest homes were designed by Lewis Giles Sr. and constructed by Deanwood builder Randolph Dodd in 1926 for white developer Joseph Tepper. The cost to build was given at $2,000 each, but this represented a priceless opportunity for homeownership for African Americans. (DCHPO.)

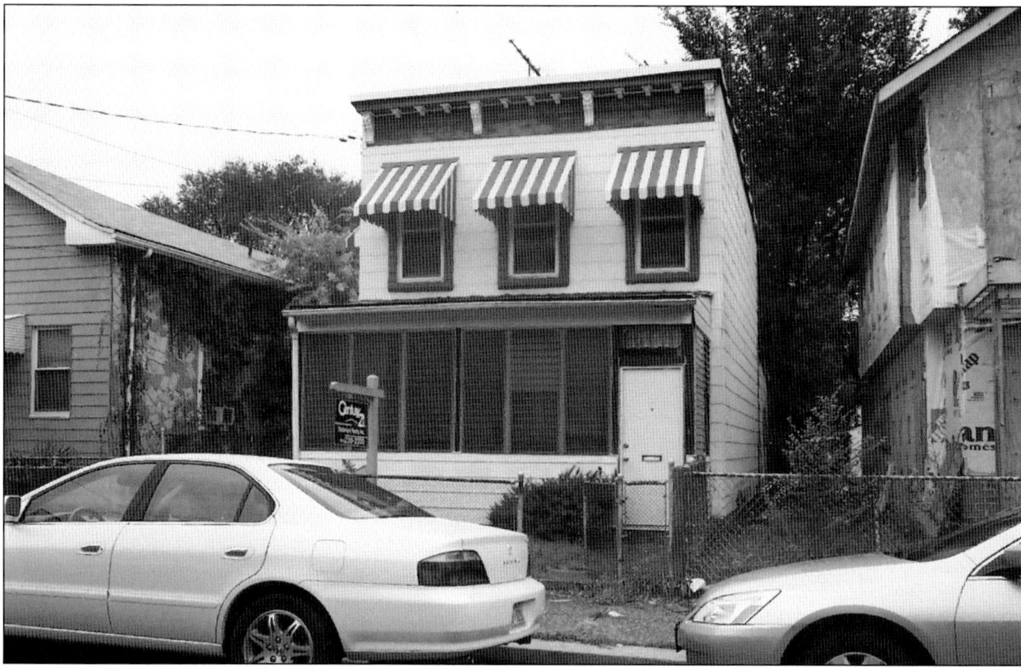

JACOB KING FAMILY HOME, 2005. King designed and built what is now 1046 Forty-fifth Street just after the beginning of the 20th century. Its Italianate row house style was popular in the community. To the left is the building erected in 1908 to serve as the second home of First Baptist Church of Deanwood. B. P. Bond was the architect and James Lacey the builder. (DCHPO.)

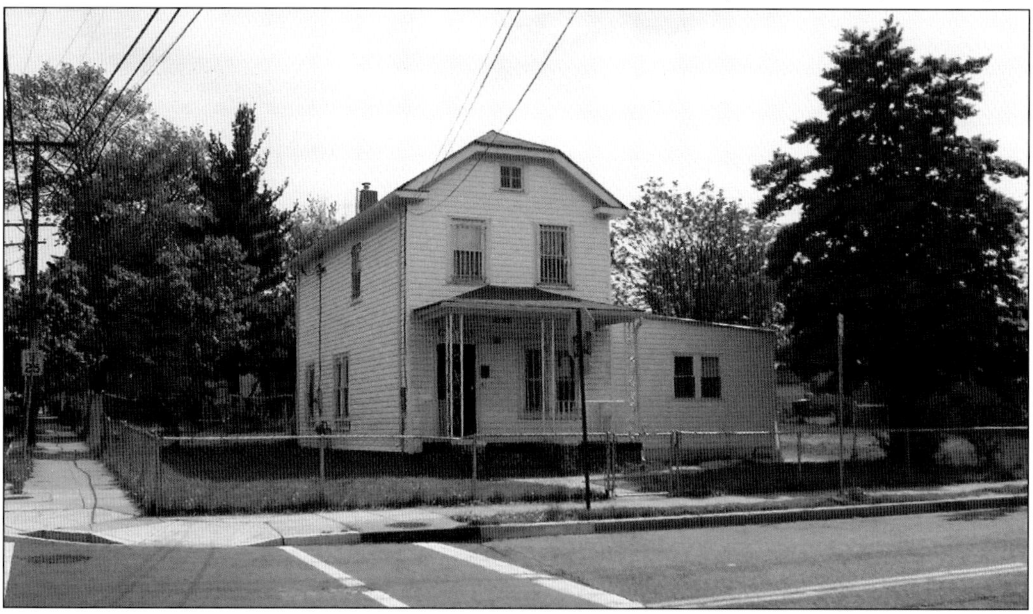

FISHING SCHOOL, 2005. The original structure at 4737 Meade Street was built in 1911 by the Municipal Building Company with Bernard Brown as the architect. The company built seven more houses on Meade, Forty-eighth Street, and Forty-eighth Place between 1910 and 1911. This building now houses the Fishing School, a faith-based, after-school family and child support center for children and youth ages 6 to 16. (DCHPO.)

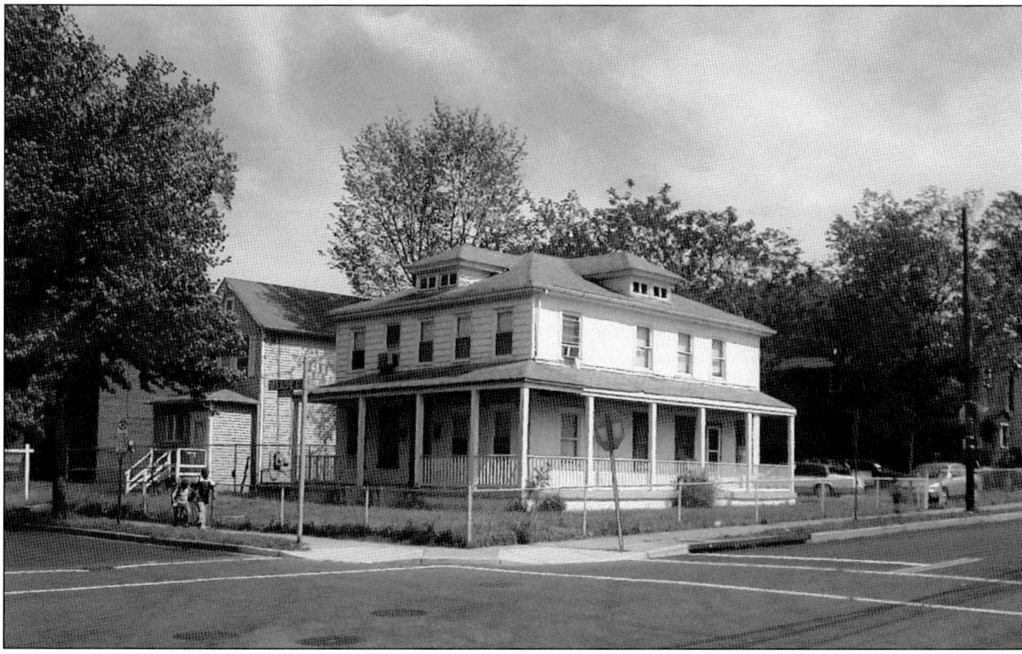

White House, 2005. The Municipal Building Company built this home at 4801 Meade Street with H. A. Riggs as the architect. The building was modified significantly in 1927 by African American architect and Deanwood favorite Horace W. Turner. Turner designed over 130 buildings between 1925 and 1949. Many were in Deanwood. (DCHPO.)

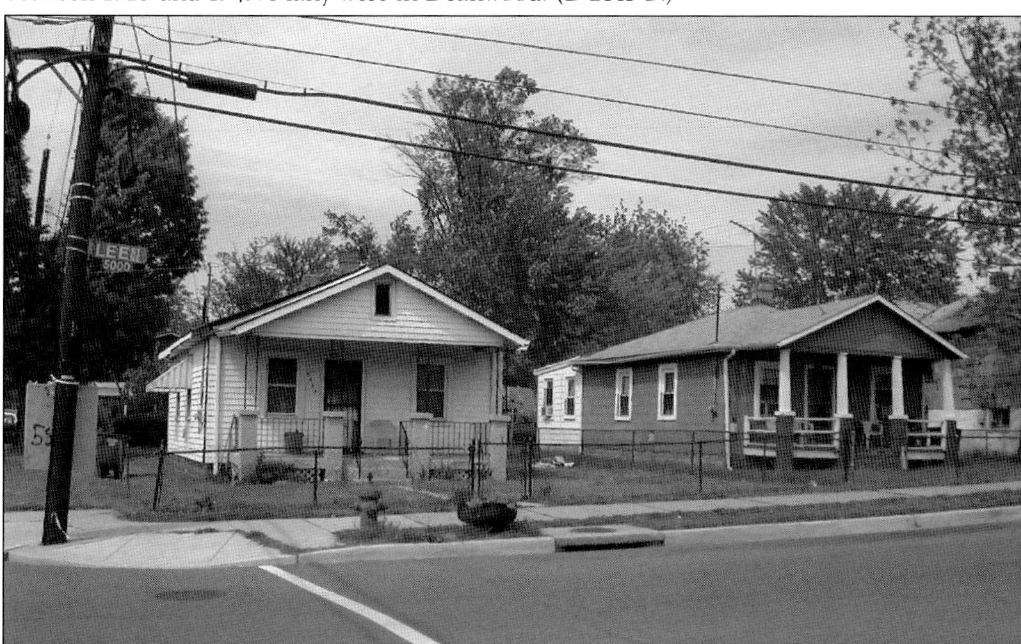

5000 Block Lee Street, 2005. This contemporary view of Lee Street shows another popular style of homes found throughout the neighborhood: 5002 and 5006 Lee Street are in the one-level Craftsman style. These houses, designed by Horace Turner and built in 1927 by owner Archie Savoy, are examples of the 1920s boom in housing construction in Deanwood. (DCHPO.)

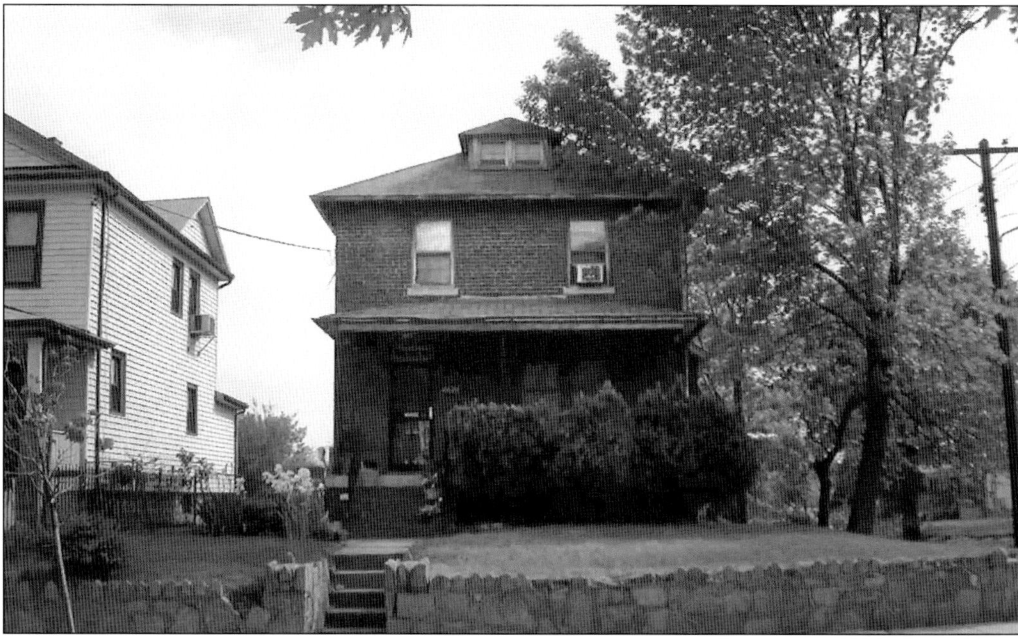

LEWIS HOUSE, 2005. This foursquare-style house at 4827 Jay Street was not one of the standard designs for Deanwood. However, its architect and builder, Lewis Giles Sr. and Randolph Dodd, were a familiar design team. Constructed in 1932 of brick, this stately home named for its original owner is evidence of the presence of upwardly mobile professional-class African Americans in the community. (DCHPO.)

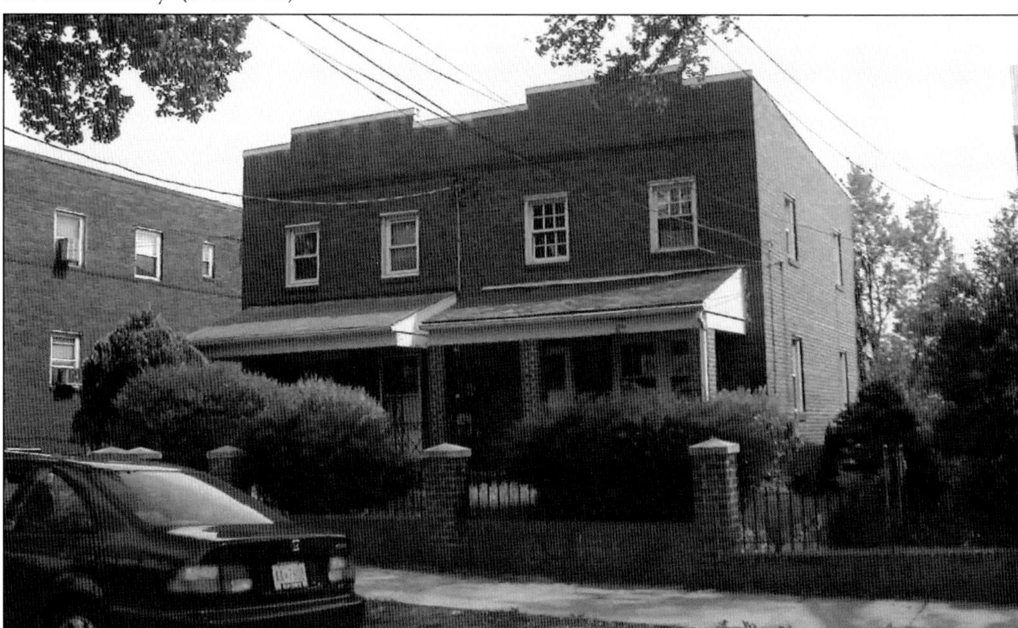

4625–4627 JAY STREET, 2005. Lewis Giles Sr. was the architect on this Joseph Tepper development along the 4600 block of Jay Street. The semi-detached brick houses are typical of 1940s housing construction along the highlands of Deanwood. Heretofore undeveloped, this area experienced intense housing construction from 1940 to the late 1950s. (DCHPO.)

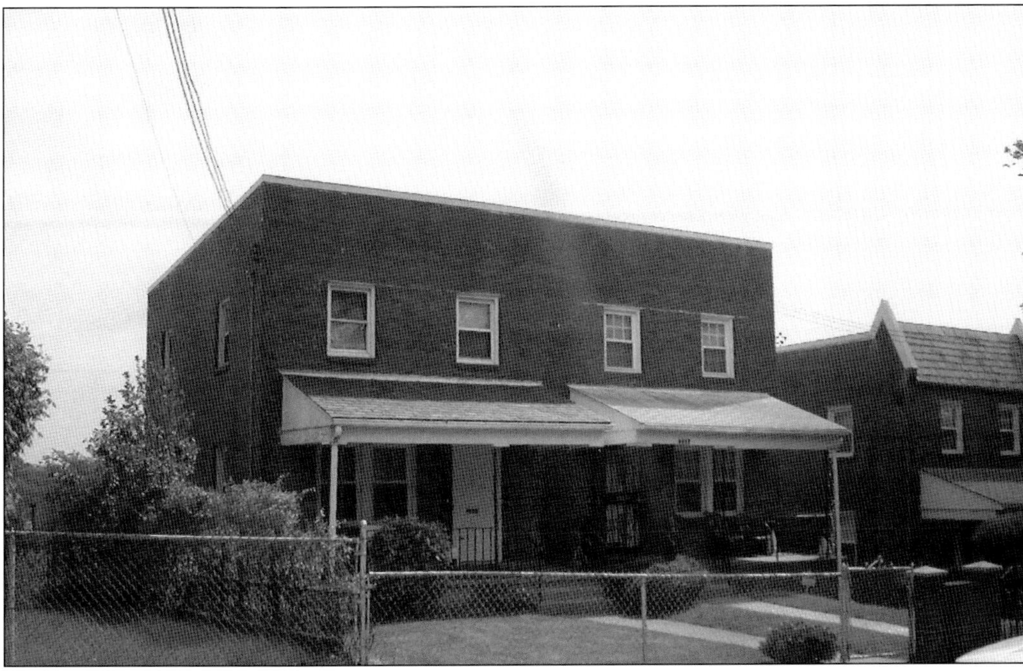

4617–4619 JAY STREET, 2005. These houses represent another style in the Giles-designed Tepper project on the 4600 block of Jay Street. Constructed in 1940, these homes furnished the opportunity for blacks to own homes during a period when many District neighborhoods had restrictive covenants. (DCHPO.)

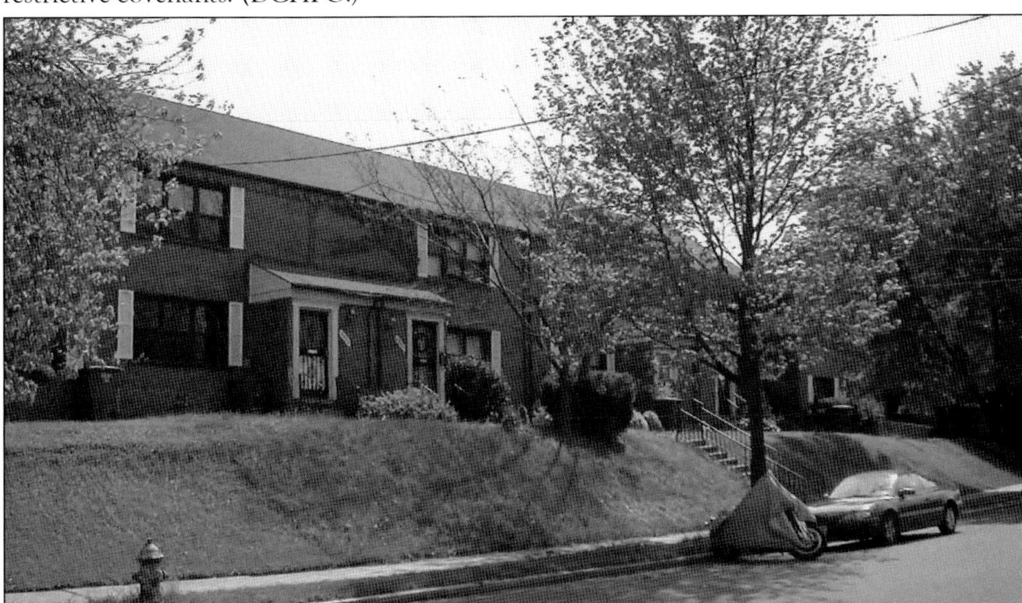

SUBURBAN GARDENS APARTMENTS, 2005. Developed by Suburban Gardens, Inc., in 1941 near the site of the old amusement park of the same name, these Colonial Revival garden apartments in the 4900 block of Just Street were designed by Harvey Warwick and built by A. Lloyd Goode. They addressed a critical shortage of decent, attractive, and affordable housing for Washington's middle-class blacks. (DCHPO.)

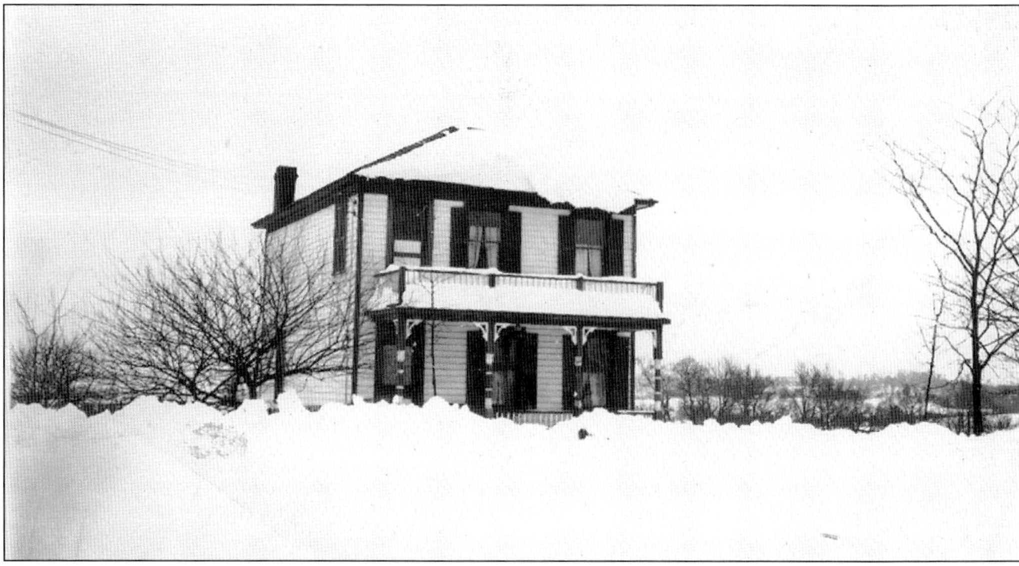

FORTY-EIGHTH PLACE AND JAY STREET, 1922. On January 27 and 28, 1922, a storm dropped 28 inches of snow on Washington, D.C., and collapsed the roof of the Knickerbocker Theater. It was the biggest blizzard to ever hit the city. It took a storm of this magnitude to shut things down in Deanwood—according to lifelong resident Helen Gordon Hasty, "[We] never closed schools for 10 inches of snow." (WF.)

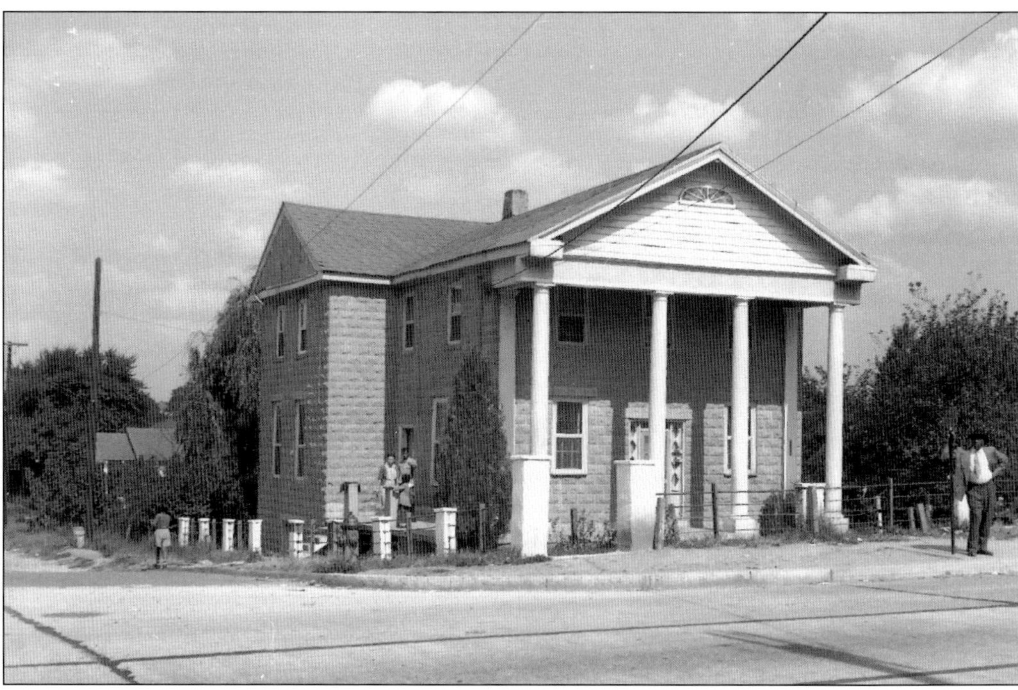

5000 SHERIFF ROAD, SEPTEMBER 25, 1948. The imposing house at 5000 Sheriff Road has been a landmark in Deanwood since its construction in 1926. Designed by Horace W. Turner, it was built by original owner J. T. Brown. The Dr. Chancellor Williams family, who owned the house for many years, were the occupants when this photograph was taken. (JTWC, HSWDC.)

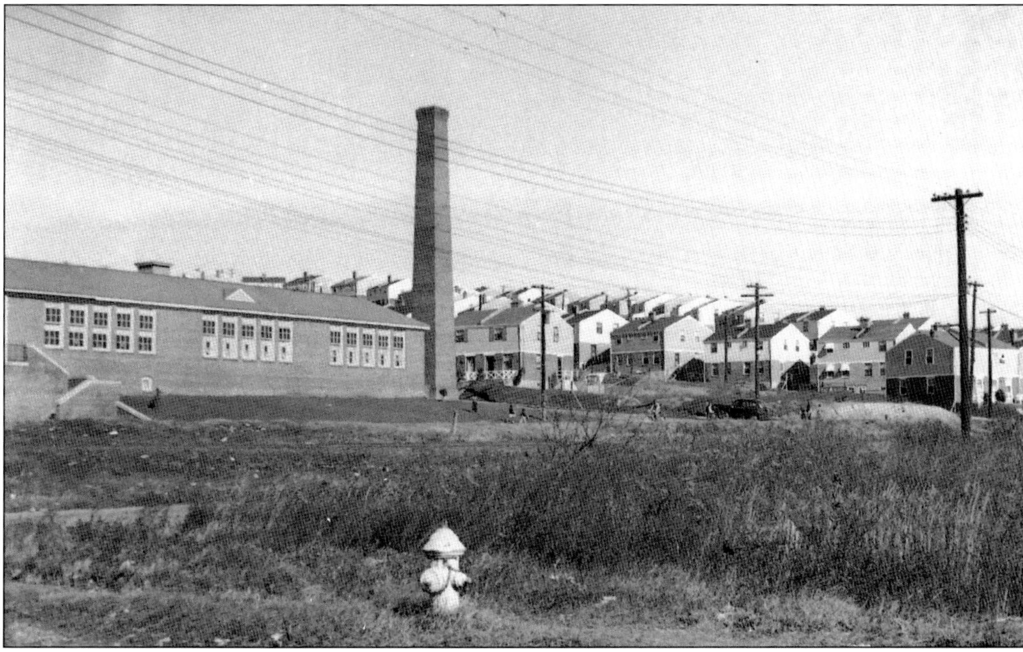

SUBURBAN HEIGHTS, NOVEMBER 7, 1948. This is a 1948 view of Suburban Heights, a World War II housing project. Suburban Heights was located northeast of Merritt Elementary School. The project was developed in 1945 by John Graham Jr., a Seattle architect who is most famous as the designer of the Space Needle for the Seattle World's Fair. (JTWC, HSWDC.)

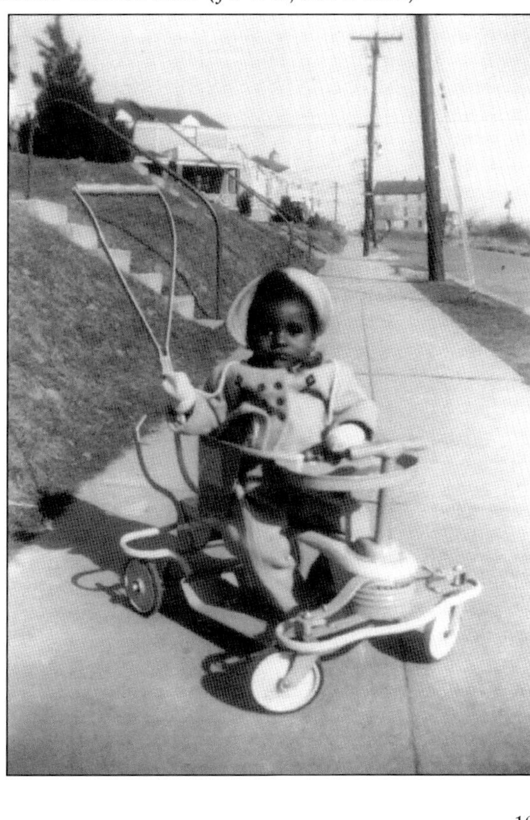

SUBURBAN HEIGHTS HOME, C. 1950. Suburban Heights offered many more families the opportunity to become homeowners. Alice Chandler is photographed in front of her family's home at 5106 Hayes Street. Just a decade earlier, the same area was home to Suburban Gardens Amusement Park, which offered blacks a place to come for fun and entertainment. (Alice Chandler.)

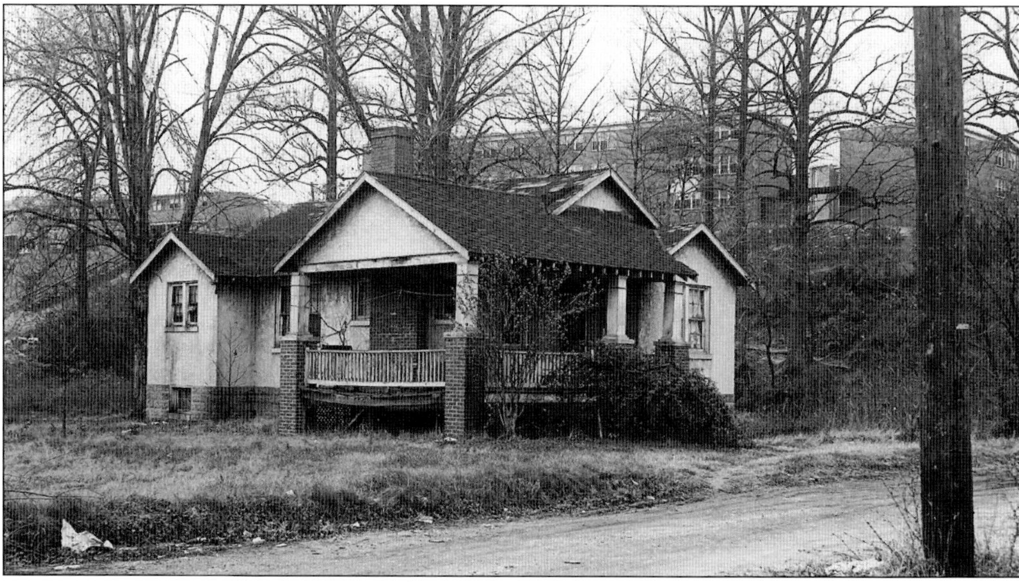

5117 Deane Avenue, 1956. Houses like this one along the Watts Branch experienced flooding in August 1933. Torrential rains caused the branch to become a raging river. Basements and roadways flooded when the water level rose to the height of the fire hydrants. Cars were stranded, and pedestrians had to wade through the debris-filled water. (NCPE, NPS.)

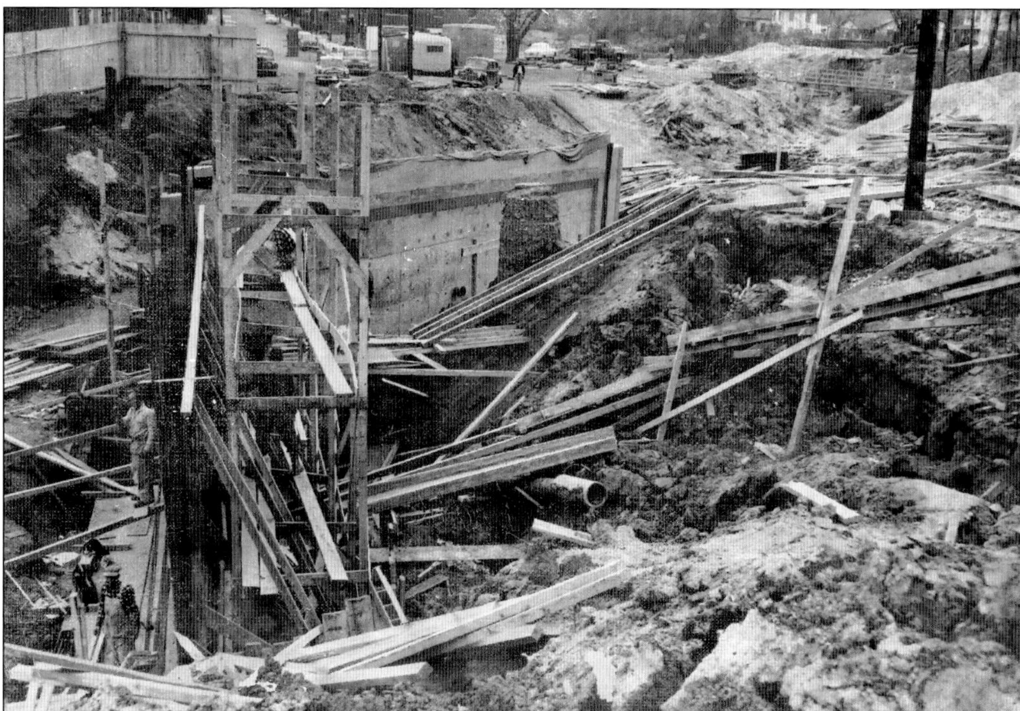

Gault Place Bridge, March 8, 1956. The Watts Branch of the Anacostia River crosses the Deanwood neighborhood from east to west, making it true waterfront property. Here the northwest wing wall of the Gault Place Bridge across the branch is being constructed to allow traffic to flow from Forty-second to Forty-fourth Streets NE. (D.C. Department of Transportation Archives.)

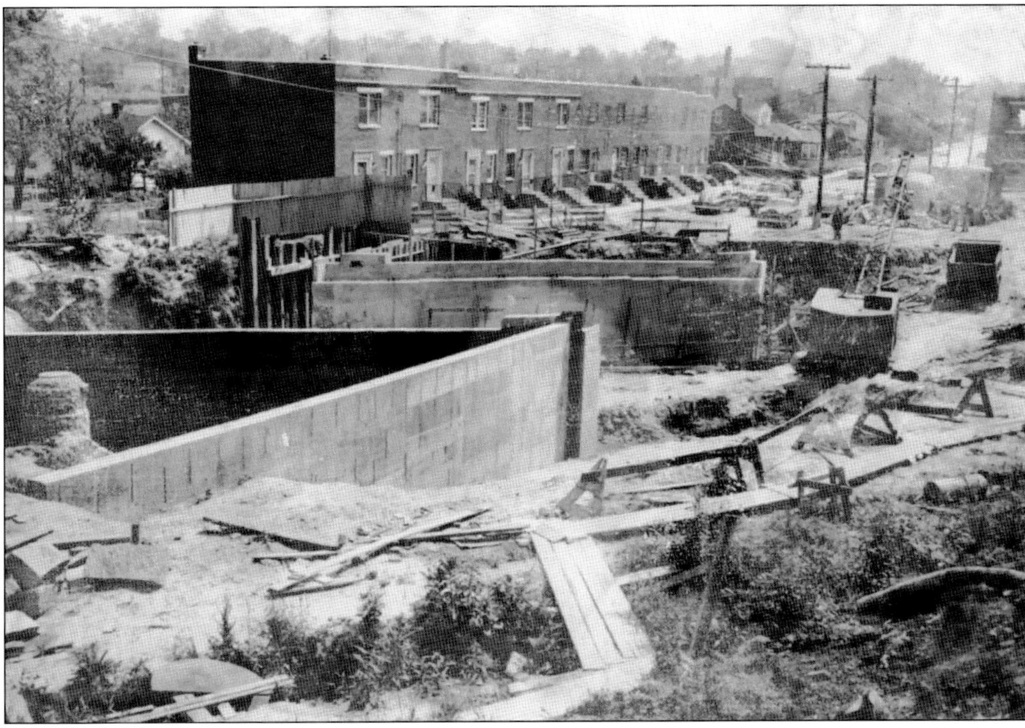

Gault Place Bridge, June 7, 1956. The D.C. Department of Transportation took pictures of their projects to chronicle their work throughout the city. This view, looking east of Gault Place, reveals the progress of city crews. Many neighborhood infrastructure improvements such as this did not come to Deanwood until the late 1950s. (D.C. Department of Transportation Archives.)

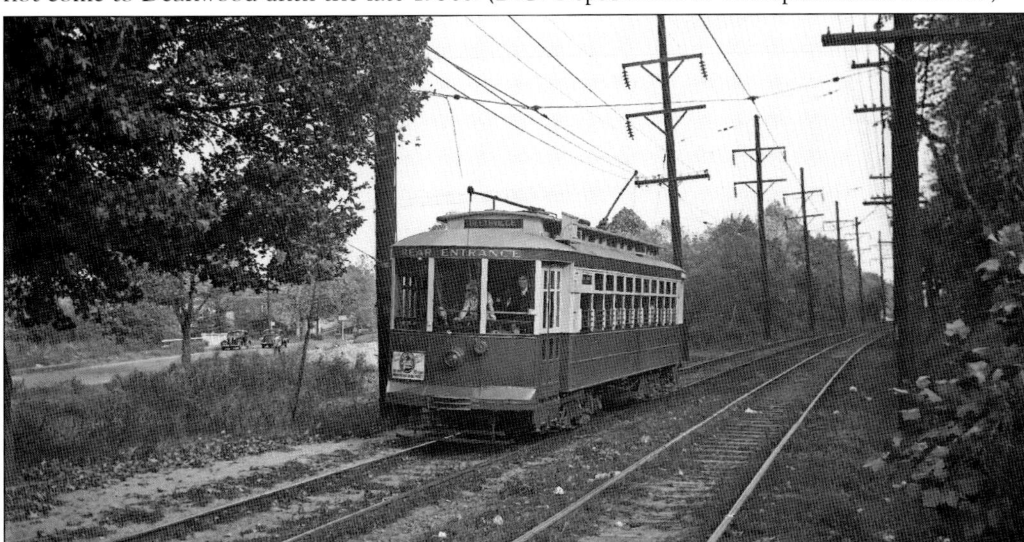

Beltsville Streetcar, 1947. Streetcars were one of the ways that Deanwood residents stayed connected to the world outside their self-contained community. Residents talked of taking the streetcars to downtown D.C., but many felt all they needed was right here in their community or in Benning, the neighboring commercial district. (Robert S. Crockett Streetcar Photograph Collection, HSWDC.)

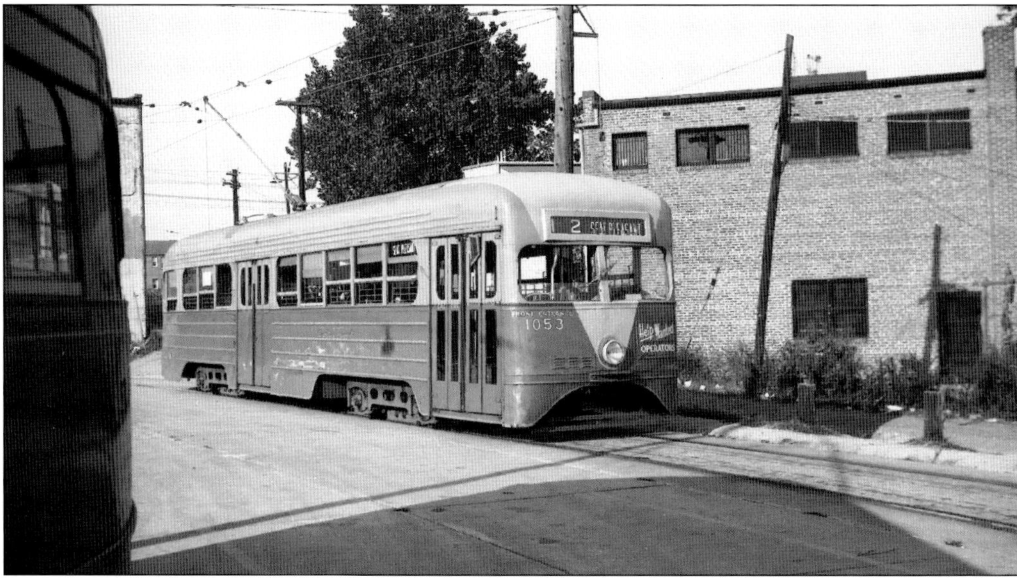

Seat Pleasant Streetcar, 1948. The streetcars were the subjects of protest activity from Deanwood and Marshall Heights residents. Led by Howard D. Woodson, president of the Northeast Boundary Civic Association, residents were successful in stopping an increase in the fares in the 1930s from 30¢ for four tokens to 35¢. (Robert S. Crockett Streetcar Photograph Collection, HSWDC.)

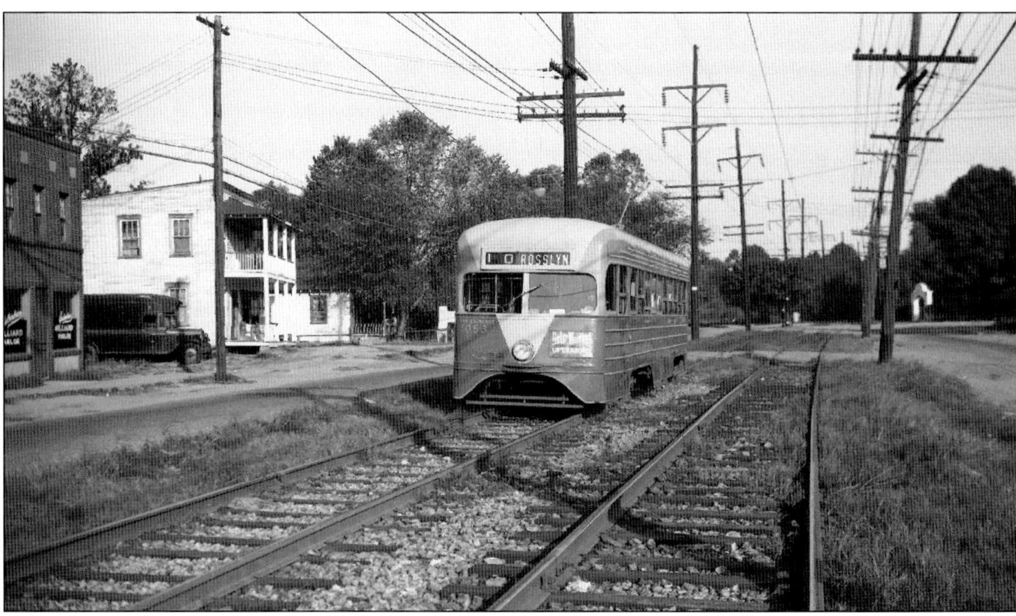

Rosslyn Streetcar, 1948. To visit Suburban Gardens from Washington, D.C., one could catch the Chesapeake Railroad, which ran along Deane Avenue, and disembark at Lowrie Place, or one could take the trolley that traveled from the western suburbs of D.C. to Deanwood. For many years, the Deane Avenue route was the only one in the northeast corner of Washington. (Robert S. Crockett Streetcar Photograph Collection, HSWDC.)

Two

Sons and Daughters of Deanwood

In the 19th century, Washington, D.C., was known as the Federal City, and the area east of the Anacostia River was known as Washington County. It was rural and underdeveloped and had a sense of being set apart from the rest of the District. Longtime residents of Deanwood remember being called "those folks living in the country."

It may have been this sense of being set apart that helped make the community bonds so strong and encouraged people to call it home for generations. Homes have been passed from parents to children and sometimes even grandchildren. In Deanwood, it was not uncommon for the same families to be neighbors for decades and for scores of relatives to live within blocks of one another.

This longevity among neighbors and deep roots in the community created an environment where the term "family" extended beyond one's bloodlines and into the entire community. Residents who were children in the 1930s and 1940s recall Deanwood as a place where they were watched by neighbors as well as their parents and disciplined by both if necessary. Teachers in the community are remembered as being loving adults who not only taught academics in the classroom but showed genuine affection for their students outside of school as well.

The relationships that existed between residents and community business owners were characterized by this same sense of family. It was common practice for neighborhood physicians to go to the homes of those patients who could not make it to the office or allow patients to pay for their treatment by taking services in lieu of cash when times were hard—local carpenters provided carpentry work and electricians did electrical jobs for the doctors. Many times, supporting a local business became a community affair. According to one longtime resident's recollection, when the train stopped to deliver supplies to the F. L. Watkins lumber yard, "everyone would rush down to help stack the lumber and bricks. No one got paid, it was just the neighborly thing to do."

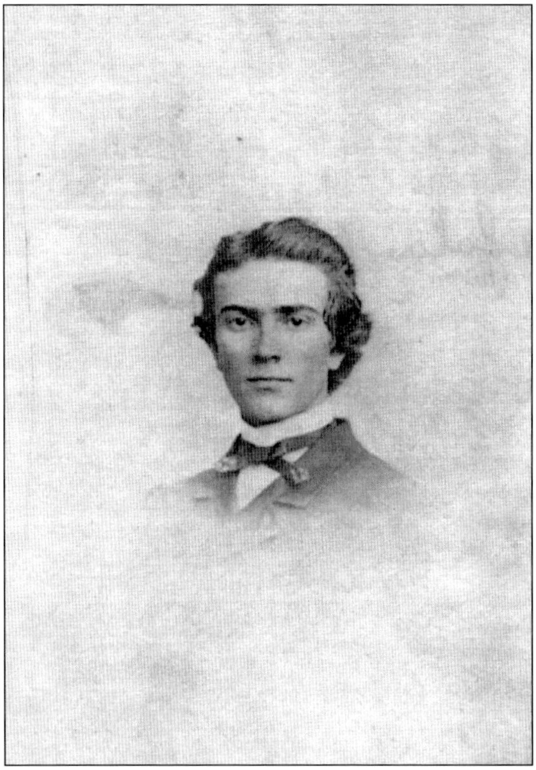

Julian W. Dean. This early picture shows a young Julian W. Dean, Levi Sheriff's grandson. He was the son of Sheriff's daughter, Mary Cornelia, and John T. W. Dean. Dean went on to become a physician and one of the few non-farmers who called Deanwood home in the 1880s. (SMKD.)

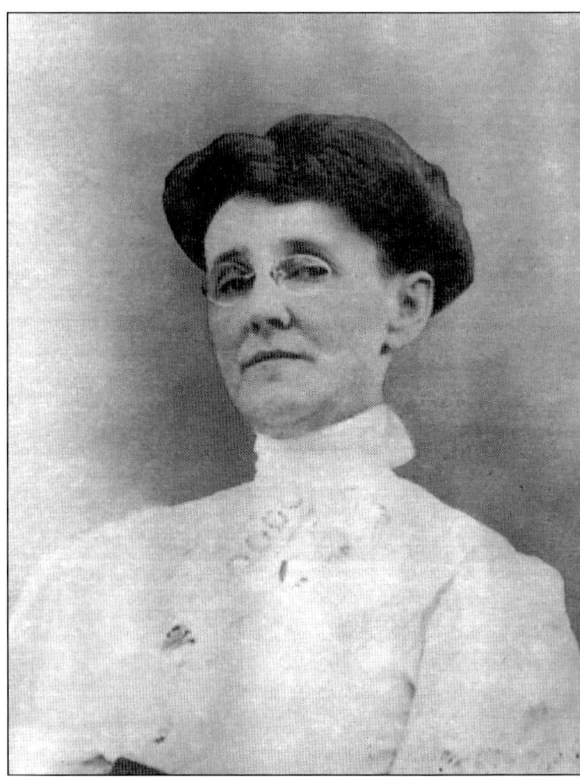

Eleanor Rehil Dean. Eleanor Rehil Dean was the wife of Dr. Julian Dean. She and Dr. Dean raised their children in the Sheriff-Lowrie-Dean family farmhouse, which was built in the 1790s. Photographs from the family album show her and her children spending time in the parlor. (SMKD.)

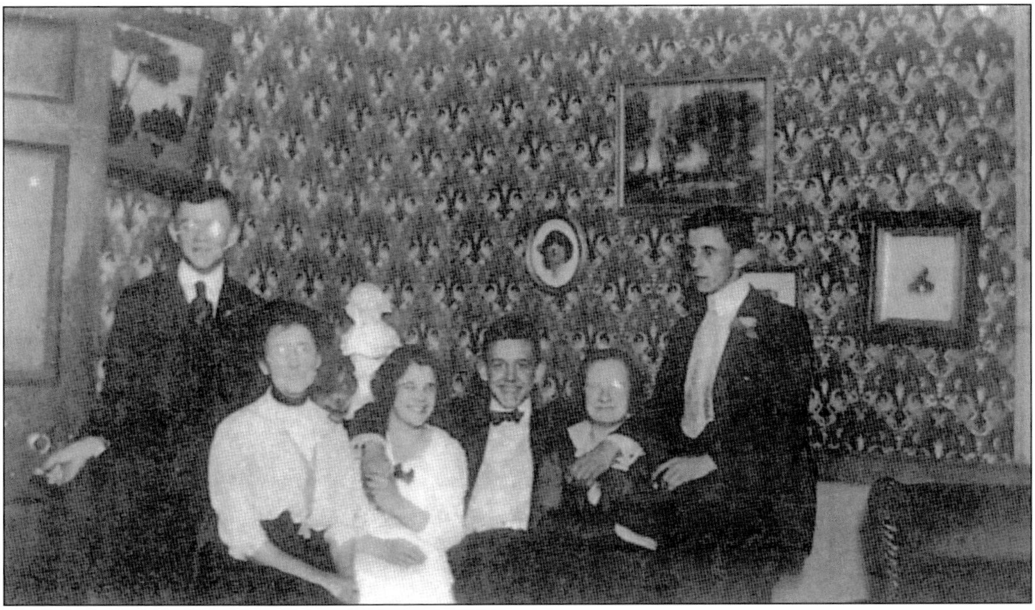

FAMILY FARMHOUSE PARLOR. Members of the Dean family pose for a picture in the parlor of the family farmhouse. Pictured from left to right are Edward Dean, Eleanor Rehil Dean, Dorothy Dean, John Dean, Dorothy White, and Henry B. Dean. (SMKD.)

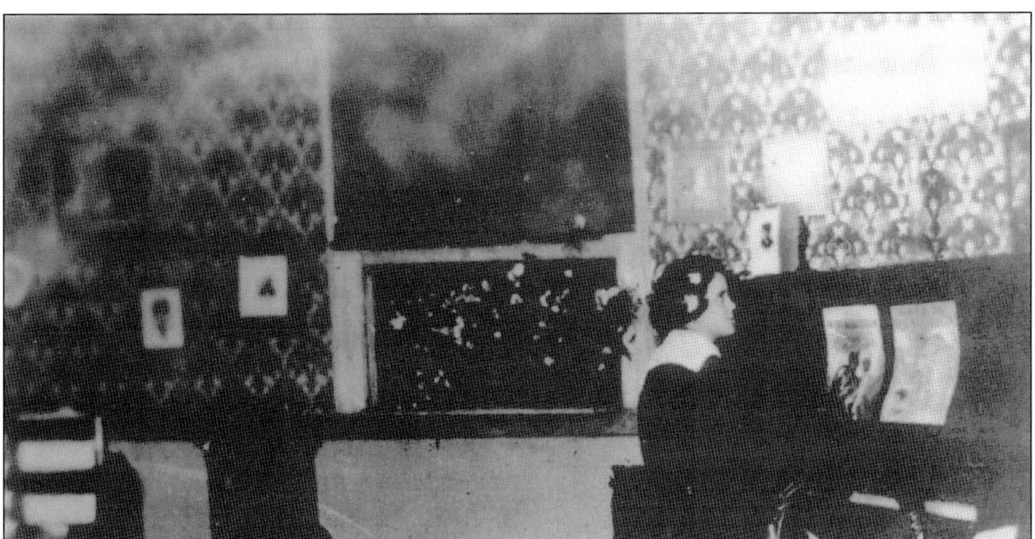

DOROTHY DEAN GRIFFIN. Remnants of the family history remained intact in the farmhouse when "The Rambler," a reporter for the *Evening Star* newspaper, visited the site in 1916. The piano where Dorothy Dean is seated was described as "an ancient square piano" with keys that once were white "and are now yellow—and tones jingle and jangle." (SMKD.)

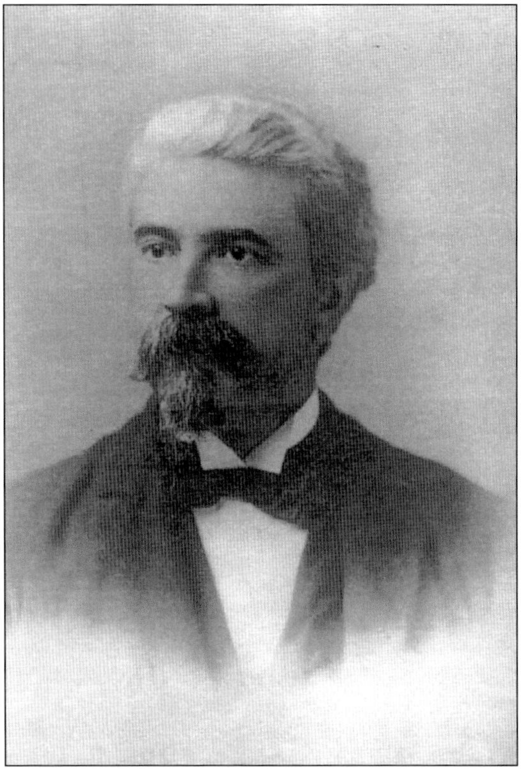

DR. JULIAN W. DEANE. Around 1888, Dean added an "e" to his name, so later generations are recorded as "Deane." He started his family with Eleanor Rehil Deane. He and his family moved away from Deanwood briefly after his land was sold at public auction in 1895. However, he returned to his birthplace, the Deane family farmhouse, about 1904 and died there in 1905. (SMKD.)

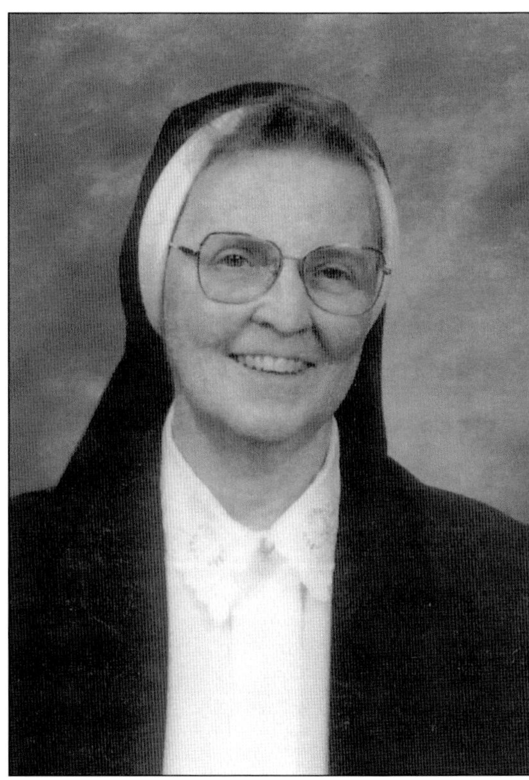

SR. MICHAEL KATHLEEN DEANE. Sr. Michael Kathleen Deane is the great-granddaughter of Levi Sheriff. Her father, Henry B. Deane, was the son of Dr. Julian and Eleanor Deane. Sister Deane represents the fourth generation of the Sheriff-Deane family, the early landowners of the area now known as Deanwood. (SMKD.)

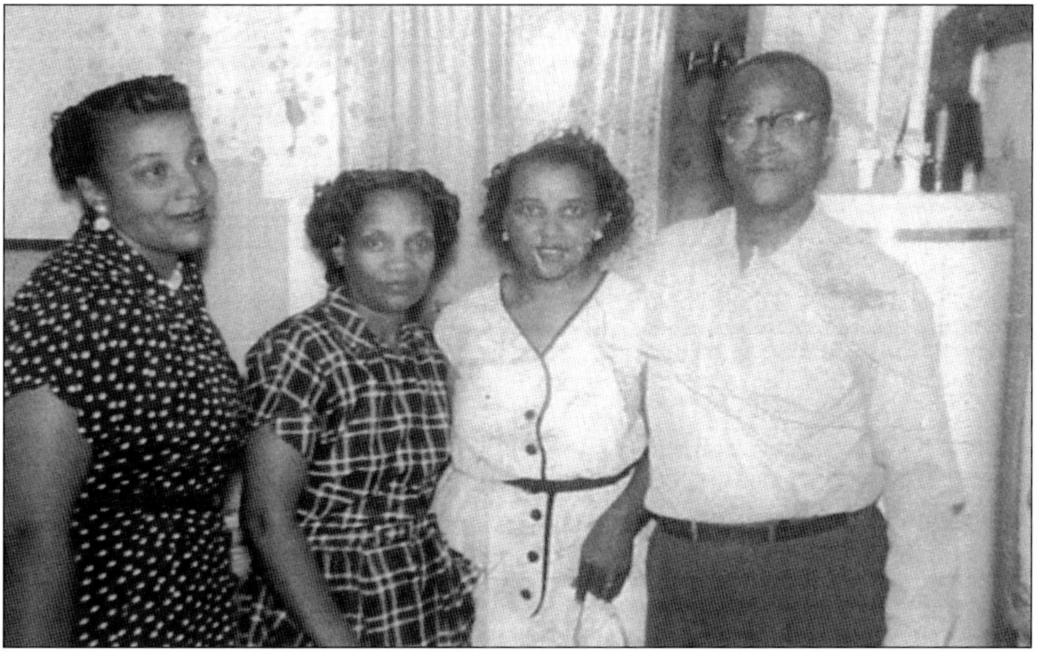

BROADUS FAMILY AND NEIGHBORS, C. 1950. James and Annie Broadus are joined by two neighbors just before the birthday party of their daughter, Doris. Pictured from left to right are Elsie Lattisaw, Teresa Harrod, Annie Broadus, and James Broadus. Annie Broadus's special homemade chocolate layer cake was always a favorite among partygoers. (EKB.)

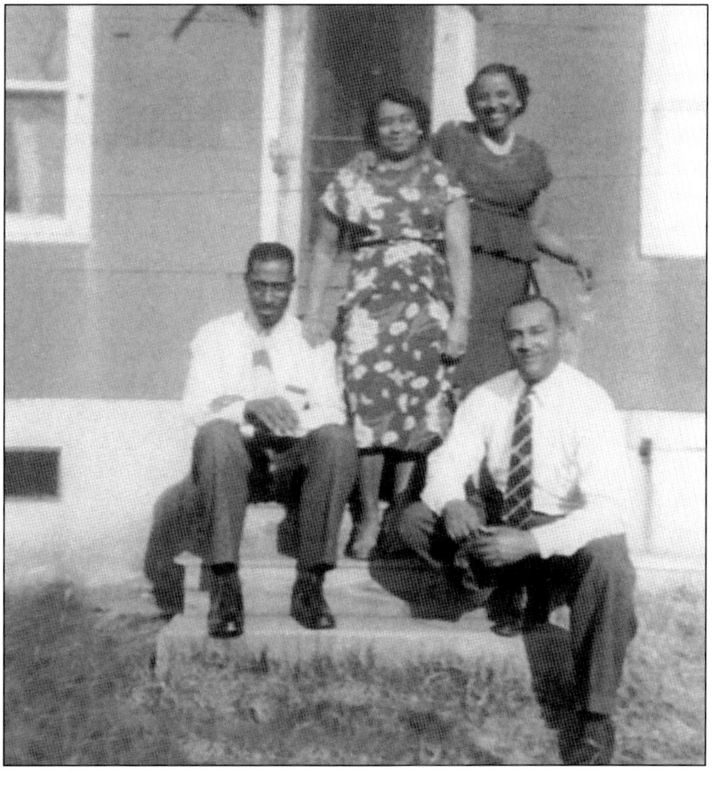

BROADUS FAMILY AND FRIENDS, C. 1950. After a new room and new steps were added to the back of their home at 908 Forty-fifth Place, the Broadus family invited friends over to celebrate. Pictured from left to right are Ellis Miller; his wife, Florence Miller; Annie Broadus; and James Broadus. (EKB.)

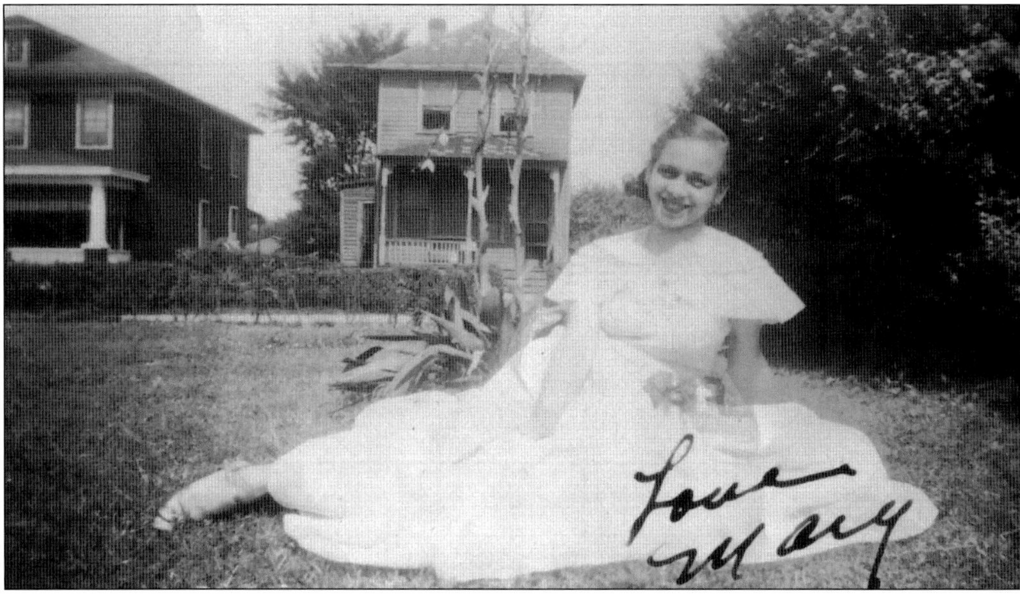

MARY JACKSON, JUNE 26, 1947. Mary Jackson poses in her front yard at 1128 Forty-eighth Place just before leaving to participate in her Class Night activities at Dunbar Senior High School. Jackson and her siblings—Joseph, Elva, Carrie, Albert, William, Charles, Theodore, and Jean—grew up in the house. (Sandra Brown.)

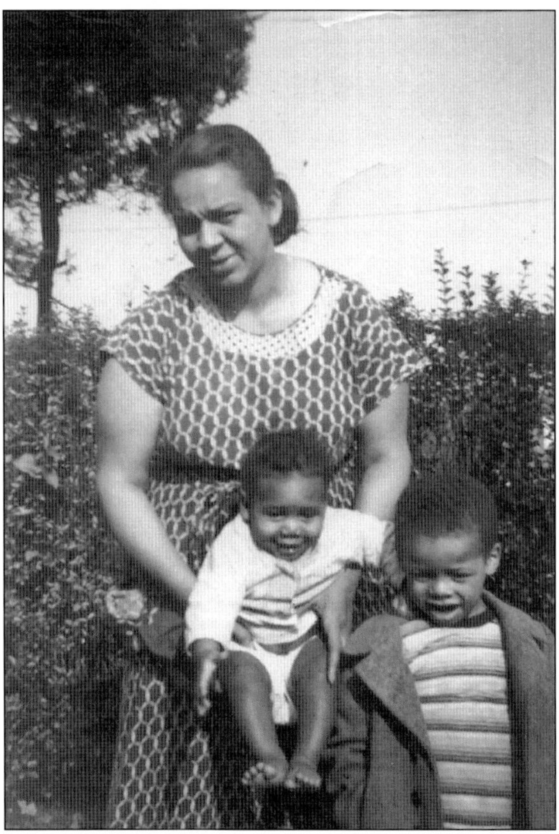

MARY JACKSON, C. 1953. Jackson felt an affinity with her childhood home and the community of Deanwood. As a mother, she continued to raise her children in the neighborhood. Here she holds her son James while his brother, Celester, stands at her side. Her daughter, Sandra, was born in the family home at 1128 Forty-eighth Place. (Sandra Brown.)

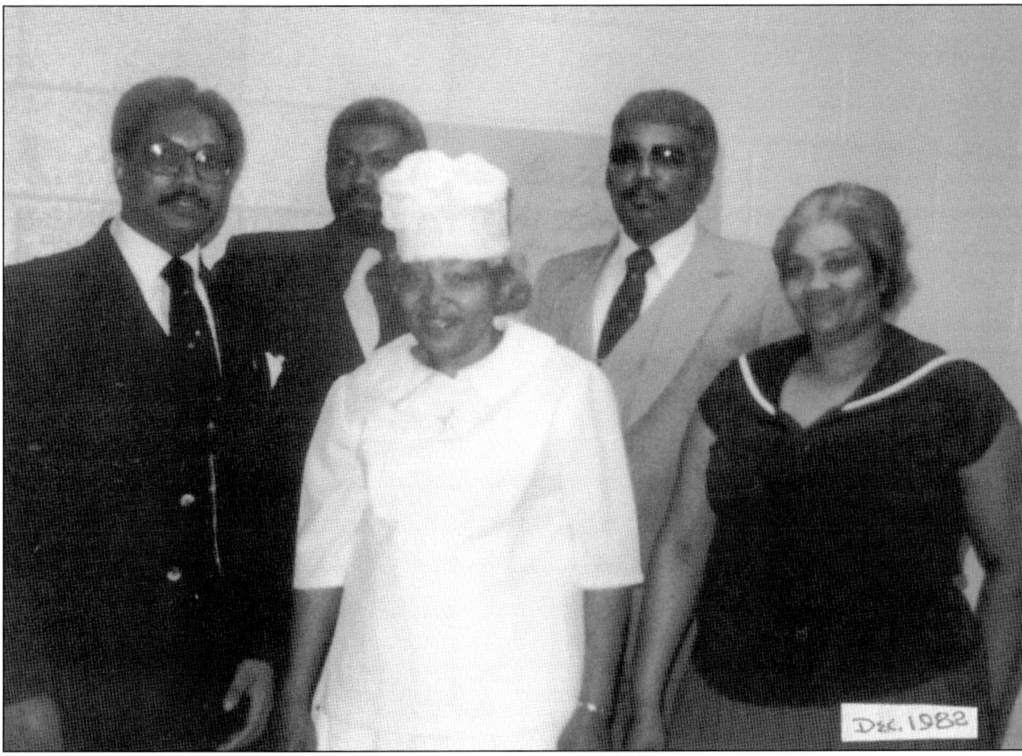

Brown Family. When people departed the U4 bus in front of 4411 Sheriff Road, Marjorie Brown was always there to pray for them and their family. She was a neighborhood icon and a longtime member of Bible Way Temple on New Jersey Avenue. She poses in her missionary uniform with her four children (from left to right), Raymond, Norman, Theodore, and Delores. (Theodore Brown.)

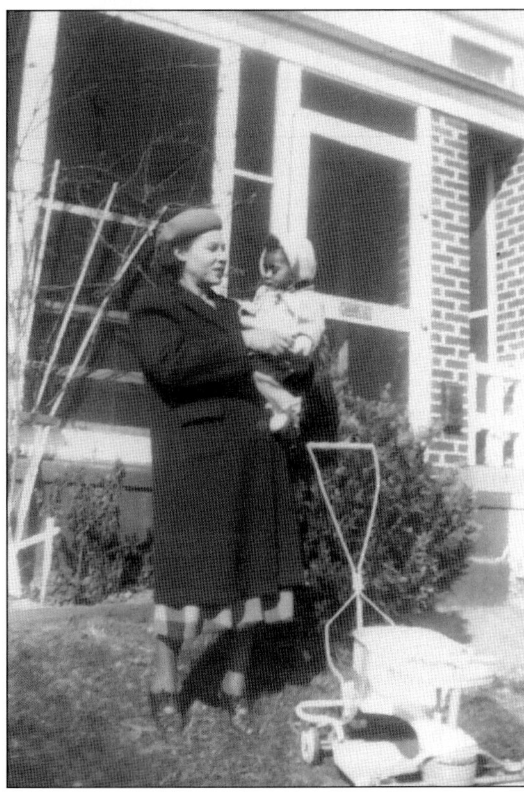

Mary and Alice Chandler, c. 1950. Mary Chandler holds her daughter, Alice, in front of their home at 5106 Hayes Street in Suburban Heights. Many young, professional African Americans moved into the development to raise their families when it was completed in the late 1940s. Decades later, some of the original families remain. (Alice Chandler.)

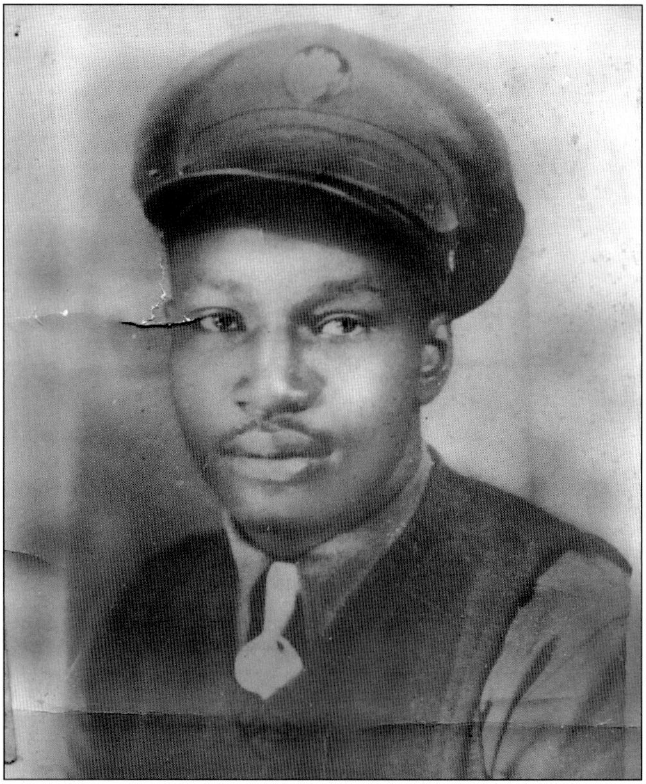

BENJAMIN E. GANTT JR., 1942. Seen here in his army photograph, PFC Benjamin E. Gantt Jr. was born and raised at 1202 Forty-seventh Place. He attended Deanwood School and was a member of the Church of the Incarnation for his entire life. After World War II, he left the army, married fellow Deanwood resident Corinne Raymond, and worked at the Naval Research Lab and Capitol Hill Hospital. (Corinne Gantt.)

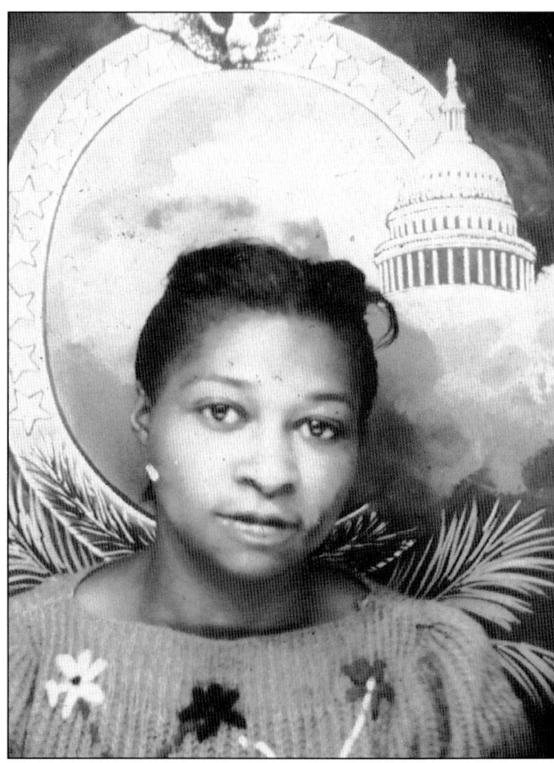

CORINNE RAYMOND GANTT, LATE 1940S. Corinne was born in 1917. Her parents, William and Lula Raymond, operated a rooming house near the Benning Race Track. During World War II, she worked at Washington Navy Yard on the assembly line adding boosters to rockets. After the war, she married Benjamin E. Gantt Jr., and they raised their family in Fairmount Heights, Maryland, but remained active in Deanwood through their churches. (Luther Raymond.)

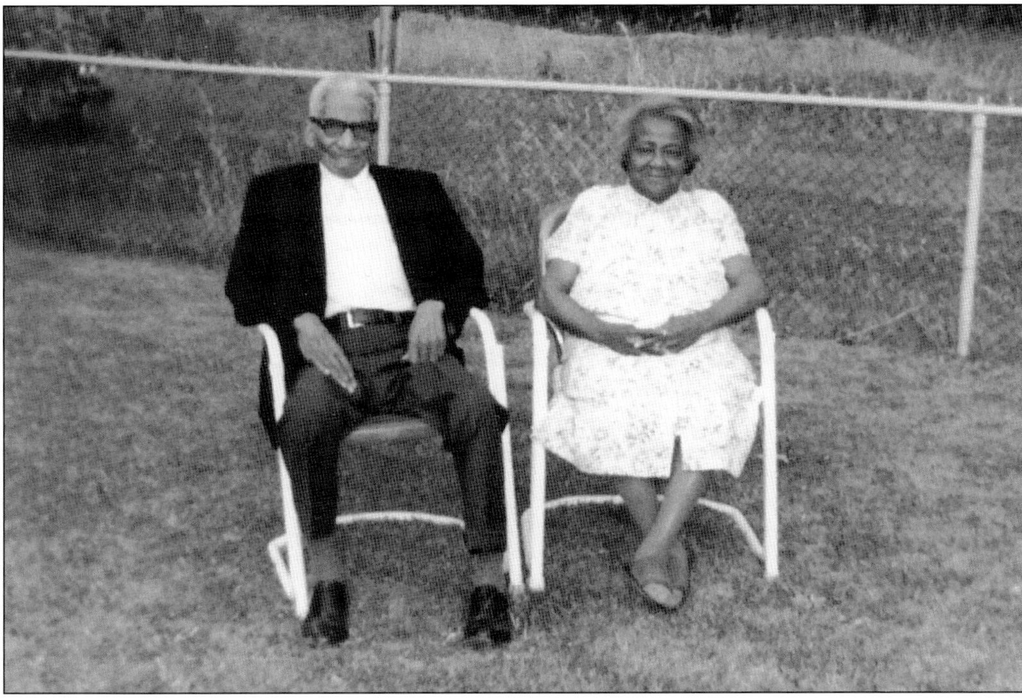

Mr. and Mrs. Gordon. Maurice J. "Mouse" and Elizabeth M. Gordon were part of the Deanwood business community. They owned and operated a tailor shop at Forty-fifth Street and Sheriff Road. The shop operated from 1940 until 1955. Maurice made men's suits, and Elizabeth did alterations. (Helen Hasty.)

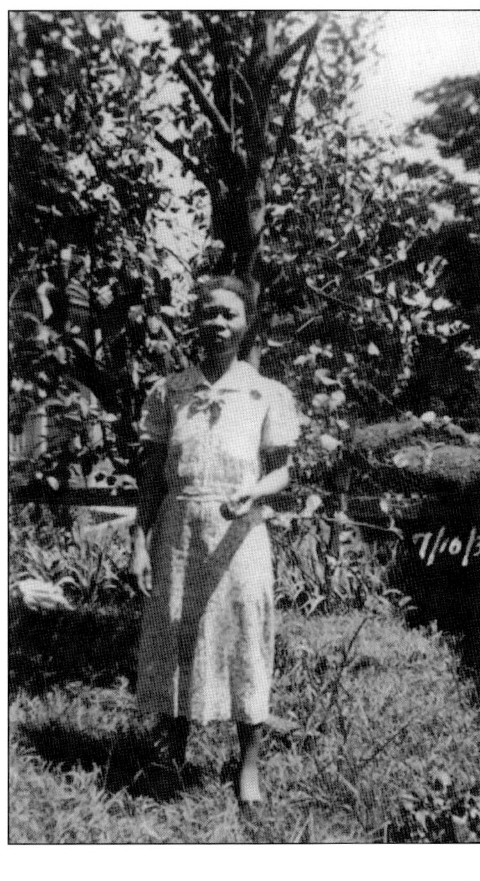

Geraldine Haywood, July 10, 1939. Geraldine Haywood enjoys a pear from the tree in her yard at 4838 Sheriff Road. The home was built by her father-in-law, Sydney Haywood, in 1926. In the early 1900s, it was not uncommon for young families to receive help from their relatives. Before their house was complete, she and her family stayed next door with her in-laws at 4898 Sheriff Road. (Geraldine Carroll.)

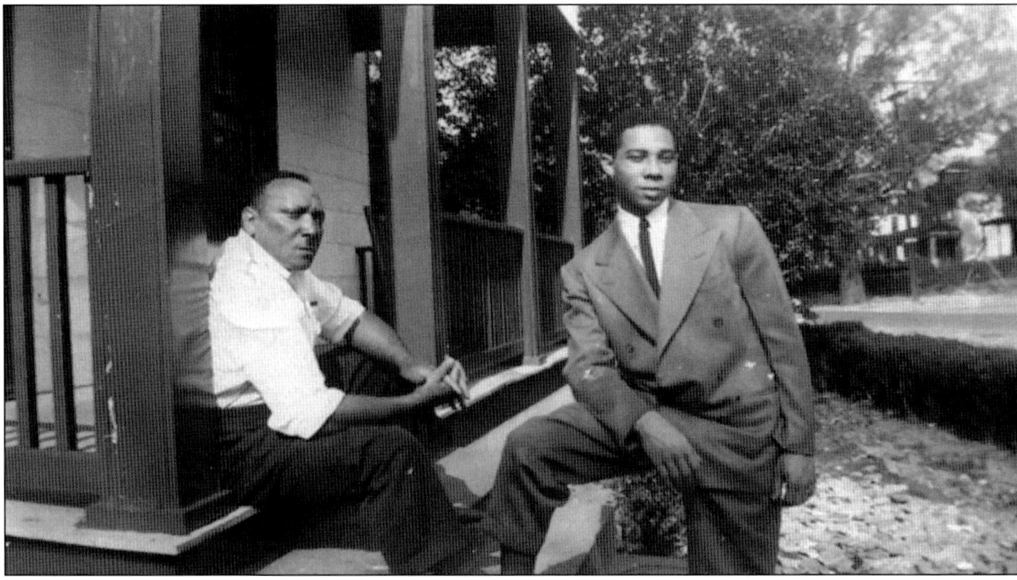

FATHER AND SON, C. 1943. Hiram Harry Haywood (left) and his son, Hiram Harry Haywood Jr., relax on their front porch. Years later, Hiram Sr.'s daughter, Geraldine (Haywood) Carroll, fondly recalled growing up in the neighborhood and the rural nature of the community. She often played with Nellie, her grandfather's horse. (Geraldine Carroll.)

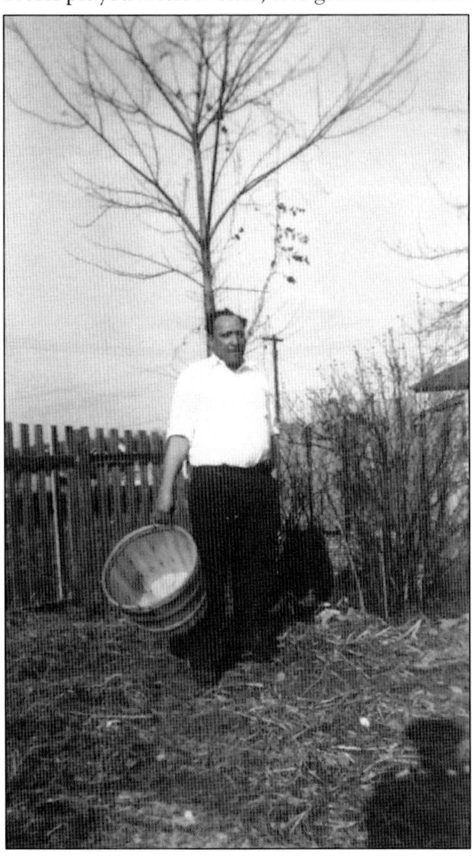

HIRAM HAYWOOD SR., C. 1947. Fruit trees graced many of the properties in Deanwood, a legacy from the community's agricultural history. The Haywood family enjoyed fruit from the pear tree in their front yard as well as from the grapevines and fig, cherry, peach, and plum trees that grew in the rear. Here Hiram Sr. prepares to harvest some of the fruit. (Geraldine Carroll.)

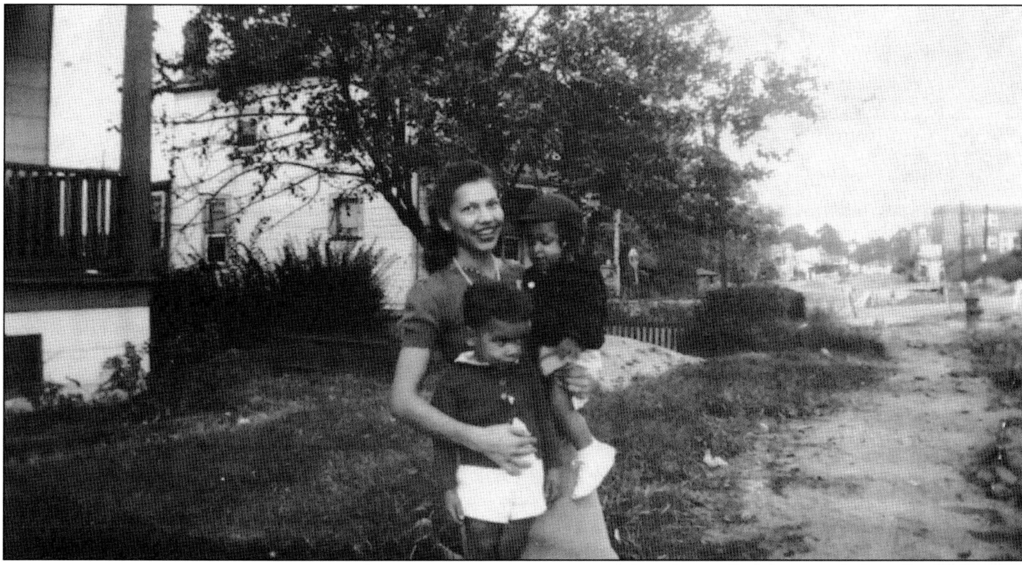

CHARLEAN HAYWOOD, C. 1947. Hiram Haywood Jr.'s wife, Charlean, holds her nephew, Alfred Q. Carroll III (right) and son, Hiram III, in front of the family home. The unpaved Sheriff Road and lack of sidewalks in the background attest to the underdeveloped nature of the community well into the middle of the 20th century. (Geraldine Carroll.)

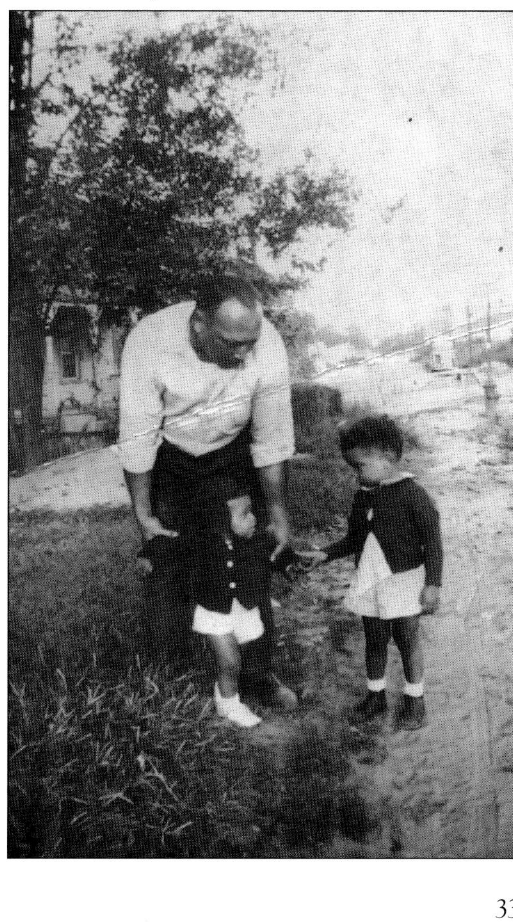

THREE GENERATIONS, C. 1947. The Haywood family has owned the home at 4838 Sheriff Road for generations. Here Hiram Harry Haywood Sr. plays with his two grandsons, Alfred Q. Carroll III (left) and Hiram Harry Haywood III, in the same front yard where, years before, he played with their parents. (Geraldine Carroll.)

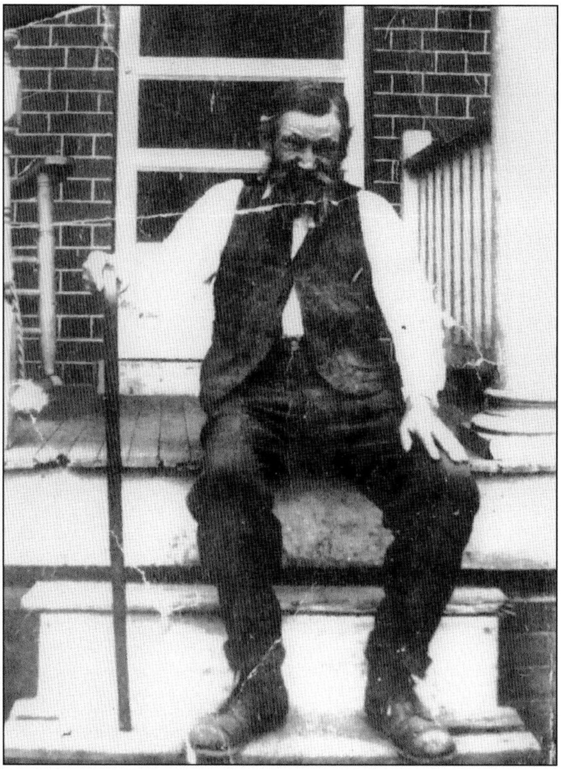

PETER KINGSBURGSON, 1900. Peter Kingsburgson was the father of Jacob C. King Sr. This picture was taken in 1900, when he came to Deanwood on a rare visit after the birth of Jacob's first born, Eva (born March 1, 1899). At the time of this picture, the street was unnamed, and the house had no address. In later years, it became 1046 Whittingham Place. (EKB.)

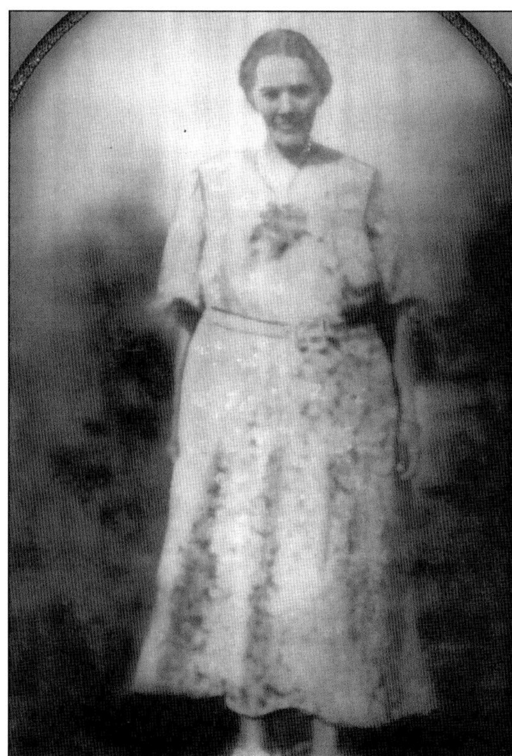

LUCY WINSLOW KING, C. 1900. Lucy Winslow King, wife of Jacob King Sr., poses in her Sunday best. She was well known among her neighbors for her delicious homemade pies, which she served daily to the men working next door on the construction of First Baptist Church of Deanwood in 1901. (EKB.)

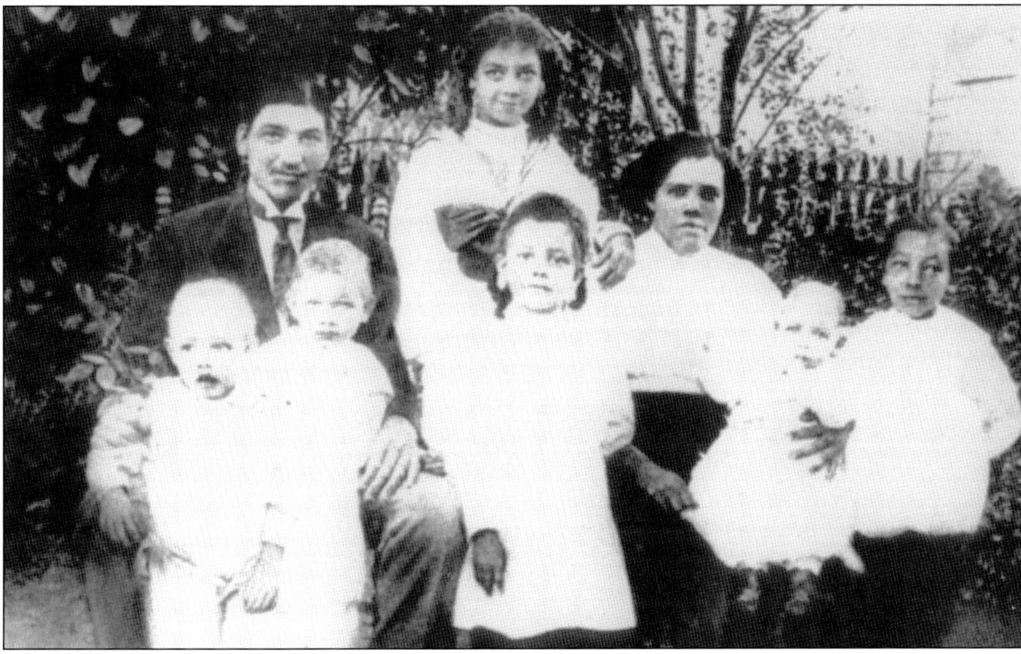

FAMILY OF JACOB KING, 1908. At 1046 Whittingham Place, six of the nine King children are pictured. From left to right are Jacob Jr., Jacob Sr., James, Eva, Callie, Mama Lucy holding Earl, and Leroy. Missing from the picture are Hugh, Esau, and Beulah (born in that order after this photograph was taken). King built the family house seen in the background. (EKB.)

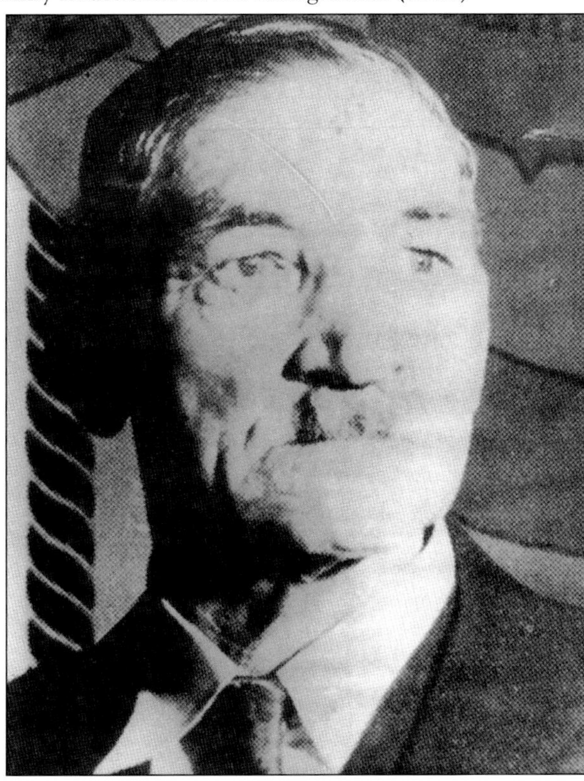

JACOB CHARLES KING SR., C. 1940. King was a self-taught contractor. He built many homes in Deanwood, including his residence—1046 Whittingham Place. He was an expert in building basements and moving homes on his flatbed truck to be installed on top of newly built basements. (EKB.)

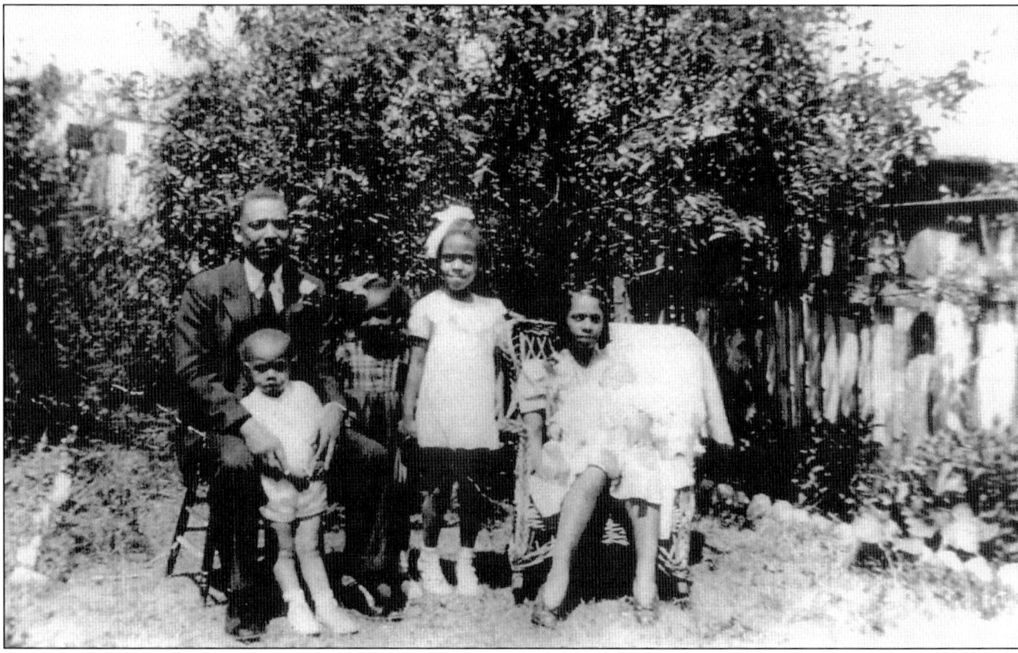

KING FAMILY HOMESTEAD, C. 1941. In keeping with a family tradition, Earl and Elizabeth King pose for their family picture at 1046 Whittingham Place. From left to right are Earl Sr. with Earl Jr., Elaine, Earlyne, and Elizabeth holding Ernest. Baby Edith completed the family two years later. (EKB.)

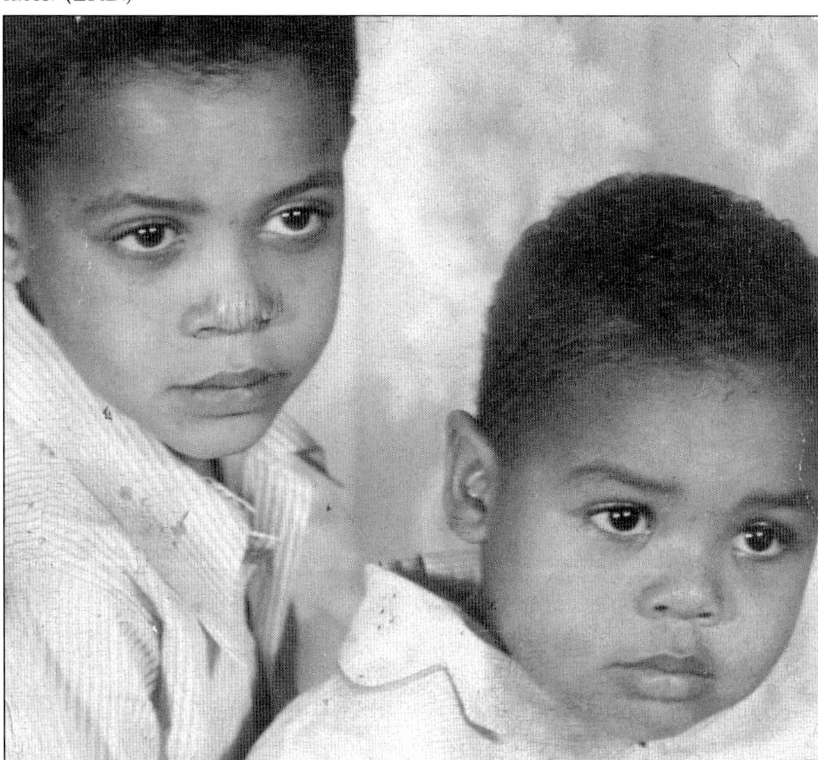

JOHNNY AND JERRY KING, C. 1949. Esau John "Johnny" King Jr. (left), age four, and younger brother Ricardo "Jerry" King, age two, look into the lens of their father's camera after getting all dressed up for a birthday party. Johnny, Jerry, Goldie, and Sylvia are the oldest children of Esau and Sarah King. The baby girl, Jackie, was born in the late 1950s. (Sylvia Brown.)

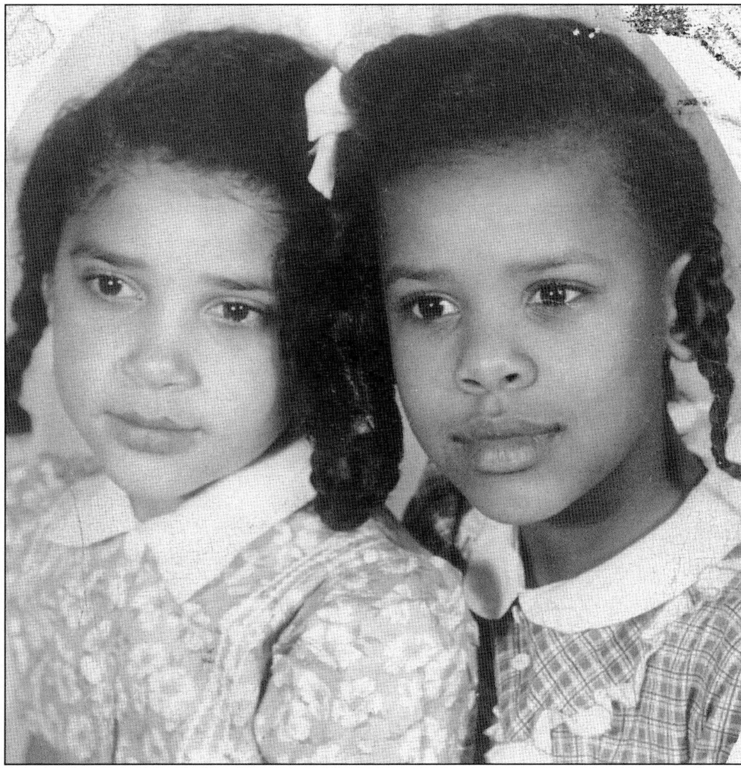

GOLDIE AND SYLVIA KING, C. 1949. Sisters Goldie (left), age 10, and Sylvia King, age 12, pose for their father. They attended George Washington Carver Elementary School (formerly Deanwood Elementary School). For generations, many siblings not only attended Carver together but also had the same teachers. (Sylvia Brown.)

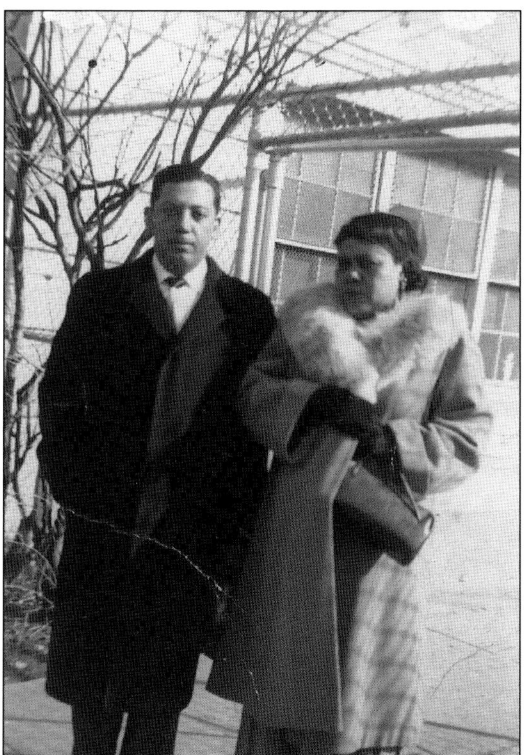

ESAU AND SARAH KING, C. 1951. In addition to homes, Deanwood Elementary School served as a popular backdrop for photographs among children and adults alike. Here Esau John King Sr. and his wife, Sarah Harrington King, stop to pose for a photograph on a beautiful fall day. (Sylvia Brown.)

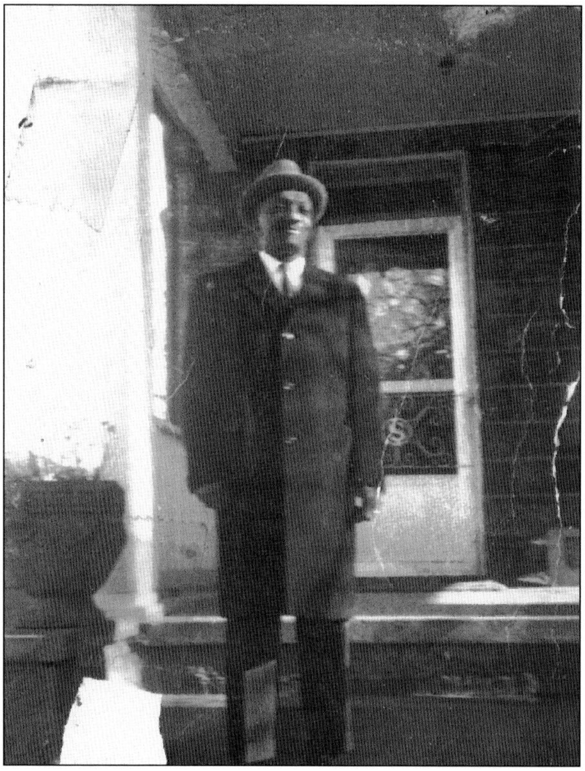

BERNARD C. LEVI, EARLY 1960S. Bernard Levi stands in front of his home at 1029 Forty-fourth Street, where he and his wife, Rosalie, raised their four children, Doris, Fannie, Bernard, and Ruth. The address was 1014 Franklin Street when the home was originally built by his wife's aunt, Fannie Sparrow. (Ruth A. Morrison Levi.)

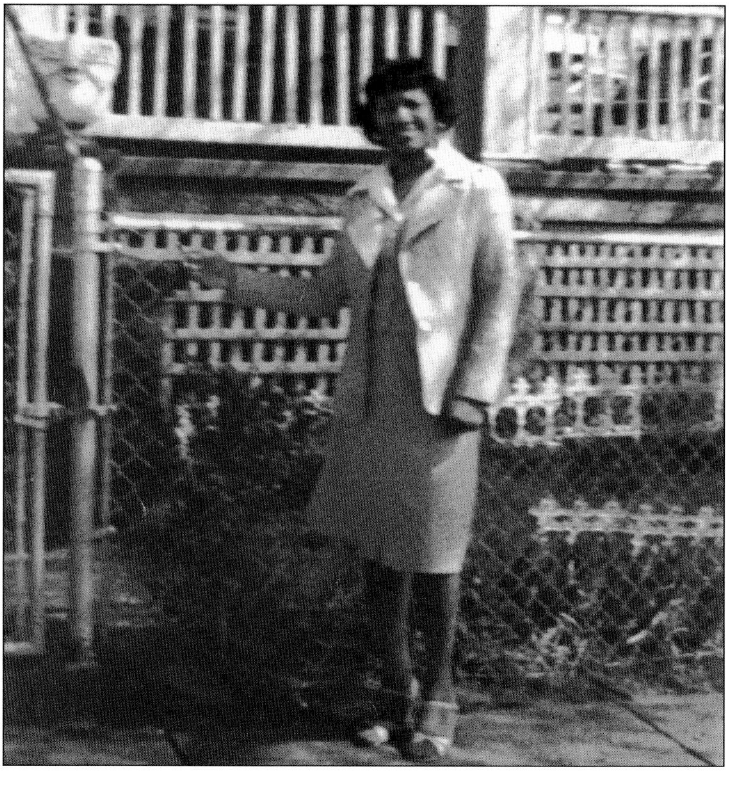

DORIS LEVI, EARLY 1960S. Doris's sisters, Ruth and Fannie, recall that their family never had to shop for fruit. They had a peach tree, a plum tree, and grapevines in their backyard, and they got cherries and pears from their neighbors' trees. Keeping with the community's rural roots, the family also kept a chicken and a rooster in their yard. (Ruth A. Morrison Levi.)

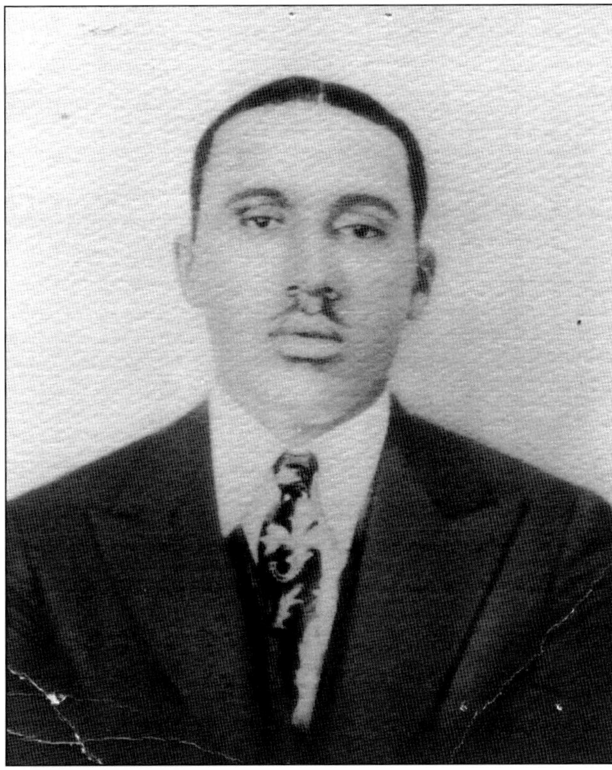

LOUIS JASPER LOGAN, 1936. Louis Logan moved into 1020 Browning Place with his wife, Ruth, in 1936. Logan was an accomplished brick mason and contributed to the masonry of many prominent buildings in D.C., including the National Catholic Shrine of the Immaculate Conception; the First Baptist Church of Deanwood; the Veterans Affairs Medical Center on Irving Street NW; the State Department; and Georgetown University Hospital. (Garland Logan.)

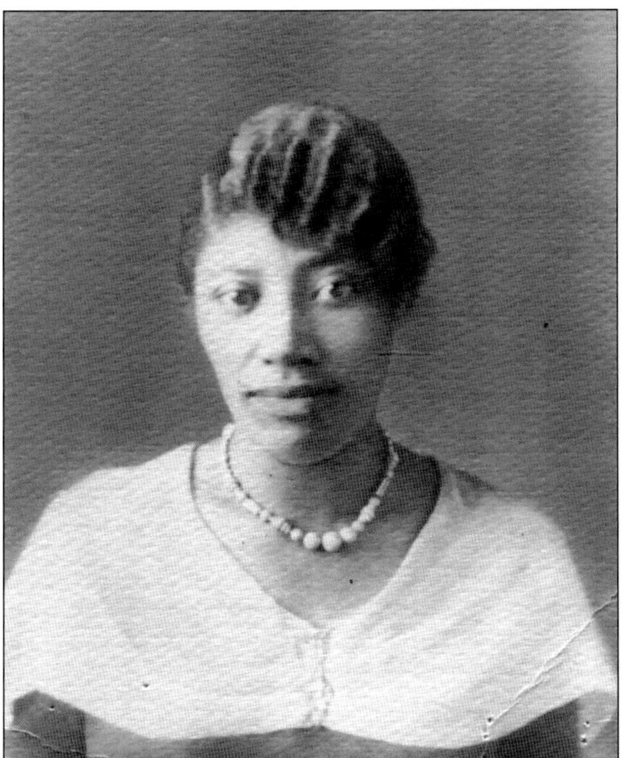

RUTH LOGAN, 1936. Ruth Mary Dickerson was introduced to Louis Jasper Logan by her cousin in 1926. The couple married on January 1, 1936, and boarded a train to D.C. to begin their new life together right after their wedding dinner. They raised four children in Deanwood: daughters Omega and Nancy and sons Garland and Kenzel. (Garland Logan.)

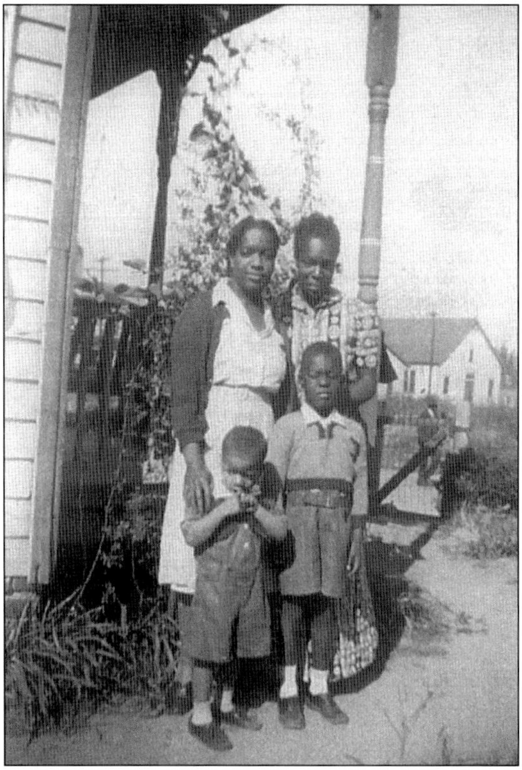

MILLER FAMILY, C. 1938. On the side of the porch at 4601 Kane Place, Arena Donahoo Leppard (left) and Josephine Miller are pictured with little Theodore Alfred Adams (left) and Henry Miller. Both Arena and her nephew Henry were born in the house, which Joseph Henry Donahoo, Arena's father, had built around 1912. (AM.)

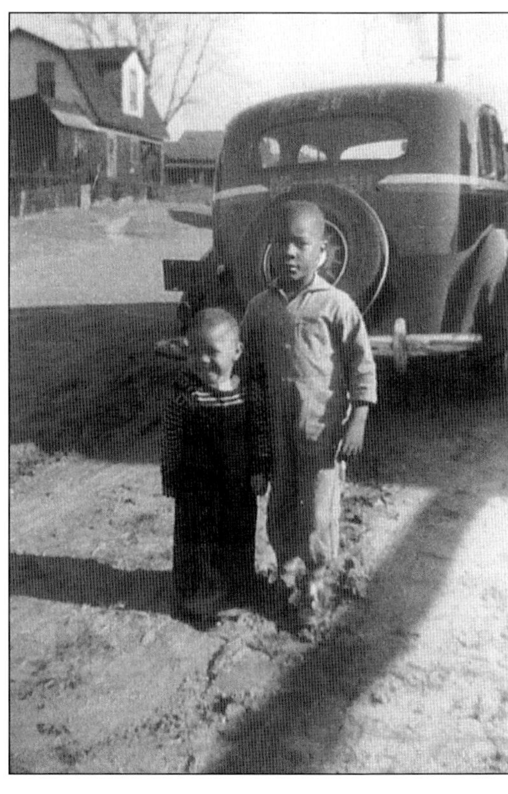

MILLER BOYS, C. 1938. Here little guys Theodore Alfred Adams (left) and Henry Miller take more pictures in front of their Kane Place home. All dressed up for an occasion with their family, the boys stand behind Henry's uncle's cab. The Turner family homestead, 1000 Westford Street (now Forty-seventh Street), can be seen in the background. (AM.)

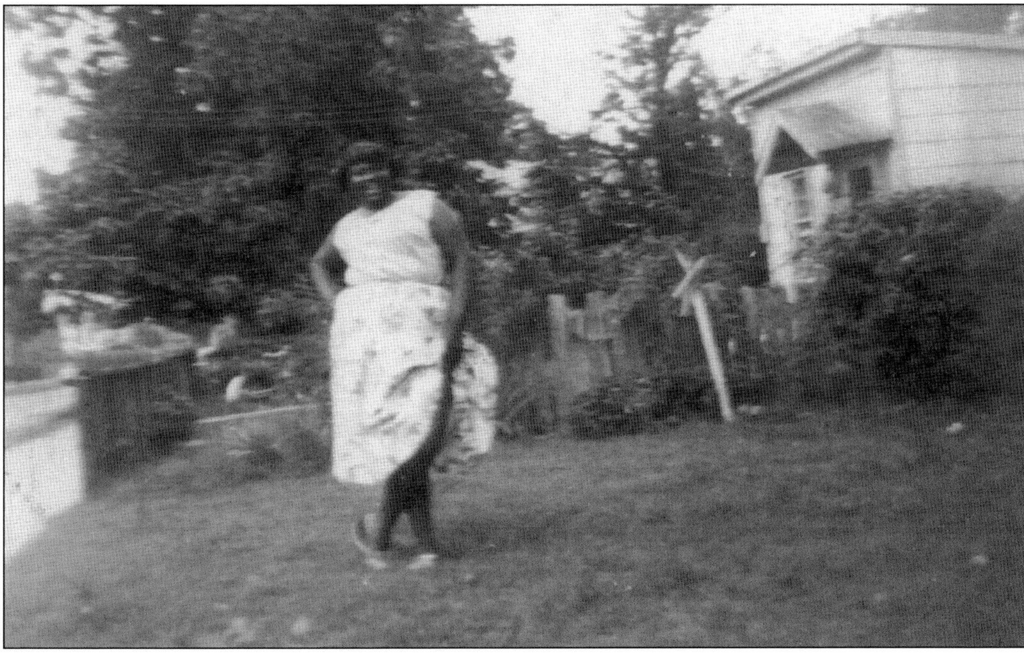

BARBARA MOORE, 1956. Residents loved to get together and have a good time. Barbara J. Moore poses in front of the home of her friend Pearl Howard at 1031 Browning Place before going to a cookout. In the background is the home of another friend, William D. Berkley, at 1035 Browning Place. (Barbara J. Moore.)

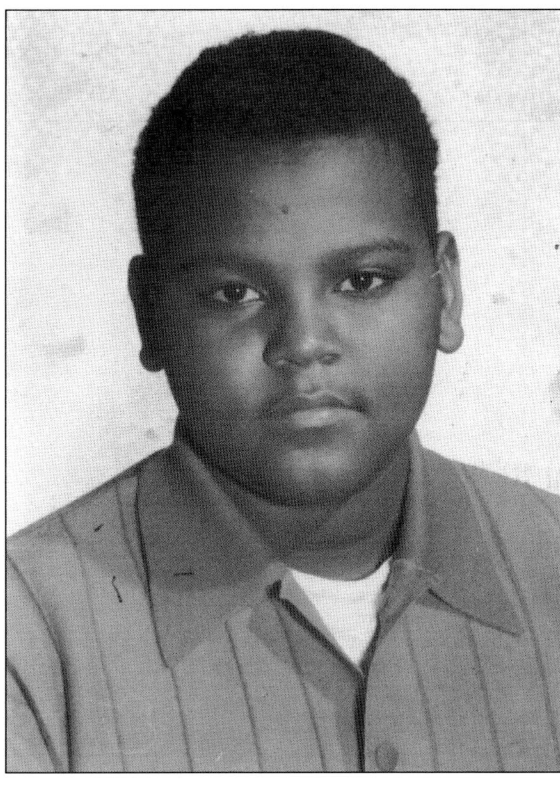

JUAN H. GADDIS, C. 1972. There was no junior high school in the neighborhood when Juan's mother, Barbara Moore, was growing up, so she attended Browne Junior High School at 850 Twenty-sixth Street. However, when Juan came of age, Deanwood could boast two junior high schools—Kelly Miller and Roper. Juan attended Roper, where he took this picture in the eighth grade. (Barbara J. Moore.)

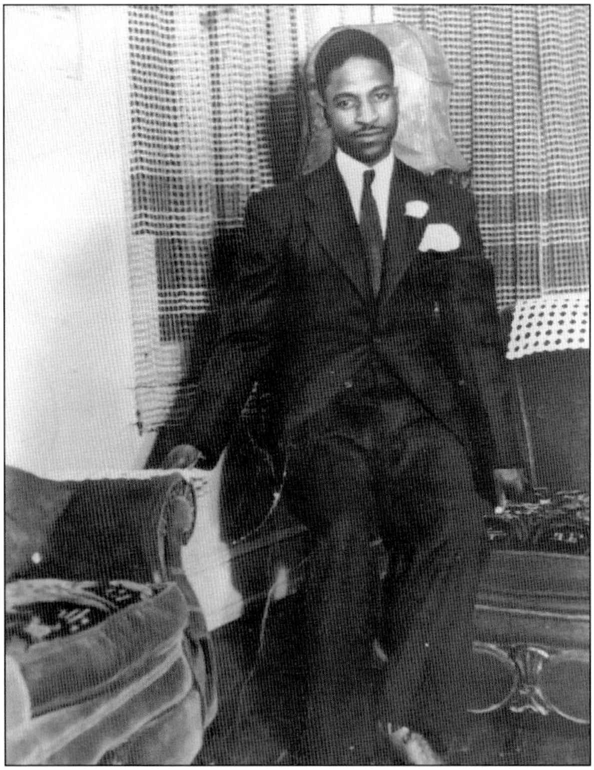

HENRY PARKER, 1940S. The Parker family owned many businesses in the neighborhood. Over the years, Henry Parker, the patriarch of the family, drove a cab, delivered ice and coal, operated a garage, and opened a filling station and grocery store in Deanwood. Here Parker is seen in his home at 4622 Clay Street. (R.P.)

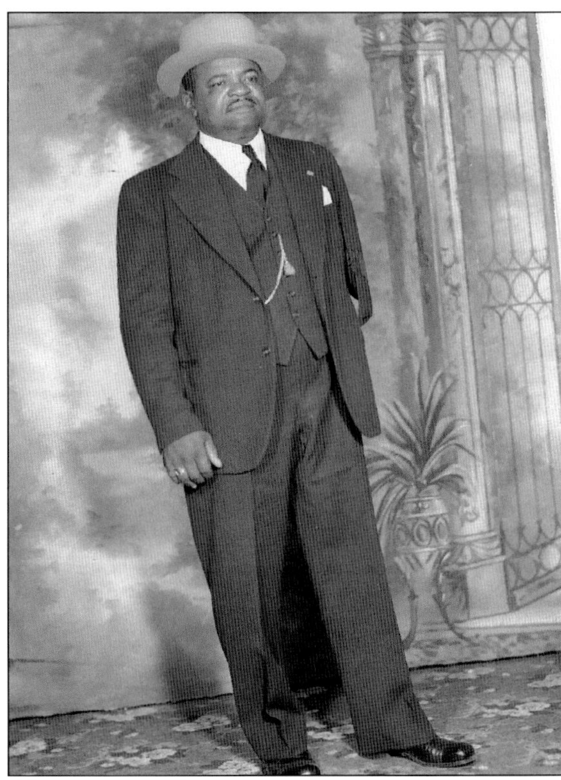

RALPH W. PLUMMER, 1930S. Ralph W. Plummer built his home in Deanwood in the 1920s. At the time, he lived in the Ivy City neighborhood and walked to Deanwood each week to store his building materials in a shed he erected on the property. He lost his arm after being struck by a car and modified his tools so that he could continue to work. (Tonya Talley Smith.)

Irene "Peggy" Plummer, 1930s. Ralph W. Plummer's wife, Peggy, was very active in her church and community. In the fall of 1929, she organized the Nurse's Unit of the First Baptist Church of Deanwood. Nurses provided comfort and aid to parishioners during worship services and supported the community during World War II by acting as air raid wardens and volunteering in local hospitals. (Tonya Talley Smith.)

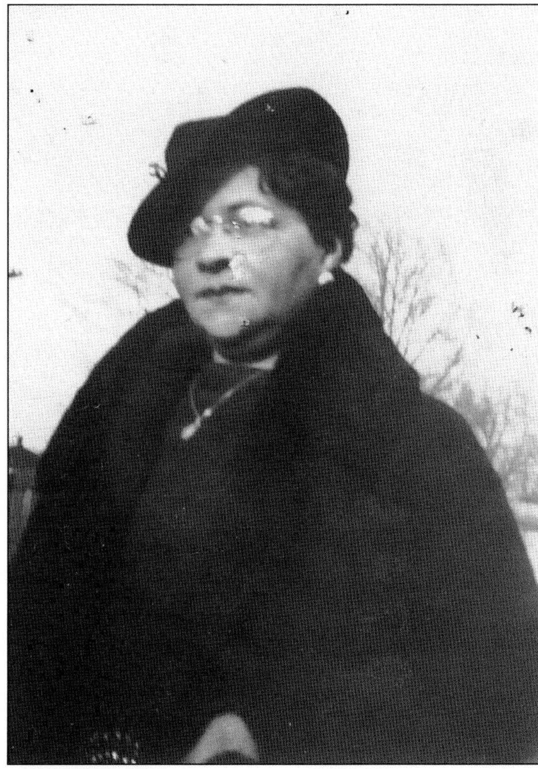

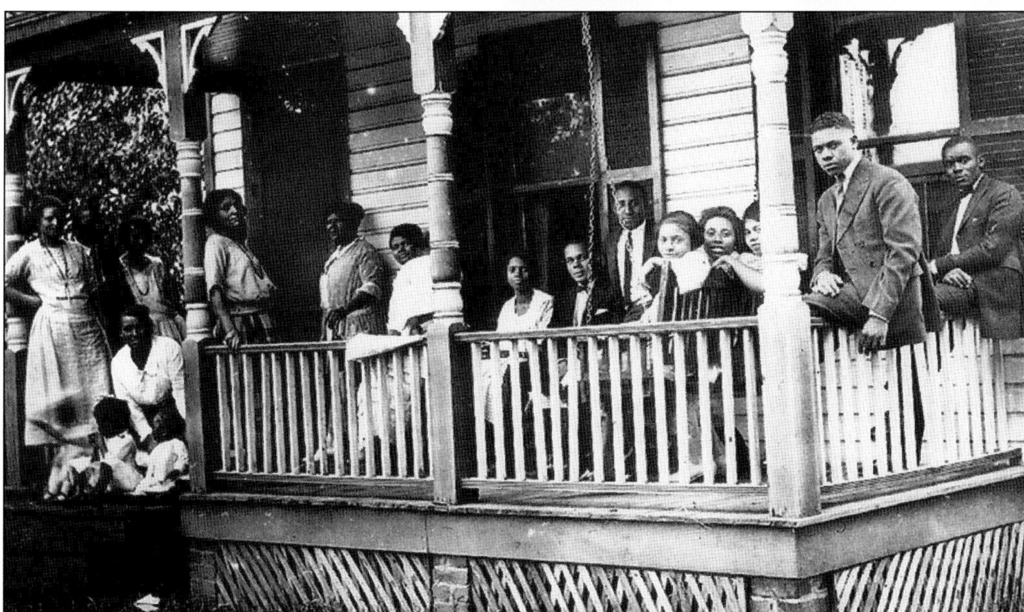

Shumate Family Homestead, c. 1930s. Like many Deanwood families, the Shumate clan has roots in the South. The patriarch of the family, Joseph Shumate, was from Meridian, Mississippi. After marrying Margaret Williams, they started their family in Deanwood and built this home at 4818 Jay Street around 1912. The Shumate family continued to live and grow in the community for generations. (WF.)

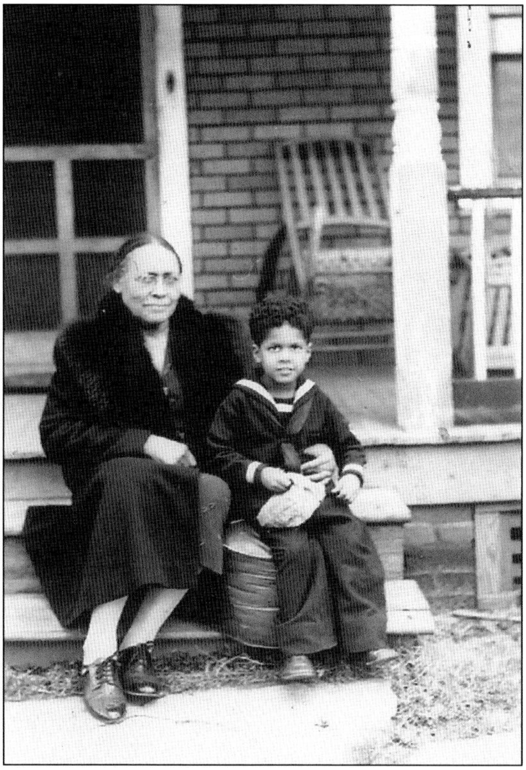

MARGARET SHUMATE, C. LATE 1940S. Joseph and Margaret Shumate had five girls: Clara, Bertie, Lela Mae, Clarice Melissa, and Josie Edwina. Bertie married Holley Reginald Wells in 1919 and had three children: Marguerite Wells, Holley Reginald Wells Jr., and Elmer Wells. Marguerite's son, Arthur DeMouy, sits on the porch of 4818 Jay Street with his great-grandmother. (WF.)

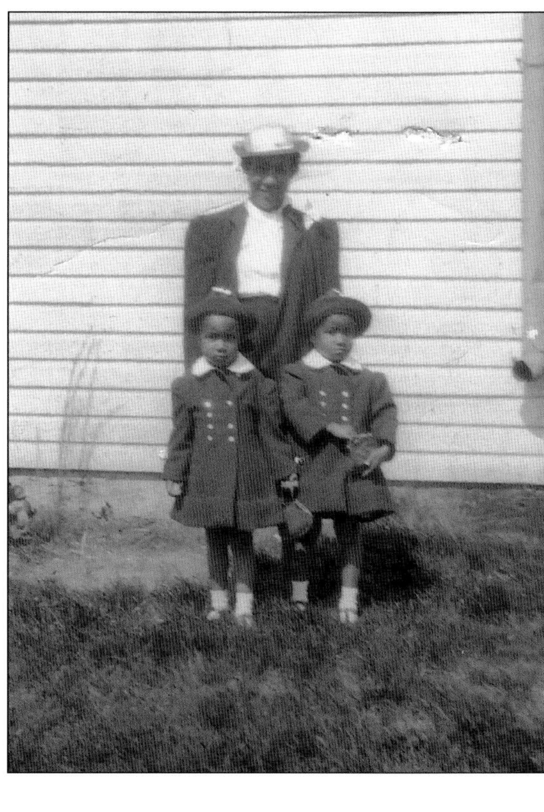

SLADE FAMILY, C. 1941. Deanwood had very few twins to boast about, so everyone looked forward to watching the Slade twins, Joan (left) and June, grow up. No one wanted to miss seeing the cute outfits their mom, Ruth, planned for a day out. Here the family poses outside of Contee African Methodist Episcopal Zion Church on Easter Sunday. (Joan Slade Gray.)

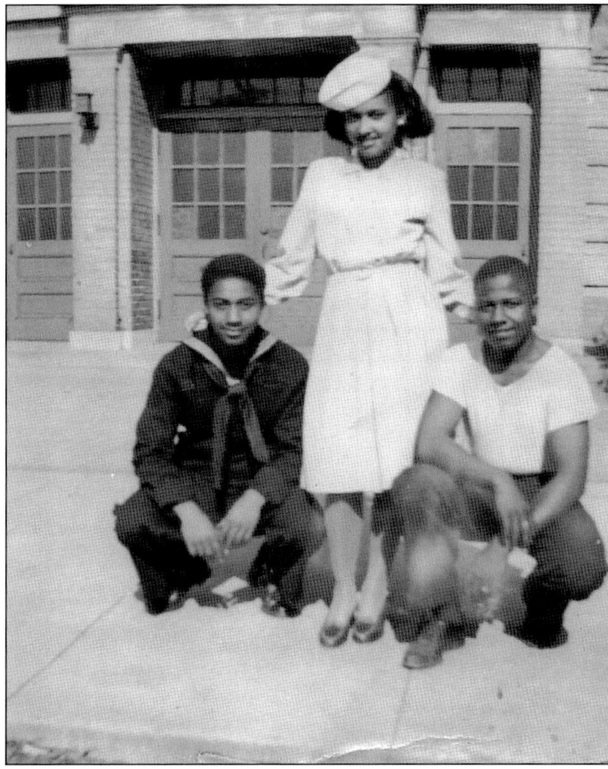

KATHERINE STOKES, C. 1947. Katherine Stokes grew up at Fifty-fifth and Blaine Streets but spent much of her free time with her best friend, Pearline Harvard, whose family lived across the street from Deanwood Elementary School. Here she poses with Pearline's cousin Cleotus Johnson (right) and Mitchell Dorsey. (Katherine Stokes.)

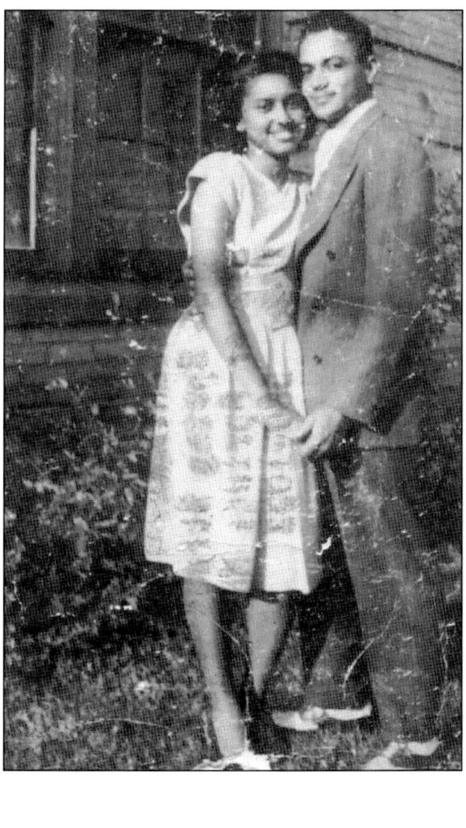

KATHERINE STOKES AND KENNER CHATMON, JUNE 1947. Deanwood School serves as the backdrop for Katherine to pose with her fiancé, Kenner Chatmon. The couple married in 1948, after she graduated from Howard University's dental hygiene program. They lived with her parents on Fifty-fifth Street for the first few years of their marriage, until they saved enough money to build a home of their own. (Katherine Stokes.)

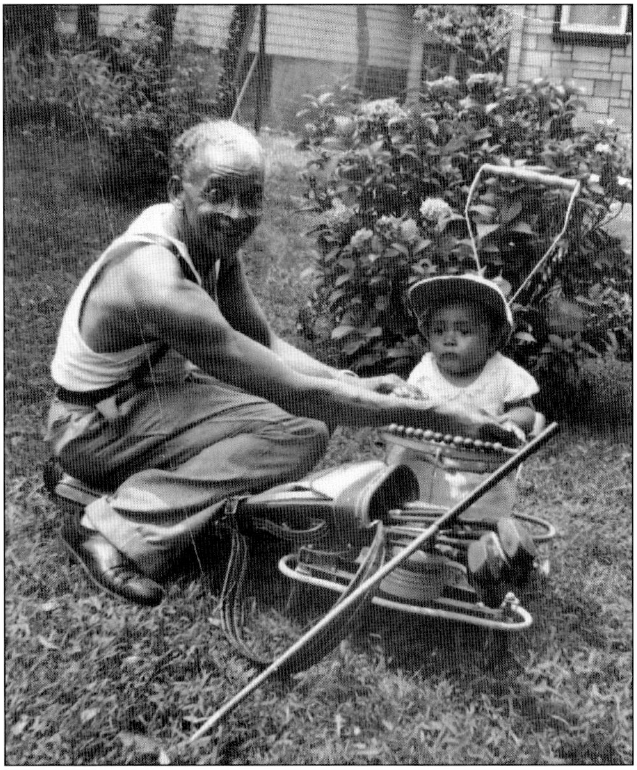

Proud Grandpa, c. 1951. Katherine Stokes's father, William Henry Stokes, sits with his granddaughter, Kendra Chatmon. The two are seen in their backyard at 309 Fifty-fifth Street. Stokes and his wife, Hazel, built their home around 1920. They smile as Kendra's father rests his golf clubs on her 1951 model baby stroller. (Kendra D. Chatmon.)

Kendra and Pete, c. 1952. Kendra Chatmon represents a third generation of the Stokes family to live in Deanwood. She and her father's hunting dog, Pete, play in the yard of her grandparents' home. Many families had rural, Southern roots, and hunting was a popular pastime among the men. (Kendra D. Chatmon.)

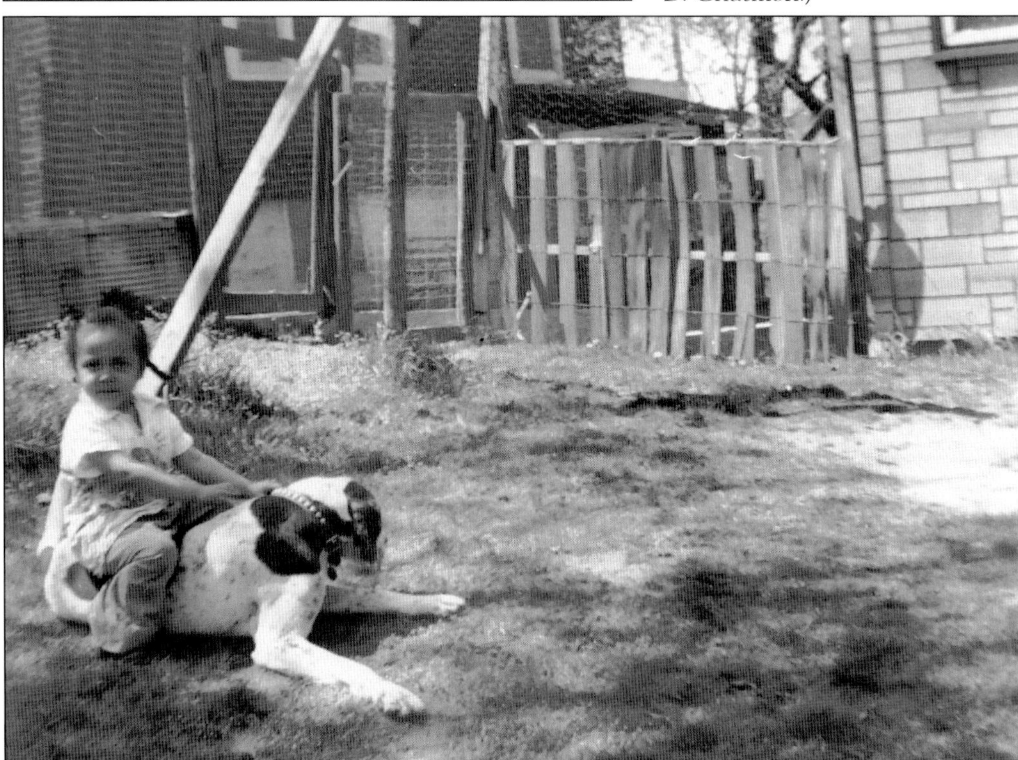

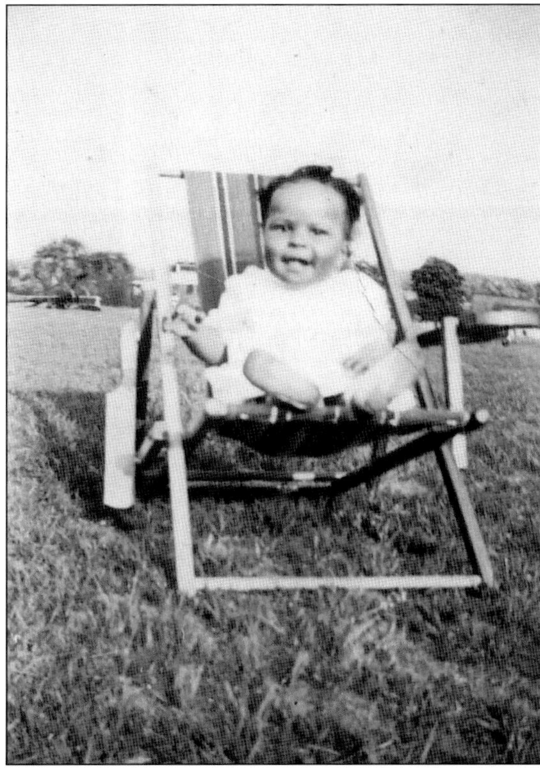

DORIS TAYLOR, C. 1934. Baby Doris smiles for the camera in her parents' yard at Fifty-first and Lee Streets. William and Grayce Taylor moved to Deanwood in the late 1920s, where they raised Doris and her brother, Charles. Both Doris and Charles attended Carver Elementary School. Afterward Doris went on to become a member of the first graduating class of Merritt School. (Doris Taylor-Collins.)

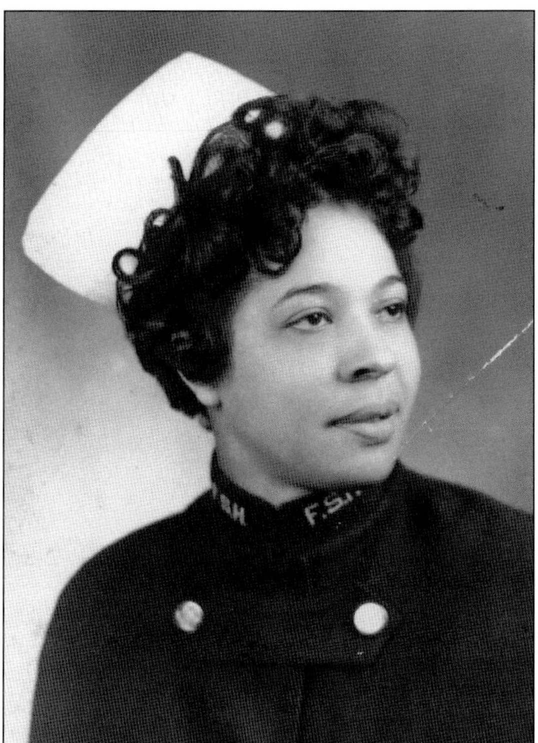

DORIS TAYLOR-COLLINS, C. 1963. All grown up and well into her chosen profession as a public health nurse, Doris Taylor-Collins makes her family and community proud in her uniform. She served as a nurse practitioner with the D.C. Department of Public Health for 27 years. For 25 of those years, she worked as a clinic and school nurse, traveling to public schools throughout the city. (Doris Taylor-Collins.)

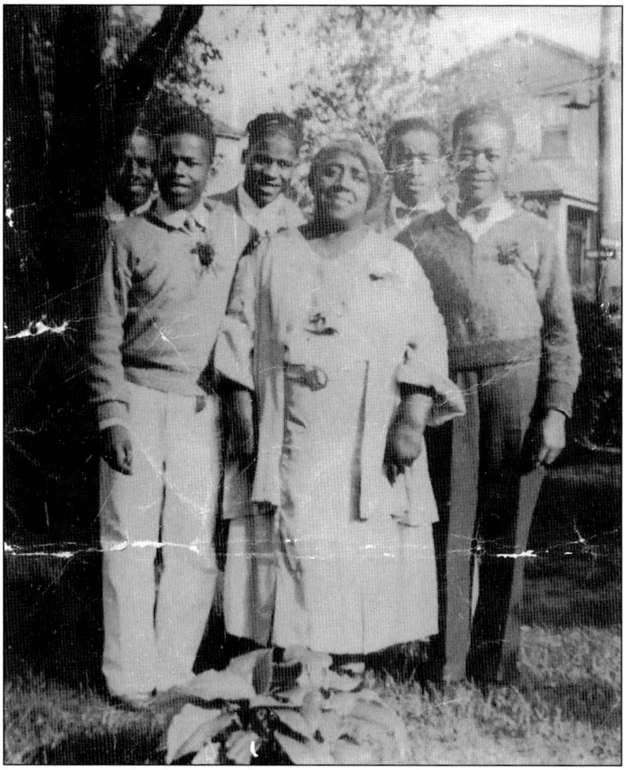

Jennie Turner and Sons, c. 1936. The Turner brothers pose in front of the family home at 1000 Westford Place (now Forty-seventh Street) with their mother, Jennie Virginia Jones Turner, just before departing for an evening activity at First Baptist Church of Deanwood. From left to right are Clarence II, Herbert, Reginald, Jennie, Thomas, and future Tuskegee airman Andrew. (Barbara Turner Botts.)

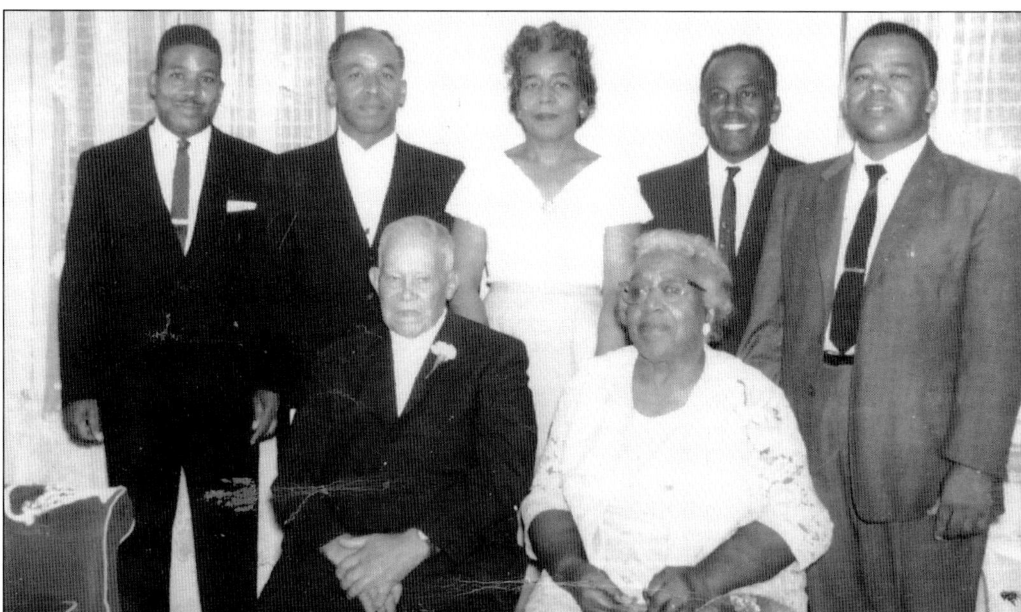

Clarence Turner Sr. Family, 1960s. Seated here are Rev. Clarence Turner Sr. and his wife, Jennie Jones Turner. The Turners were pillars of the Deanwood community and raised their children to continue this legacy. As adults, the Turner children became business owners and civic leaders in the community. Standing in their parents' home are, from left to right, Reginald, Thomas, Ella, Clarence Jr., and Herbert. (Barbara Turner Botts.)

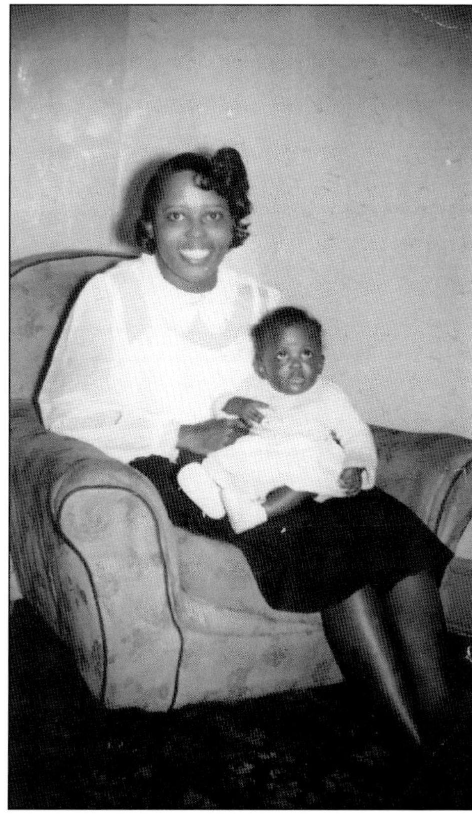

ANGELA AND DIANE TURNER, C. 1953. Angela Turner's parents, James and Harriet Slaughter, moved to Deanwood from Charlottesville, Virginia, in 1929. James was a cement finisher and came to D.C. to find greater opportunity. They raised their family at 4714 Sheriff Road. While growing up in Deanwood, Angela met Thomas Sheridan Turner and married him in 1937. (Barbara Turner Botts.)

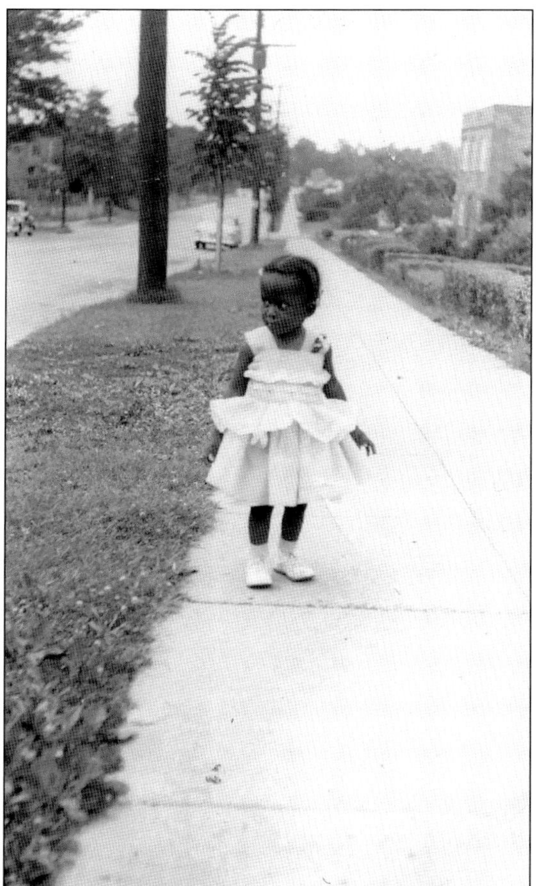

DIANE TURNER, C. 1954. Angela and Thomas Sheridan Turner had three daughters, Shirley, Barbara, and Diane. Growing up, Angela's mother made clothes and dressed her and her sisters alike. Angela continued this tradition with her daughters and made beautiful clothes for them. Diane Turner graces the sidewalk "runway" in front of her family home at 1024 Forty-ninth Street wearing a party dress made by her mother. (Barbara Turner Botts.)

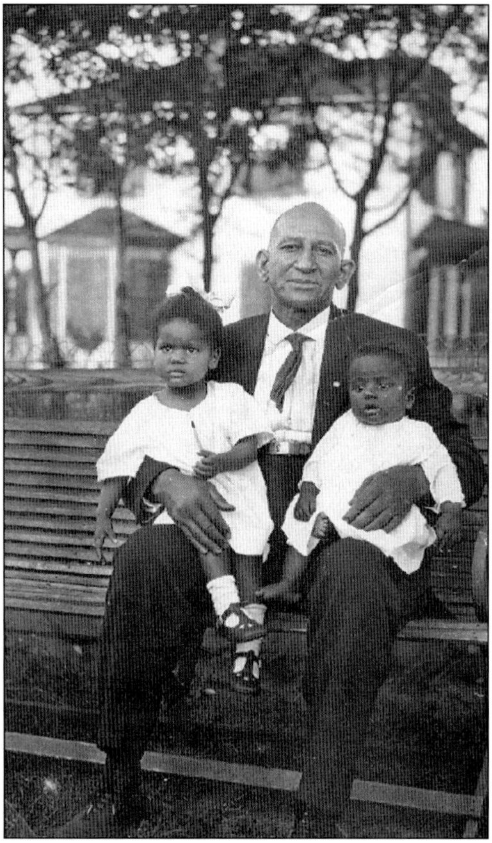

ANDERSON WELLS, C. 1923. H. Reginald Wells's father, Anderson, came to Washington, D.C., from Henton, West Virginia, to visit his son and his family. He holds his grandchildren Marguerite (left) and H. Reginald Wells Jr. while relaxing in the yard of his in-laws at 4818 Jay Street. (WF.)

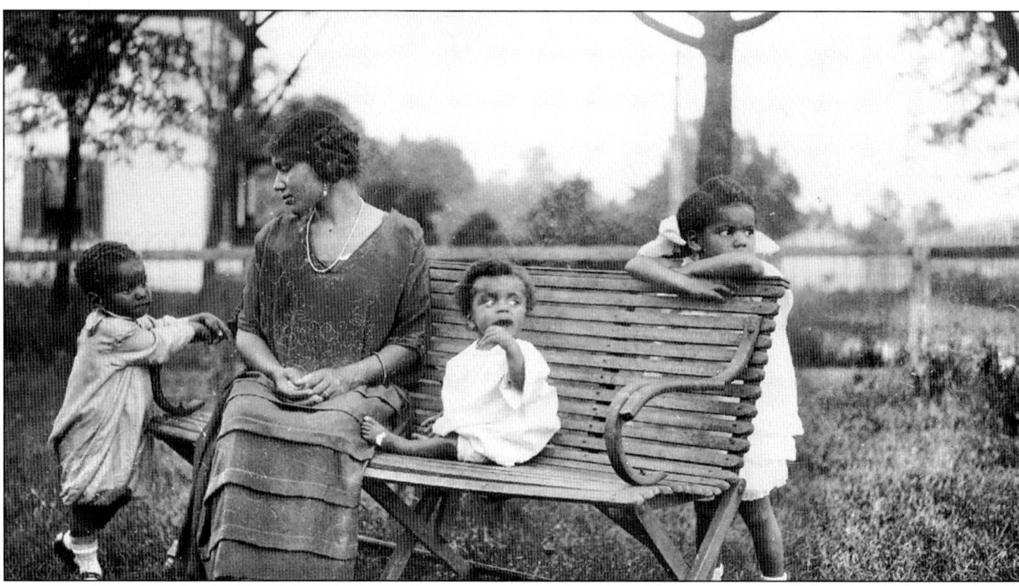

BERTIE SHUMATE WELLS, C. 1925. Bertie Shumate Wells and her husband, H. Reginald, built their house at 4831 Jay Street in 1926, right up the street from Bertie's aunt Esther's house, where the couple first met. They had three children (from left to right), Holley Reginald Jr., Elmer, and Marguerite. (WF.)

Three

Earning Our Daily Bread

In addition to creating a family-like feel among its residents, Deanwood's sense of being set apart may have also contributed to the strong sense of self-sufficiency that existed among its residents. Its distance from downtown kept it semi-rural until after World War II. The city government did not provide many services taken for granted in other parts of the District like paved streets, sewers, curbs, and sidewalks, which were not installed until the 1950s. However, conversations with longtime residents reveal that they never experienced a sense of lack, because everything they needed could be found in their own backyards.

Helen Hasty recalls that her great uncle, Frank Makel, who lived at 1121 Browning Place, owned a horse-drawn huckster wagon from which he sold fruits and vegetables. If residents wanted fish, "there used to be a fish man, Mr. Barber, that came to Deanwood every Friday to sell fish. As he drove slowly through the community, he would holler, 'Fresh fish and watermelons red to the rind.' " Many independent entrepreneurs conducted their business door-to-door and sold items such as clothes, ice, and coal and even offered knife and scissor sharpening.

Sheriff Road was one of the main business corridors of Deanwood and was home to many black-owned businesses and some operated by Jewish proprietors. One such store was Al and Ida Mendelson's Certified Market, located at 4401 Sheriff Road. Ida Mendelson also owned a hat store where the ladies went to purchase their hats for church. The Mendelsons later sold their grocery store and opened Murry's Steaks, which eventually became Murry's Family of Fine Foods, a mid-Atlantic chain. Like the Mendelsons, many other Jewish proprietors lived above their stores and were a part of the community.

Sandra Madden's recollections of her community in the 1940s and 1950s show that residents had access to goods and services relevant to almost every facet of life: "My father owned and operated the Madden Real Estate Company on Grant Street. We were a part of Deanwood's business district, which included besides us, a cleaners, beauty shop, grocery, mortuary, and pool hall."

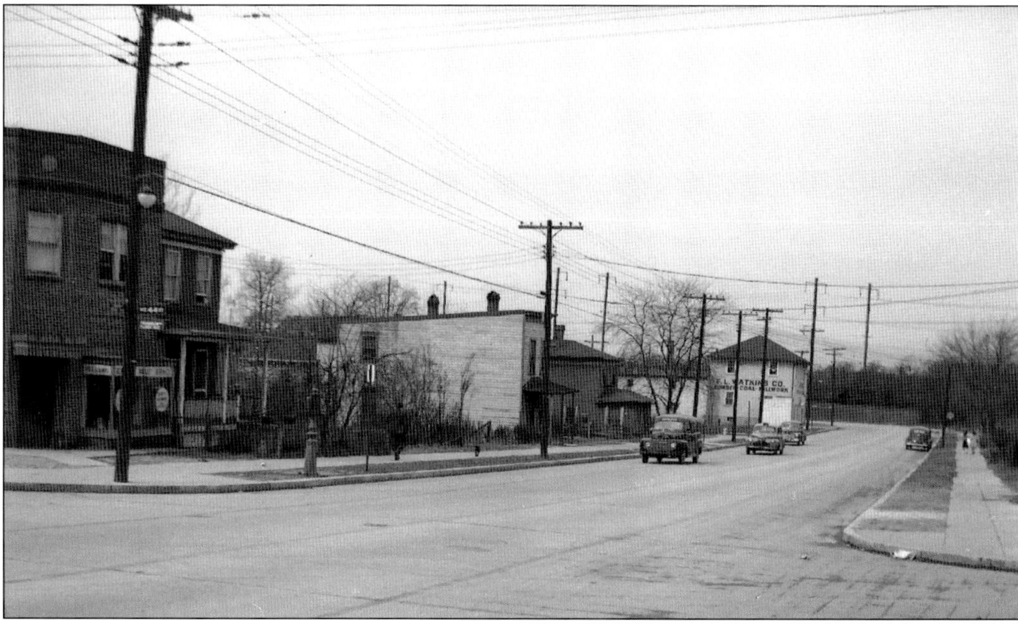

Sheriff Road, March 27, 1948. In the 1940s, people knew they had reached Sheriff Road, Deanwood's main street, when they saw F. L. Watkins and its yard full of lumber. When the train brought supplies, unloading it became a community affair. Another community anchor, Battle's Religious Book Store, was established a few doors up the road at 4311 Sheriff Road in 1961 by Lucious C. Battle. (JTWC, HSWDC.)

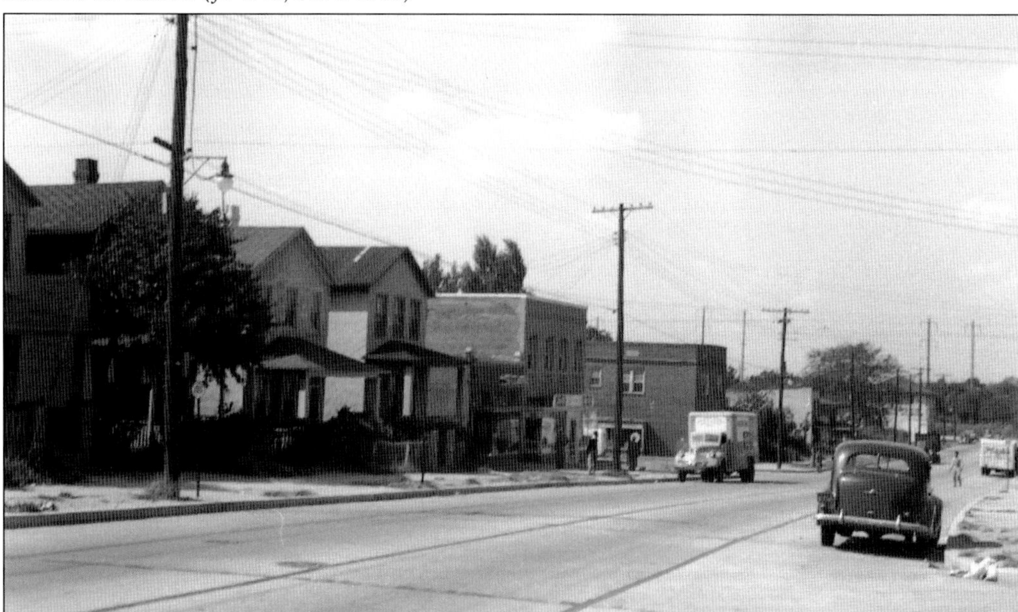

Sheriff Road, September 25, 1948. The street was a mixture of residences and small businesses. A closer look reveals 4401 Sheriff Road, the Certified Market (forerunner to Murry's Family of Fine Foods), and its refrigerated truck. Next door was Northeast Billiards (also known as the Deanwood Pool Hall), where numbers were played. Across the street was High's Dairy, a favorite for ice cream. (JTWC, HSWDC.)

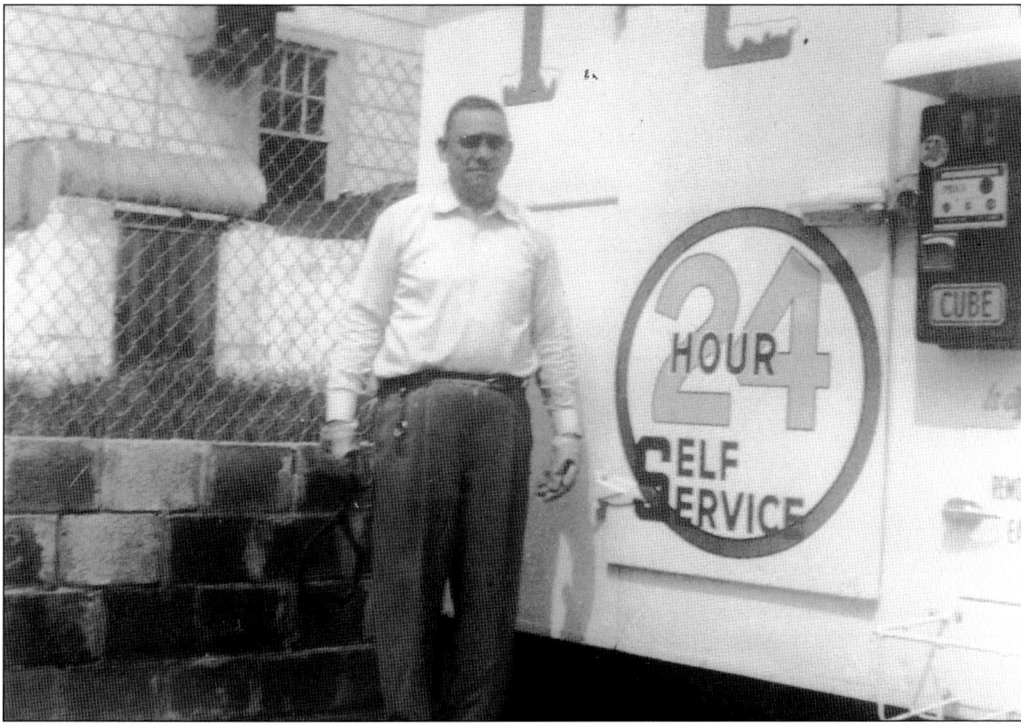

EARL E. KING SR., 1950. After starting his ice business in 1925, Earl King Sr. expanded it by buying and operating the first coin-operated ice machine east of the river. Here he proudly shows off his new 24-hour, self-service machine. Residents of the neighborhood knew they could always go to 4501 Sheriff Road to get their ice whenever they needed it. (Earlyne K. Turner.)

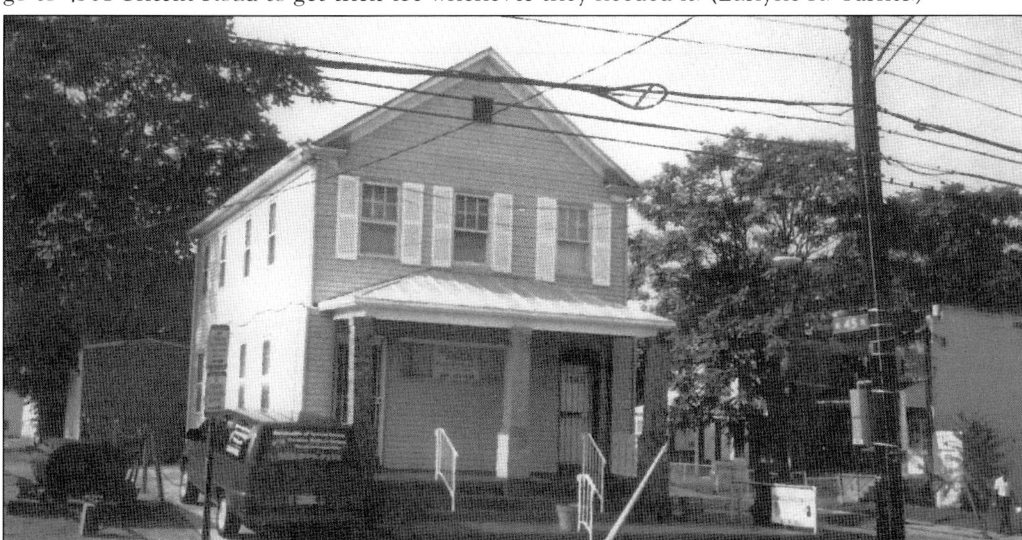

4501 SHERIFF ROAD, 2005. This building on the corner of Forty-fifth Street and Sheriff Road is a community business landmark. Many businesses have been housed there. From 1950 to 1958, it was the 4501 Soda Bar and Grill. Joe's Valet replaced it in 1959, and Mack's Shoe Shop operated there from 1965 to 1988. In 1990, Edith King Thomas opened Memorable Affairs, a party decorating business. (Edith King Thomas.)

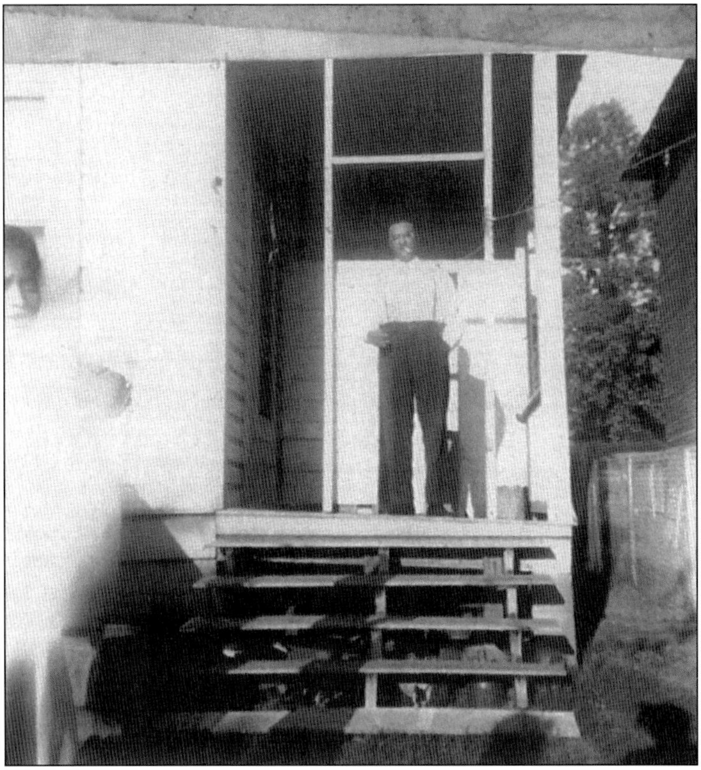

James Broadus, late 1940s. In the 1950s, Deanwood residents had beautiful wallpaper in every room. The neighborhood wallpaper hanger was James Broadus. He started his business in the 1940s and stayed in business until wallpaper became unpopular. Here he stands on his back porch at 908 Forty-fifth Place, where his daughter, Willestine, loved to spend her time playing jacks. (Annie Broadus Bailey.)

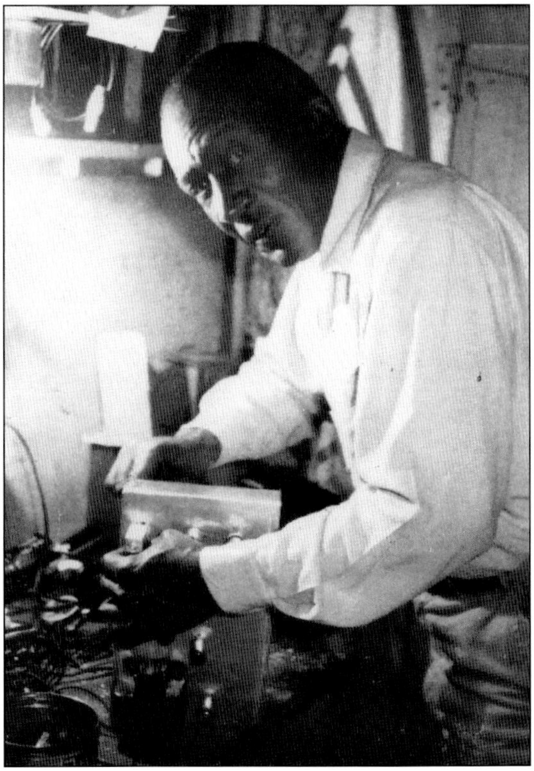

Edward L. Wright, c. 1960. Wright, a licensed citizen's band (CB) radio operator, was one of Deanwood's many expert craftsmen and independent businessmen. Because of segregation, licensed tradesmen among the "colored" citizens of Deanwood didn't exist. However, individuals continued to offer their services to neighbors and succeeded in many areas. Their work ethic and commitment represented what older residents say was the core of this community. (Jeanette Wright.)

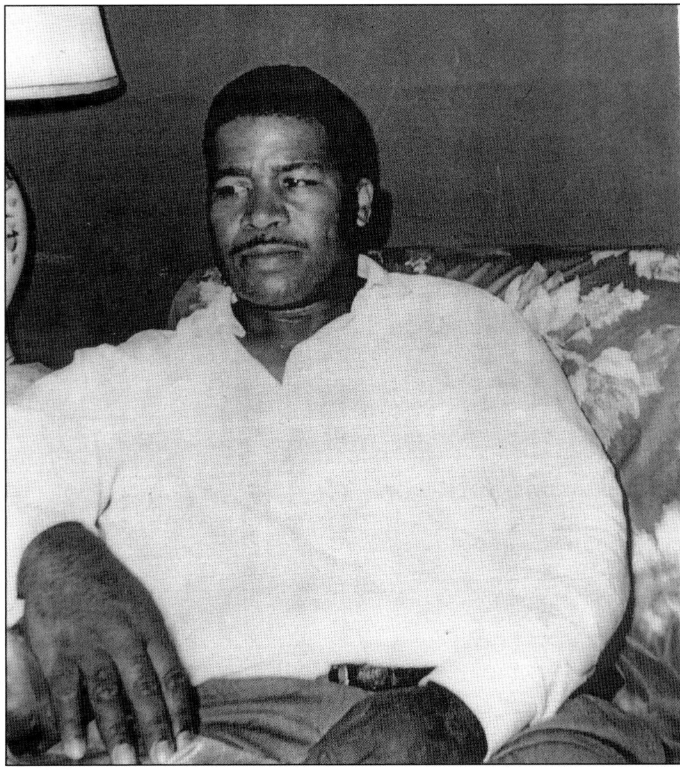

REGINALD TURNER, C. 1959. Reginald Turner owned and operated the first Laundromat in Deanwood, located at Forty-seventh Street and Sheriff Road. He was a pioneer in this business and was one of the first in the city to offer drop-off service. Many Deanwood residents dropped off their laundry before work and picked up clean, folded clothes the same evening. (Earlyne K. Turner.)

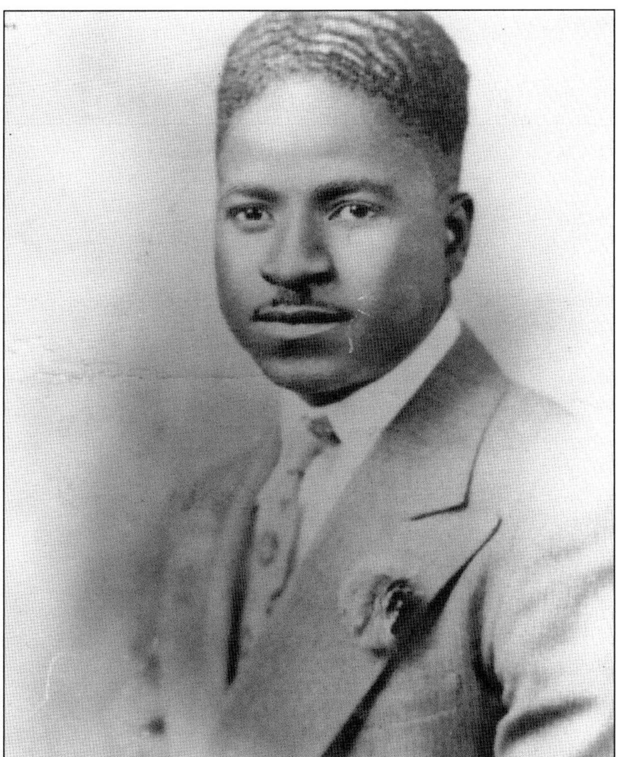

HENRY PARKER, 1940S. Henry Parker was a well-known entrepreneur in the community. He, his brother, and later his sons, Reginald and Irving Parker, operated many businesses that met the needs of Deanwood residents. The Suburban Market, located at 4600 Sheriff Road, has served the neighborhood for decades. (RP.)

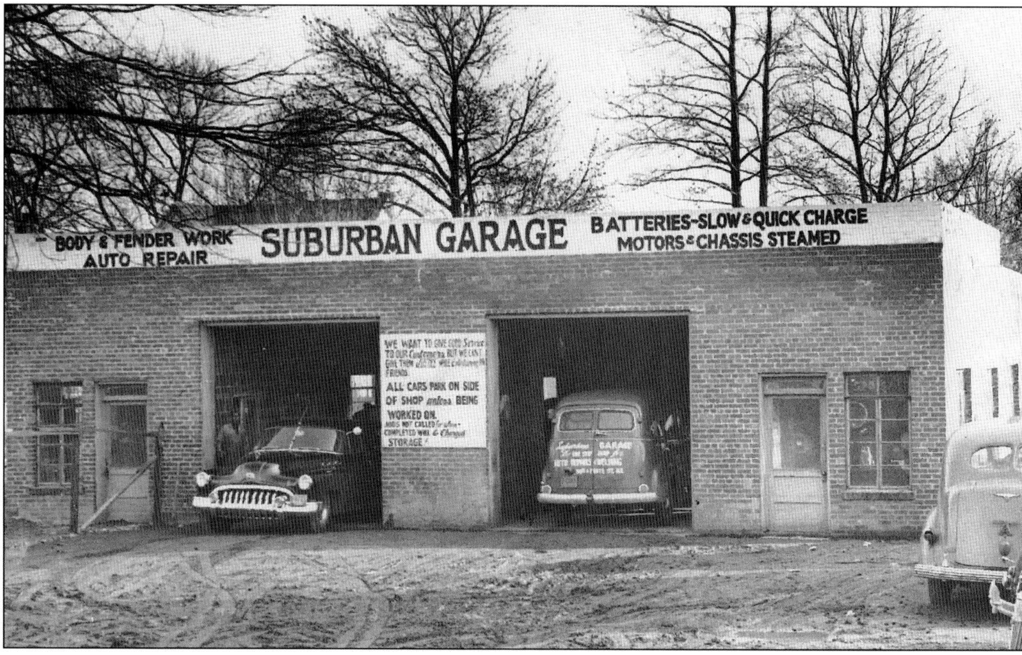

SUBURBAN GARAGE, 1950S. Henry Parker originally opened Suburban Garage for his brother, Virgil Parker, who acted as the head mechanic. Like many Deanwood residents, Henry Parker was all about family and also employed his brother-in-law, Bill Monday, as a mechanic. The garage, located at 1945 Dix Street, operated from 1945 to 1957. (RP.)

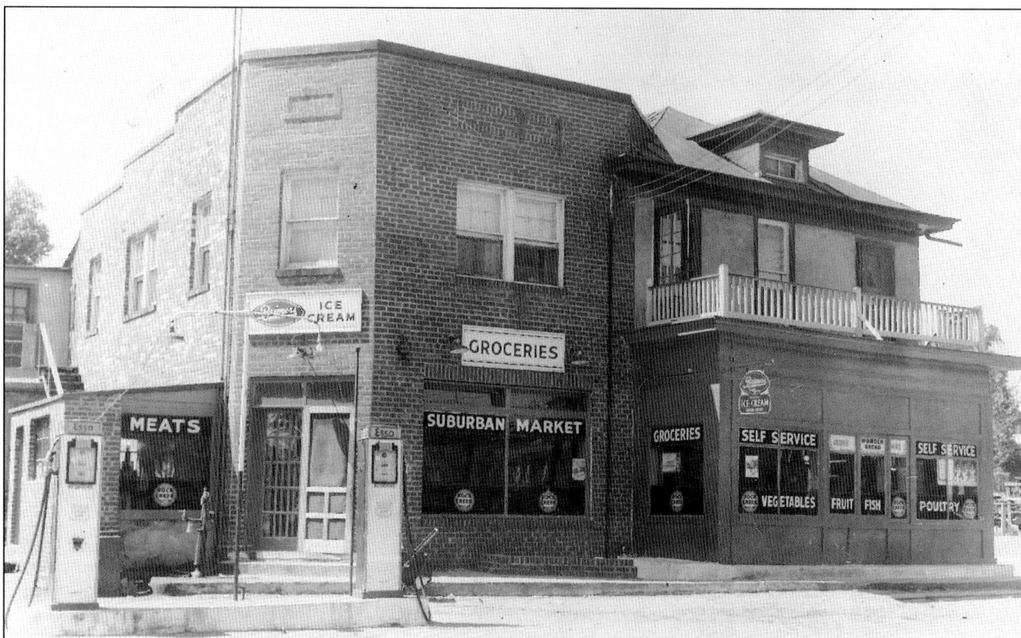

ORIGINAL SUBURBAN MARKET, 1940S. The original Suburban Market was a combination filling station and grocery store. It was located at Castle Place (now Forty-ninth Place) and Grant Street and operated for nearly two decades, from 1944 until 1963. When the land was sold, Henry Parker moved his business up the street to Sheriff Road. (RP.)

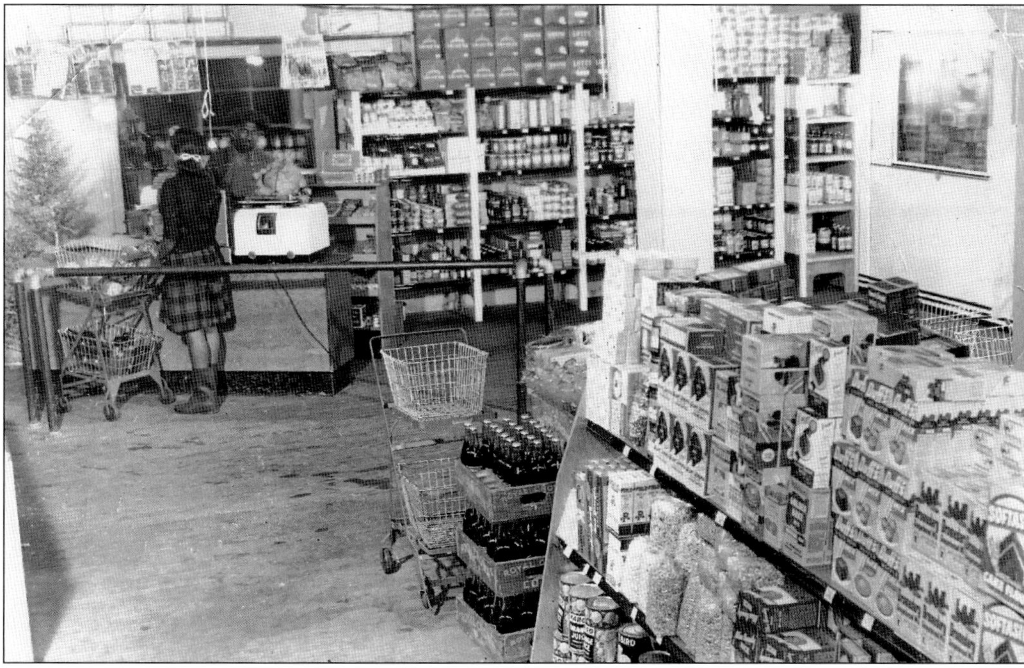

SUBURBAN MARKET, MID-1940S. Henry Parker serves his niece, Sarah Gay, at the counter of Suburban Market. As the interior shows, it was a full-service market. Community members could come to not only fill their gas tanks but also to purchase meats, canned goods, and supplies for their baking needs. (RP.)

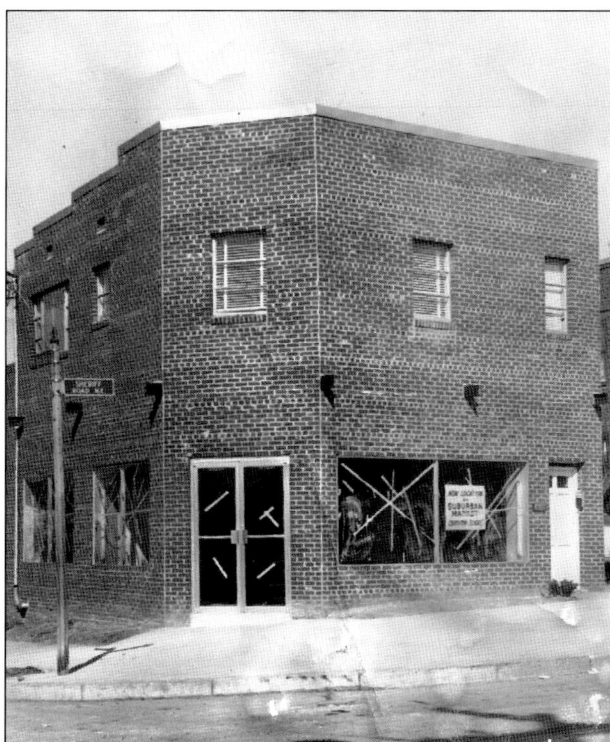

NEW SUBURBAN MARKET, C. 1962. When the land on which the original Suburban Market stood was sold, Henry Parker moved his business here to 4600 Sheriff Road. Many of the craftsmen from the neighborhood, including James Hall, Clinton Price, and Louis Logan, helped Parker to build his new store. (RP.)

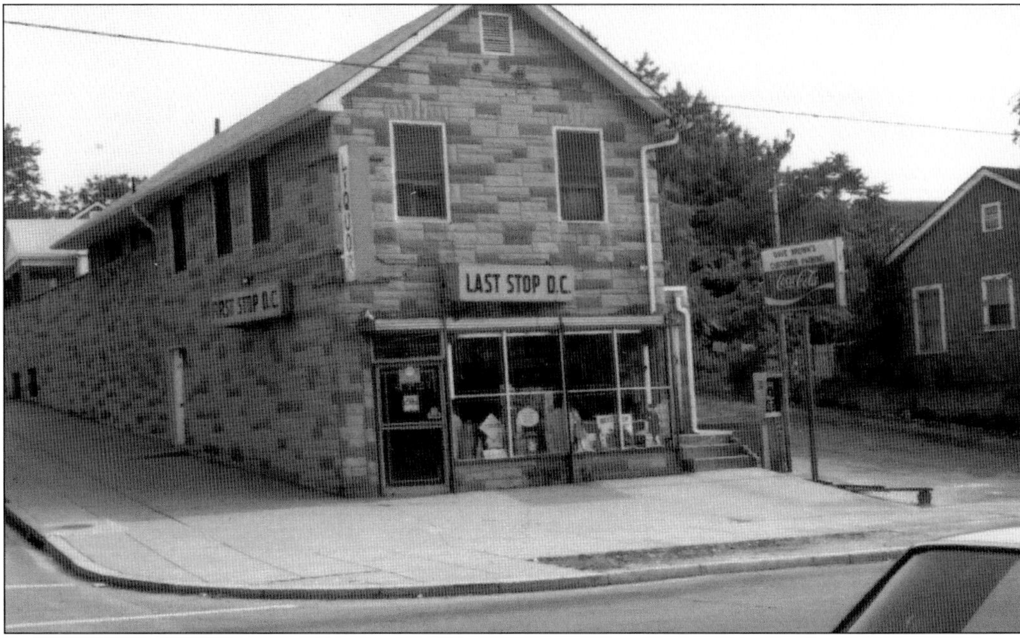

LAST STOP D.C., 1964. Dave Brown purchased his store in 1964. Brown wanted to own a business in the Deanwood neighborhood. He placed the sign "Last Stop" on the front of the building to alert passersby that it was the last stop for wine and spirits before they crossed into Maryland. (Kevin Brown.)

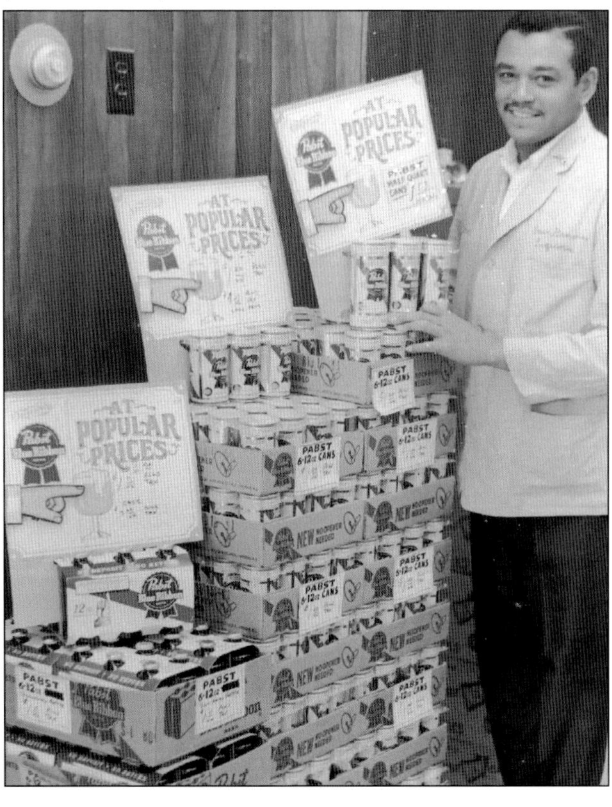

DAVE BROWN LIQUOR INTERIOR, 1969. Located at 4721 Sheriff Road, Dave Brown Liquor carried popular beverages of the day at competitive prices. It was frequented not only by Deanwood residents but also by motorists as they took Sheriff Road back to Maryland. It was truly a family affair, as sons Kevin and David came on board to help their father run the business. (Kevin Brown.)

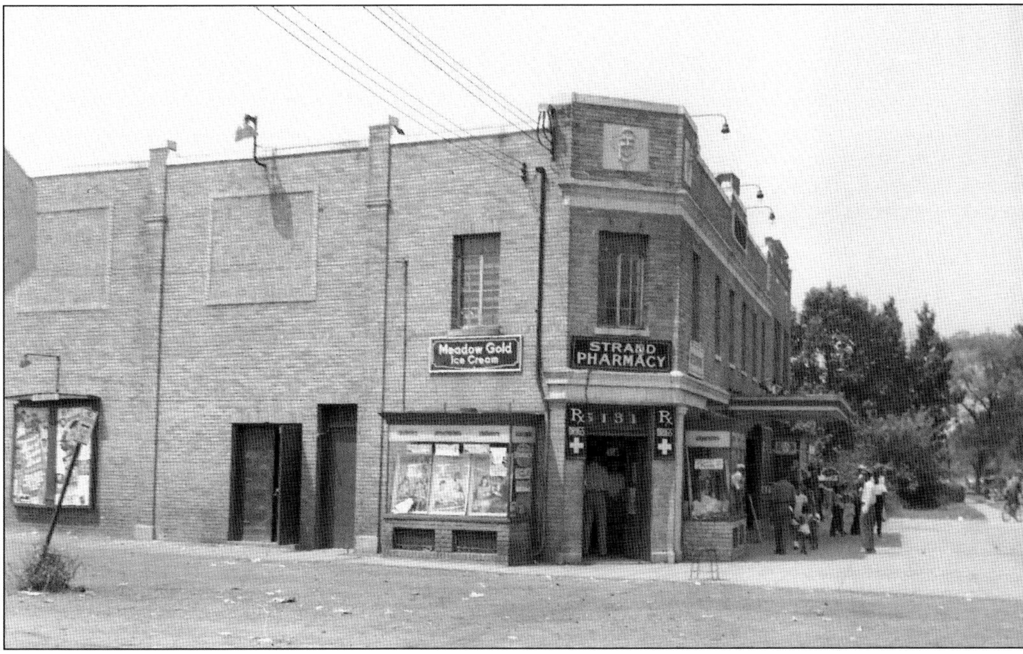

STRAND THEATER, AUGUST 8, 1948. In 1948, the Strand Pharmacy occupied the lobby of the Strand Theater, the first and only movie theater in Deanwood. This was convenient for patients visiting Dr. Wilbur F. Jackson, whose office occupied the top floor. Around the corner, patrons stand at the theater's box office to purchase their tickets. (JTWC, HSWDC.)

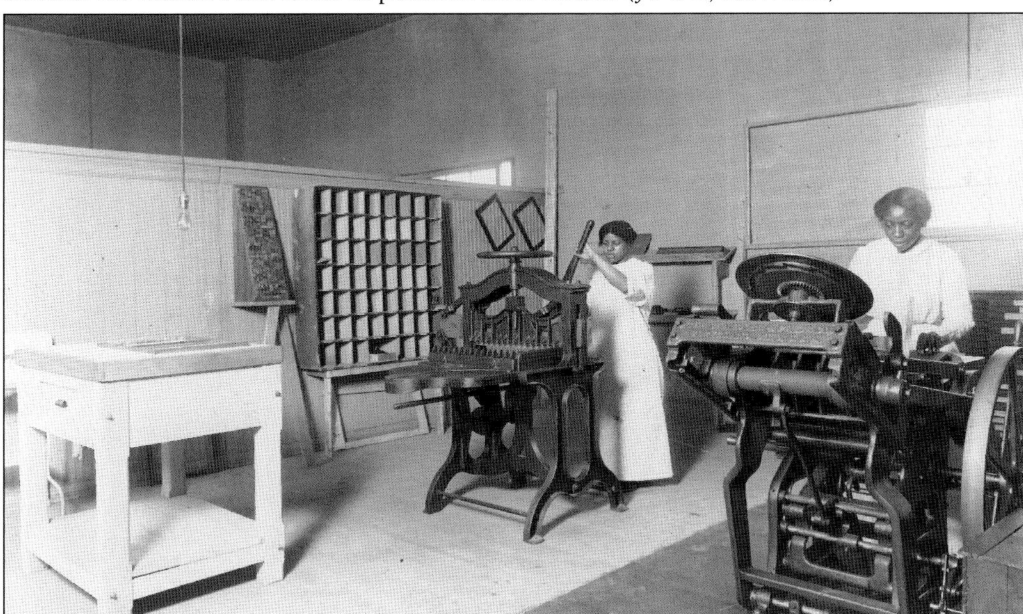

PRINT SHOP, C. 1910. When Nannie Helen Burroughs, educator and activist, was growing up, the majority of black women in cities worked as domestic servants. They maintained homes and performed what was considered unskilled labor and were paid low wages. Burroughs established the National Training School for Women and Girls to offer them professional training that might help them earn higher wages. Here students learn printmaking. (NHBS.)

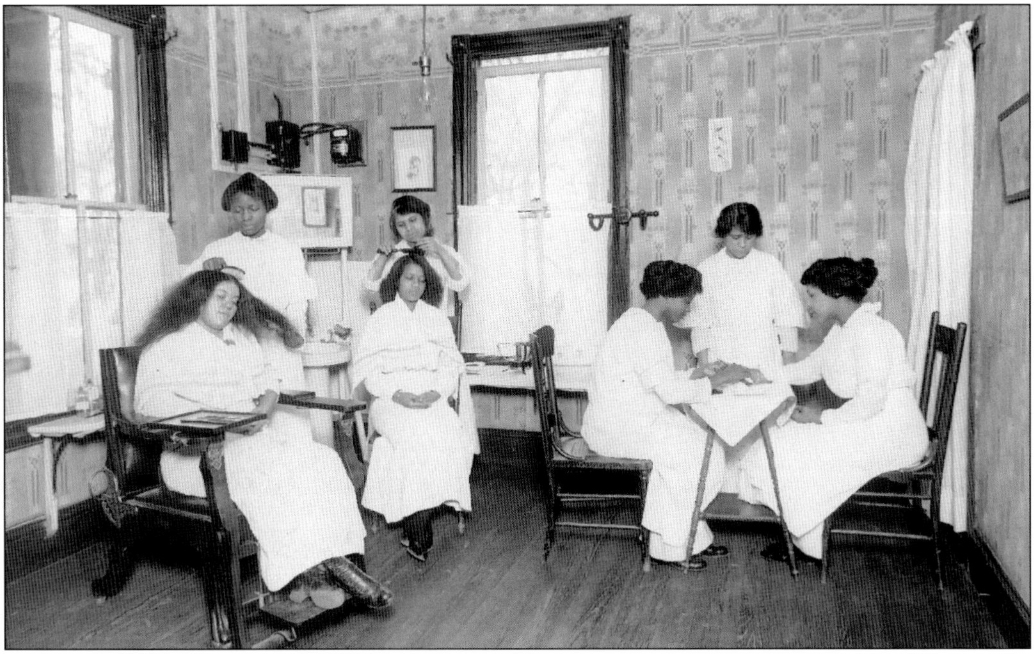

COSMETOLOGY CLASS, C. 1910. The school's first motto, "Work, Support Thyself, to Thine Own Powers Appeal," reveals the importance Burroughs's curriculum placed on the development of self-reliance and self-sufficiency. It is not surprising that she chose to locate her school in Deanwood, a community that shared these core values. Here students practice their hairdressing and manicuring skills on one another in preparation for becoming cosmetologists. (NHBS.)

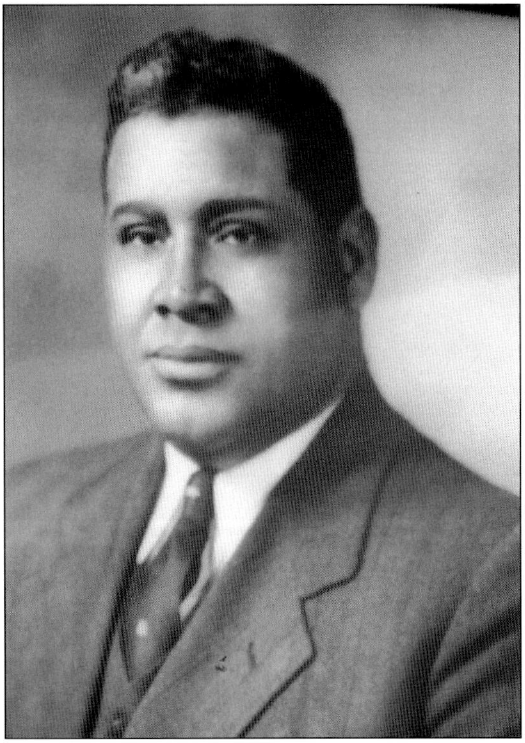

REV. HENRY S. WASHINGTON, MID-1930S. Reverend Washington was one of the "Sons of the Church" and an active member of the First Baptist Church of Deanwood. Community records show his family came to Deanwood around 1884. Washington and Sons Funeral Home opened in the 1920s, incorporated in 1939, and had three locations—467 N Street NW; an S Street NW location; and 4925 Deane Avenue. (Bruce Sellers.)

GEORGIA I. WASHINGTON, MID-1930S. Georgia Washington's husband, Henry S. Washington, opened Washington and Sons Funeral Home at 4925 Deane Avenue (now Nannie Helen Burroughs Avenue) in the 1930s. Upon his death in January 1941, Georgia took over the family business until her death in May 1959. (Madlyn E. Fox.)

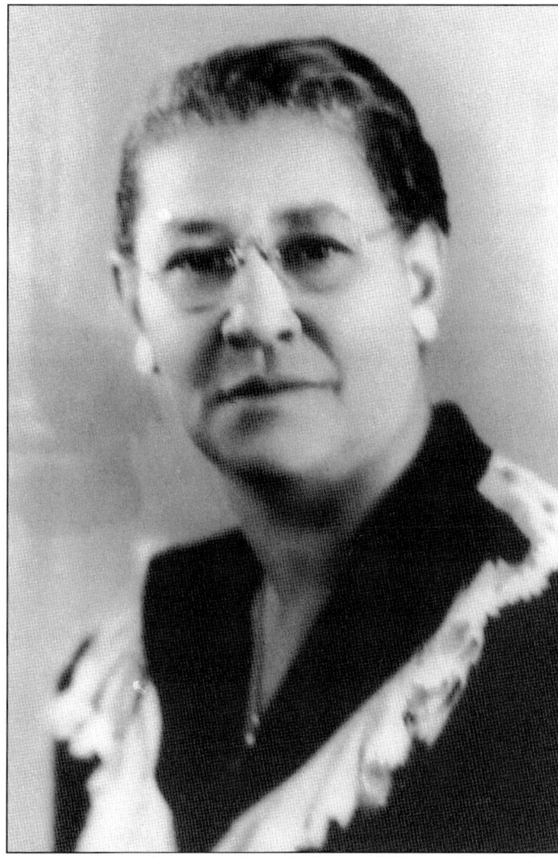

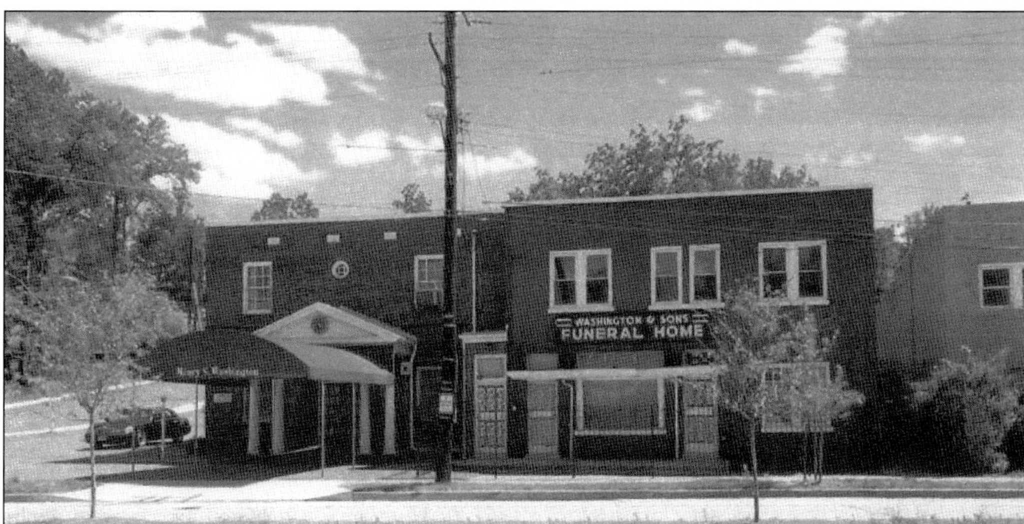

ORIGINAL FUNERAL HOME, C. 2005. As business increased, so did the need for more space. Not interested in leaving the community, the Washingtons built an addition to the original structure in August 1959 (to the left with the awning) at 4927 Deane Avenue. The business has survived into the family's third generation. The current president, Mazie Sellers, is the granddaughter of Henry S. and Georgia I. Washington. (Madlyn E. Fox.)

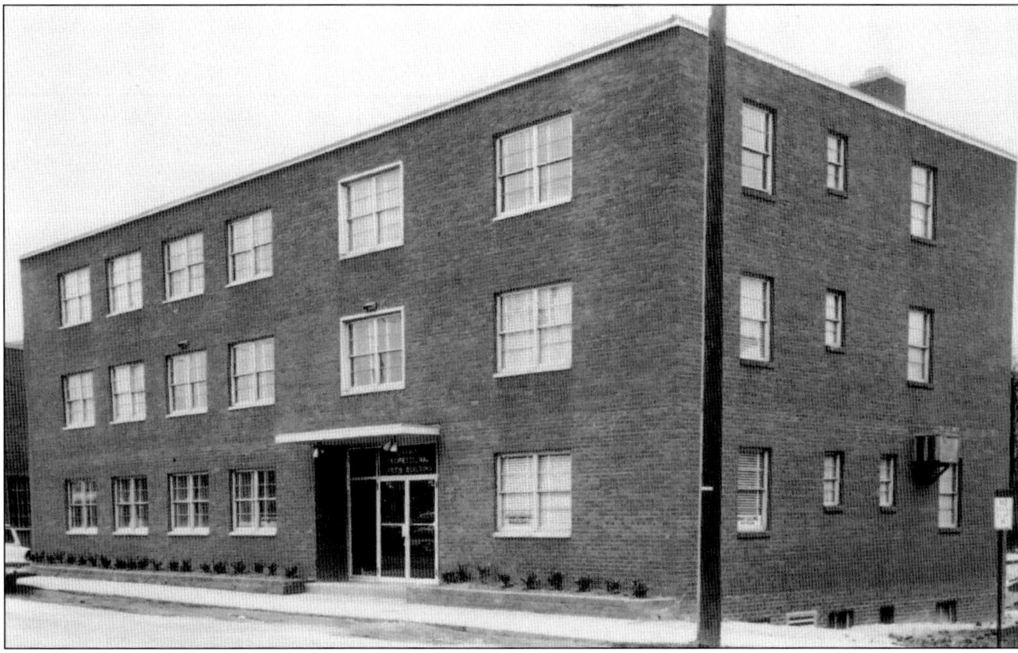

DEANWOOD PROFESSIONAL ARTS BUILDING, C. 1957. The building was erected at 4645 Deane Avenue in 1957. Dr. William K. Collins, a dentist, owned it. Lewis W. Giles Jr. was the architect, and McKissack and McKissack were the builders. When it opened, it housed a dentist, two physician's offices, a dental and medical laboratory, an architect's office, a beauty salon, and five two-bedroom apartments. (*Star* Collection, DCPL; @*Washington Post*.)

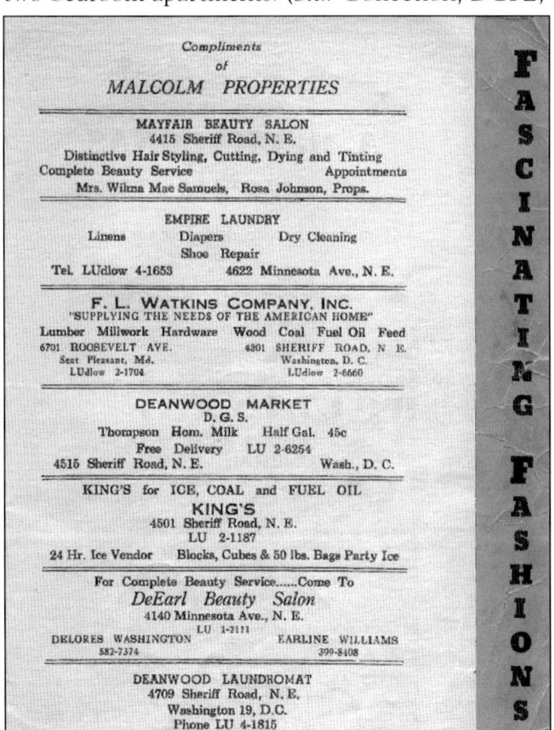

Compliments
of
MALCOLM PROPERTIES

MAYFAIR BEAUTY SALON
4415 Sheriff Road, N. E.
Distinctive Hair Styling, Cutting, Dying and Tinting
Complete Beauty Service Appointments
Mrs. Wilma Mae Samuels, Rosa Johnson, Props.

EMPIRE LAUNDRY
Linens Diapers Dry Cleaning
Shoe Repair
Tel. LUdlow 4-1653 4622 Minnesota Ave., N. E.

F. L. WATKINS COMPANY, INC.
"SUPPLYING THE NEEDS OF THE AMERICAN HOME"
Lumber Millwork Hardware Wood Coal Fuel Oil Feed
6701 ROOSEVELT AVE. Seat Pleasant, Md. LUdlow 2-1704
4301 SHERIFF ROAD, N. E. Washington, D. C. LUdlow 2-6660

DEANWOOD MARKET
D. G. S.
Thompson Hom. Milk Half Gal. 45c
Free Delivery LU 2-6254
4515 Sheriff Road, N. E. Wash., D. C.

KING'S for ICE, COAL and FUEL OIL
KING'S
4501 Sheriff Road, N. E.
LU 2-1187
24 Hr. Ice Vendor Blocks, Cubes & 50 lbs. Bags Party Ice

For Complete Beauty Service......Come To
DeEarl Beauty Salon
4140 Minnesota Ave., N. E.
LU 1-2111
DELORES WASHINGTON 582-7374
EARLINE WILLIAMS 399-8408

DEANWOOD LAUNDROMAT
4709 Sheriff Road, N. E.
Washington 19, D.C.
Phone LU 4-1815

FASCINATING FASHIONS

BUSINESS ADVERTISEMENTS, 1964. These advertisements from the "Fascinating Fashions" program for the George Washington Carver Elementary School give a snapshot of the variety of businesses that existed in Deanwood. Most of these merchants were located along Sheriff Road and provided everything from grooming to home heating needs. It also shows how they supported community endeavors by purchasing advertising space and assisting with the school's fund-raising efforts. (Erin Gantt.)

Four

Founded on Faith

The churches in Deanwood have deep roots in the rich soil of spirit-filled visions, God-directed courage, and African American unity. Christian rituals and church traditions evolved as Deanwood's population grew. Sacred gatherings united the community in far-reaching ways: connecting like-minded people, instilling black faith and pride, and defining culture and values. In addition to teaching the word of God, the early places of worship in Deanwood left a legacy of dedicated Christian leadership, educational guidance, and financial wisdom.

Members of the community shared common Christian values and the desire for suitable accommodations for religious worship. While there were many commonalities, Deanwood residents and church leaders also honored religious diversity, as seen in the variety of denominations that have called the community home. Among the earliest churches was Contee African Methodist Episcopal Zion Church, built in 1885 on Division Avenue. The First Baptist Church of Deanwood was organized in the 4700 block of Sheriff Road in 1901 and erected its first building at 1044 Whittingham Place NE (now Forty-fifth Street). While it now stands on Kenilworth Avenue, Zion Baptist Church was originally built on Sheriff Road in 1908. Beulah Baptist Church of Deanwood Heights was built in 1910 at Fifty-eighth and Dix Streets, followed a year later by Tabernacle Baptist Church at Division Avenue and Gay Street. In 1912, Randall Memorial United Methodist Church, Deanwood's first Methodist church, and the Church of the Incarnation, the first Catholic church in the community, both opened on Browning Place (now Forty-sixth Street). Two more Baptist churches joined the community, with Antioch Baptist Church on Fiftieth Street in 1924 and the New Mount Olive Baptist Church at Fifty-eighth and Grant Street in 1935. Since that time, the church presence in Deanwood has continued to grow.

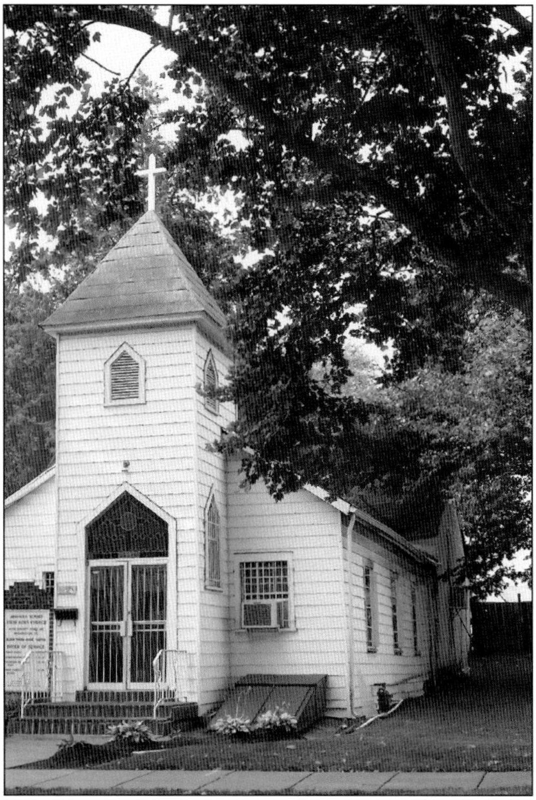

ZION BAPTIST CHURCH, 2005. This picture shows the Zion Baptist Church building (now occupied by Joshua's First Born Temple). It was the first church encountered entering Sheriff Road from the east and held all the services of a Baptist church. The church was designed by African American architect Sidney Pittman and built in 1908. Zion is now known as Zion Baptist Church of Eastland Gardens. (DCHPO.)

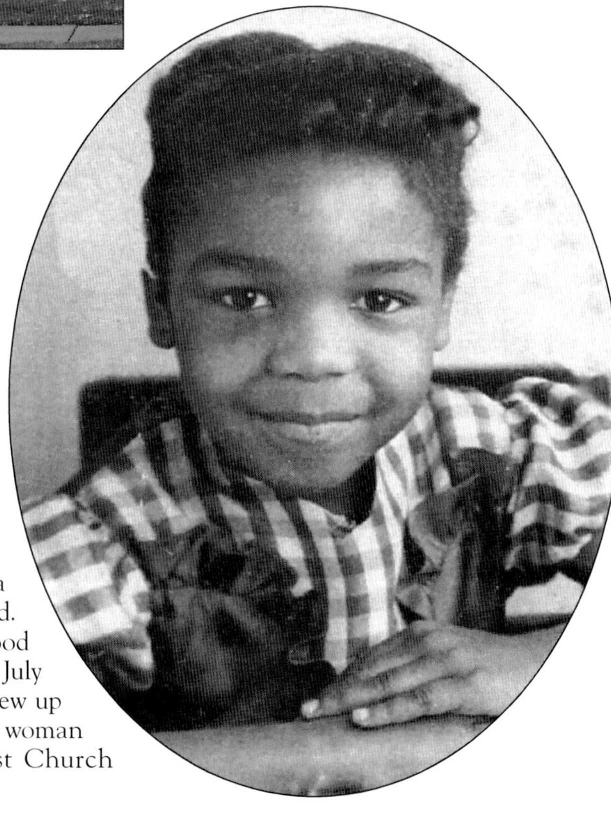

FROM PARISHIONER TO PASTOR, C. 1950. In January 1901, a Sunday school was organized in a Deanwood residence. Later services moved to a house in the 4700 block of Sheriff Road. The First Baptist Church of Deanwood was incorporated on May 17, 1906. On July 20, 2002, Rev. Sarah C. Britt, who grew up in Deanwood, was appointed the first woman pastor of the church. (First Baptist Church of Deanwood.)

REV. E. THOMAS BROADUS. Thomas Broadus was an original member of the group that worshipped at the First Baptist Church of Deanwood when it was located on Sheriff Road. He was a leader in the church and was selected as superintendent. Broadus was instrumental in helping to raise money for the first church building. (DCPL, WD Collection 5.)

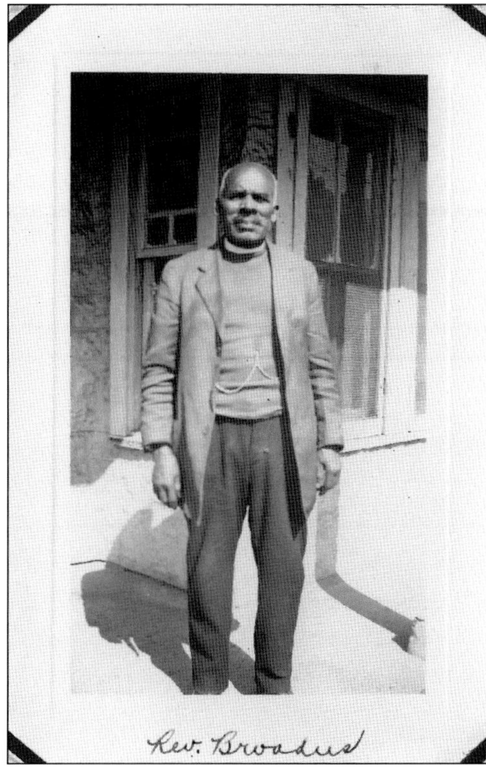

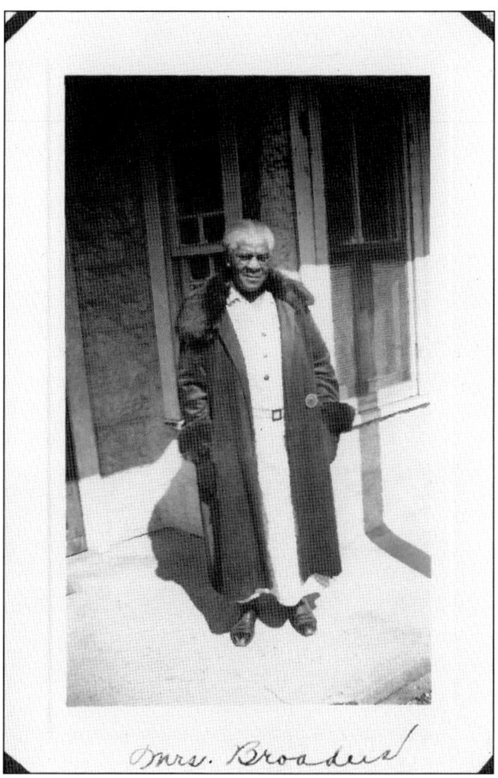

LUCY J. BROADUS. Like her husband, Lucy J. Broadus was an original member of the group that worshipped in the First Baptist Church of Deanwood. She was also a leader in the church, serving as one of the Sunday school teachers. (DCPL, WD Collection 5.)

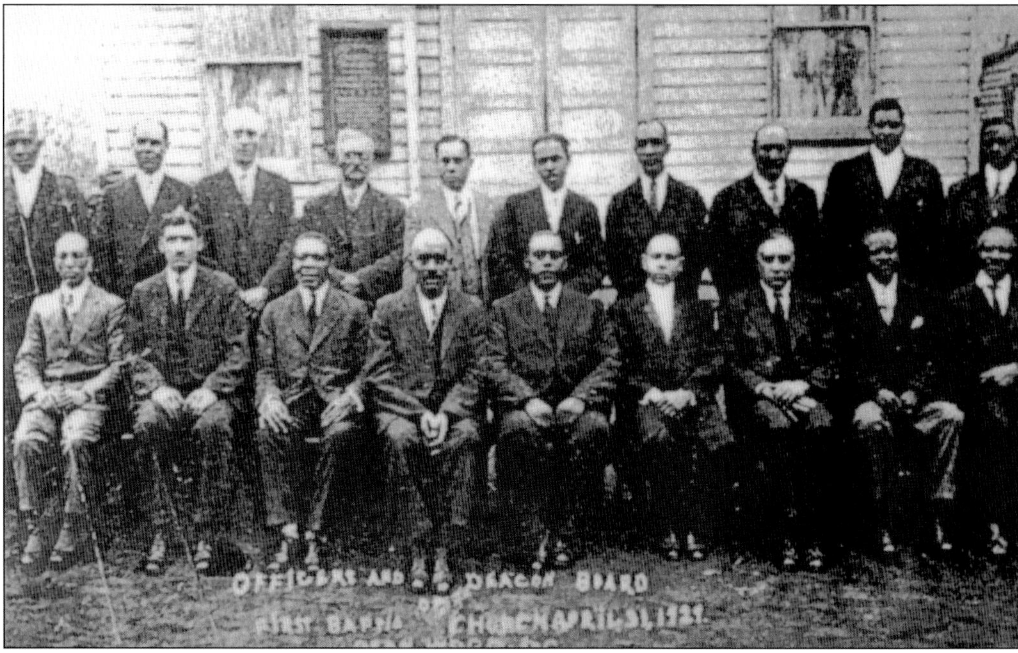

ORIGINAL BOARD, 1921. The church leadership shown here is, from left to right, (first row) Rev. T. Roebuck, J. King, F. Groomes, W. Hopkins, Rev. G. Brent, T. Warren, G. Doctor, R. Plummer, and N. Carson; (second row) H. Harris, C. Proctor, T. Stokes, S. Butler, S. Morse, W. Gaines, L. Wormley, L. King, H. Washington, and G. White. (Juanita Deskins.)

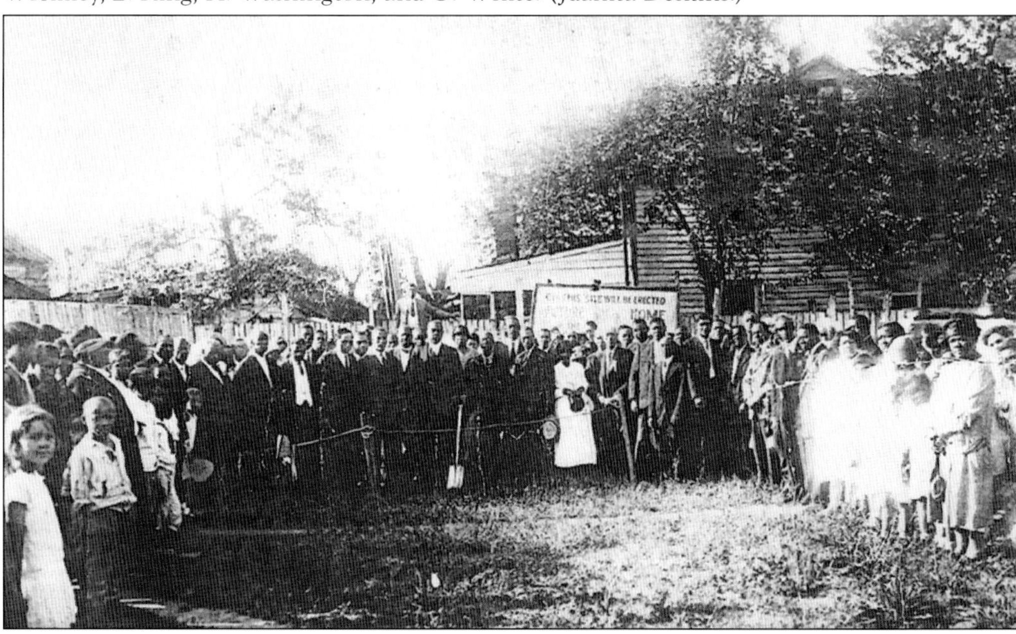

GROUND-BREAKING, MAY 30, 1929. Rev. George W. Brent began his pastorate at the First Baptist Church of Deanwood in July 1914. He had a vision for a large, beautiful building worthy of being a place of worship for his congregation. His dreams came true on May 30, 1929. The church was built entirely on donations of material and labor and never carried debt of any kind. (Juanita Deskins.)

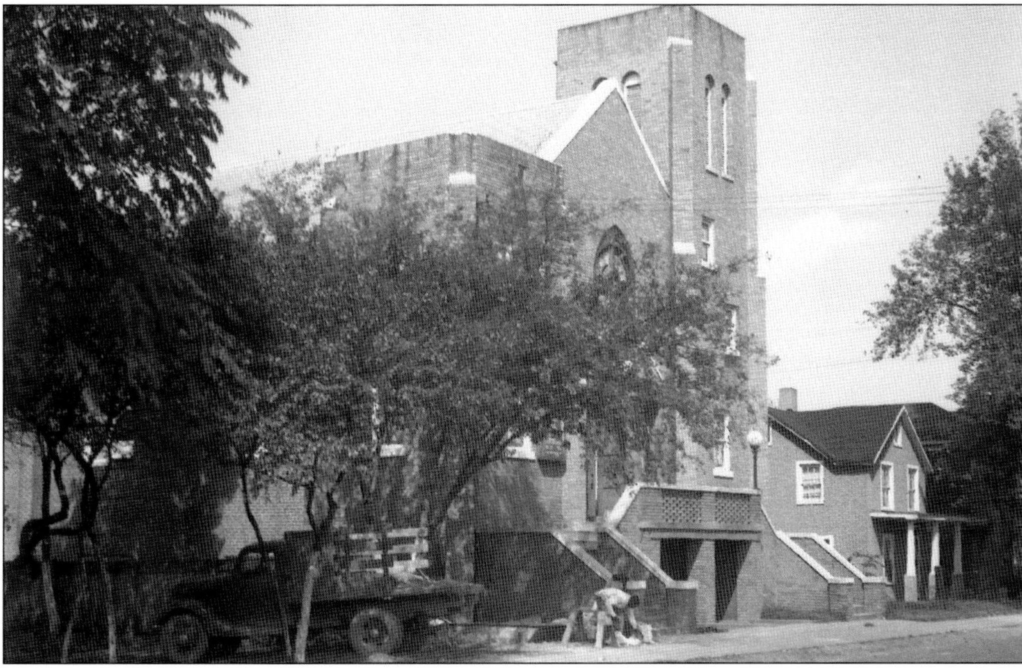

FIRST BAPTIST CHURCH OF DEANWOOD, 1948. A parishioner shows his dedication by using his equipment and supplies to make repairs to the church. At that time, it was not uncommon for members to step in when the church needed repairs. The church has since been expanded, and the new sanctuary now faces Sheriff Road. (JTWC, HSWDC.)

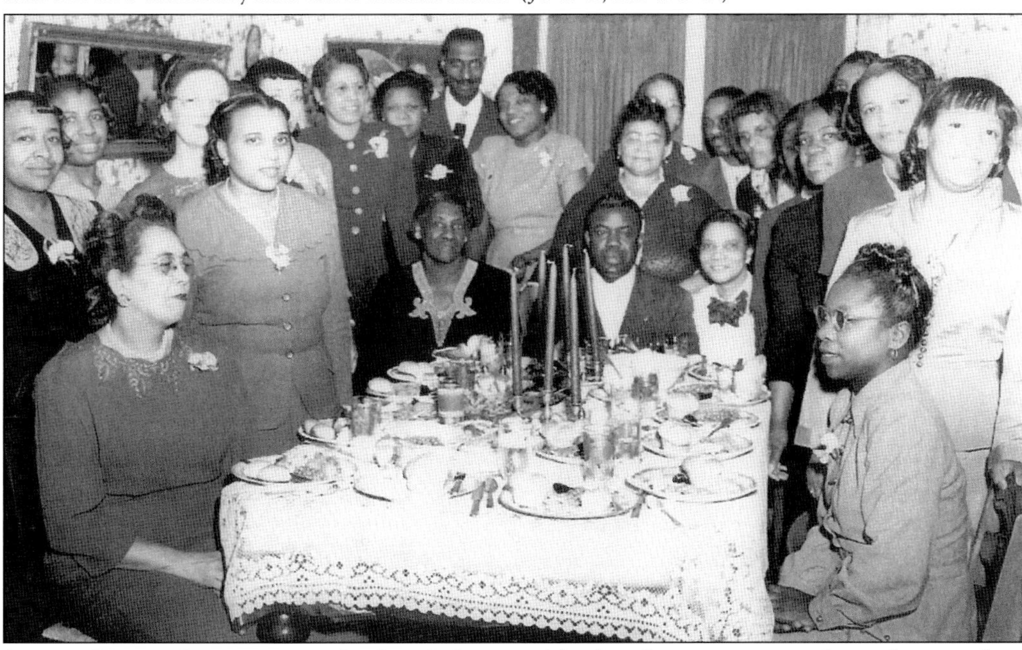

SENIOR USHER BOARD, 1949. In the 1940s, monthly church meetings were hosted in members' homes. The special guests were always the pastor and his wife. Everyone had a special recipe for sweet potatoes, the pastor's favorite dish. The competition was the talk of the church. Here Rev. Andrew J. and Gertrude Allen (white blouse) are seen at the head of the table. (EKB.)

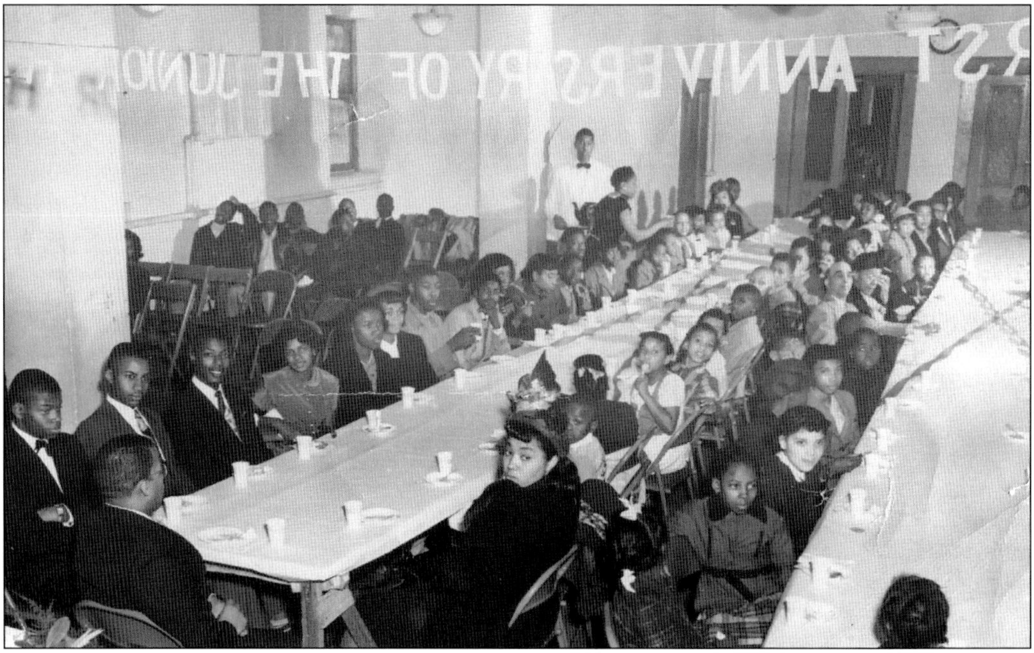

JUNIOR CHURCH ANNIVERSARY, C. 1949. The Junior Church was an innovative program established by Rev. Andrew J. Allen in 1948. Its goal was to train the youth in all aspects of running a church service and to increase their leadership abilities. It had the same offices as the adult church, except the positions of pastor and advisors, and all were held by youth. Advisors were adult members appointed by the pastor. (AM.)

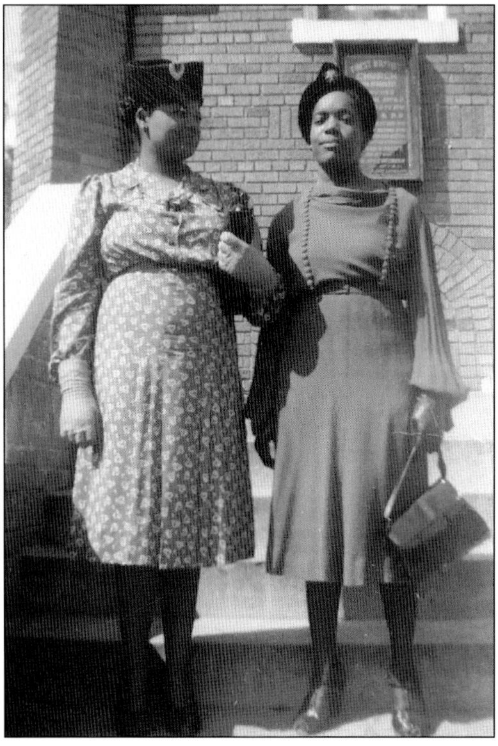

JUNIOR CHURCH ADVISORS, 1930S. Marie Plummer Talley (left) and Arena Leppard were dedicated longtime members of the First Baptist Church of Deanwood. They were chosen by Reverend Allen to establish programs and act as advisors in the Junior Church. In 1949, Leppard organized the Junior Nurses, who were modeled after the Nurses Unit in the adult church, and Plummer was appointed to organize the Junior Ushers. (AM.)

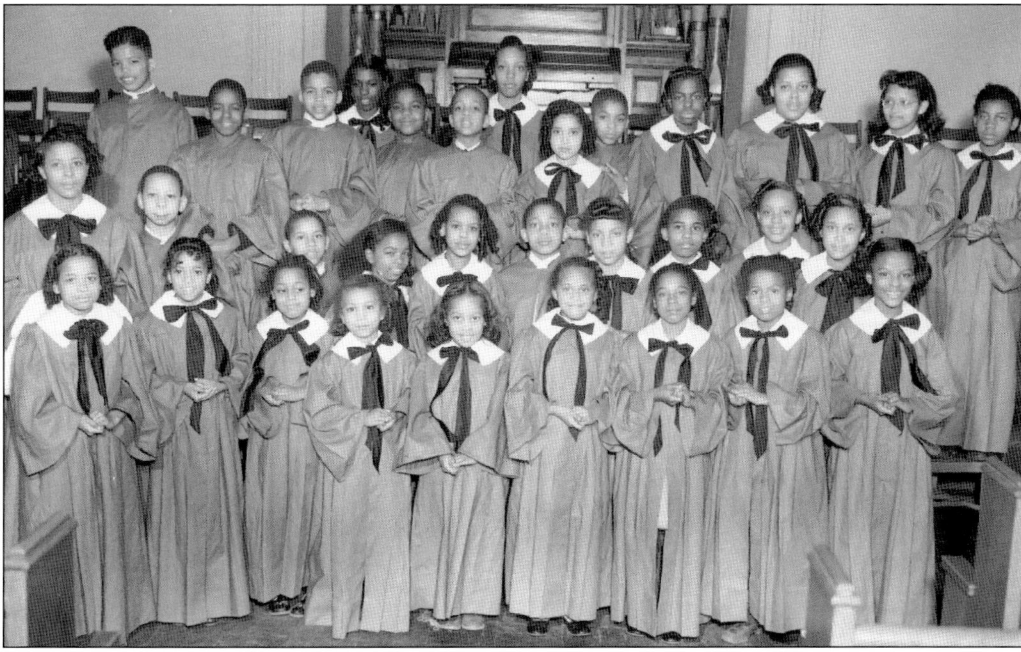

JUNIOR CHOIR, 1950S. The Junior Choir was the first choir organized in the Junior Church. It provided the youth the opportunity to share their vocal talents with both the junior and the adult church. The Junior Choir was established under the leadership of Martha Turner. Groups formed in later years included the Youth Fellowship Chorale, the Choraliers, and the Cherubs. (EKB.)

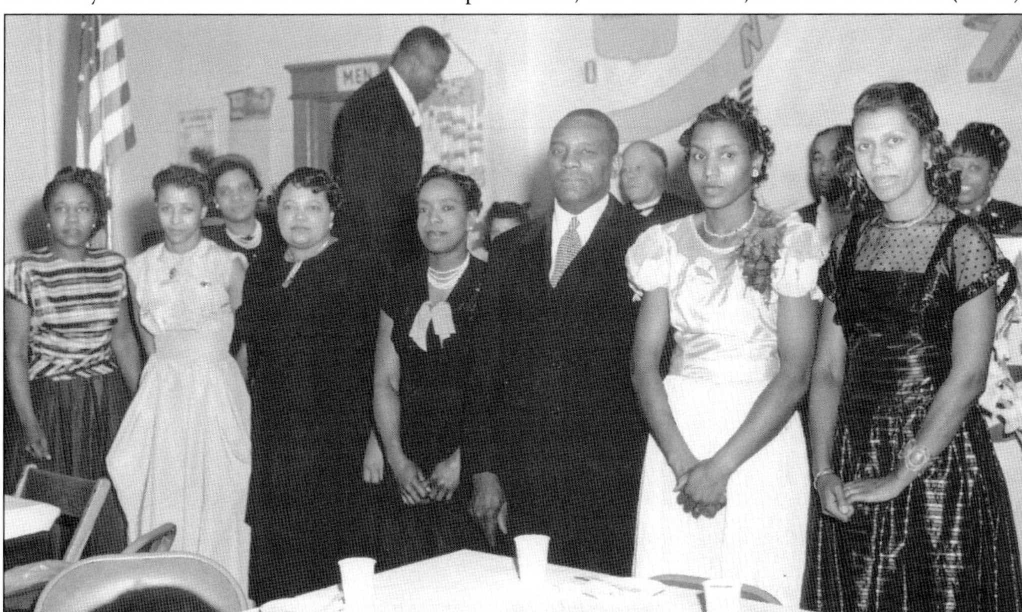

AFTER-SERVICE CELEBRATION, C. 1950. After each anniversary or special program, the church always served food. Here members pose before sitting at the homemade tables for a meal. From left to right are (first row) Martha Turner, Gertrude Allen, Marie Talley, Arena Leppard, Rev. Andrew J. Allen, and two unidentified; (second row) unidentified, Deacon Odie Williams, Rev. Clarence Turner Sr., Rev. Thomas Turner, and Rev. Angela Turner. (Audrey Williams Burke.)

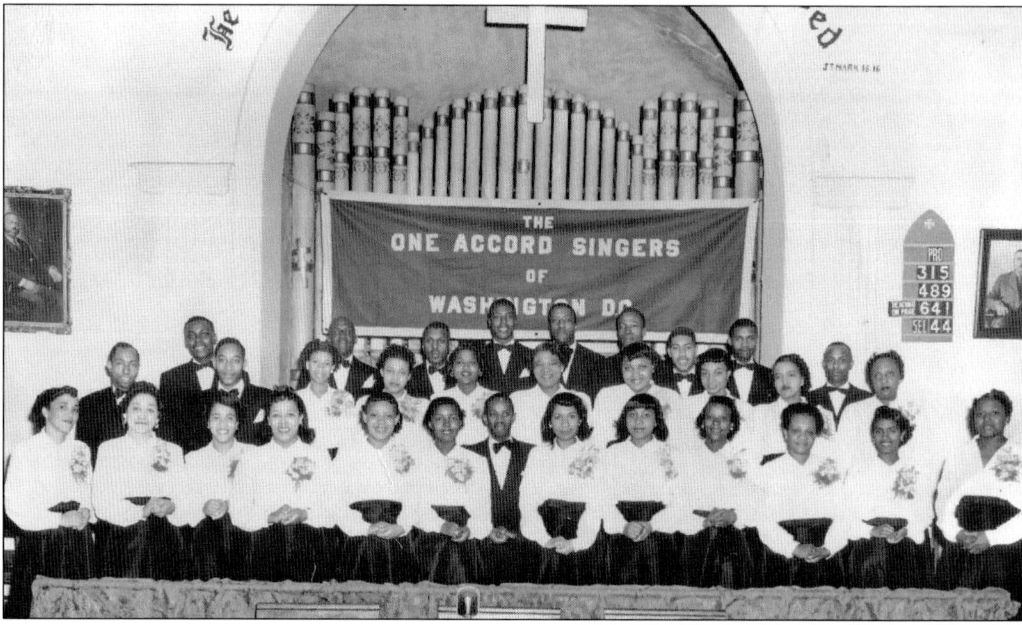

ONE ACCORD SINGERS, C. 1950. The One Accord Singers of Washington, D.C., was one of the choirs started under the direction of Rev. Andrew J. Allen. It was made up of singers from all over the city, although the majority came from the First Baptist Church of Deanwood. The group's name came from the Scripture (Acts 1:14) and the church's belief in worshipping "with one accord." (AM.)

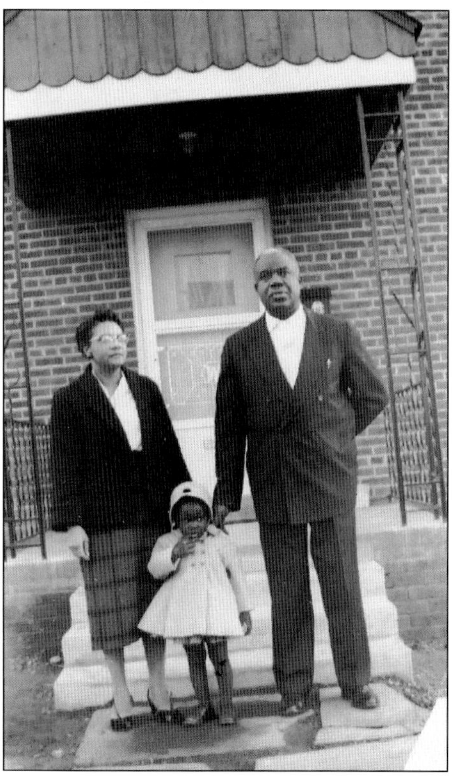

REVEREND AND MRS. ALLEN, 1958. Rev. Andrew J. Allen pastored the First Baptist Church of Deanwood from 1947 to 1979. Many innovative programs were started under his leadership. He and his wife, Gertrude, always had time to visit with members of the church. While visiting Deacon Odie and Virginia Williams's home, the pair took time to take a picture with Gail Barton Mullen, the daughter of Audrey Williams Burke. (Audrey Williams Burke.)

Deacon Odie Williams and Wife, Virginia, 1960s. The late Deacon Odie Williams and Deaconess Virginia Williams were very active members in the First Baptist Church of Deanwood. Rev. Andrew J. Allen appointed Deacon Williams as the first adult advisor to the Youth Deacons of the Junior Church. The Williamses had four children: Doris, Odie Jr., Audrey, and Charles. (Audrey Williams Burke.)

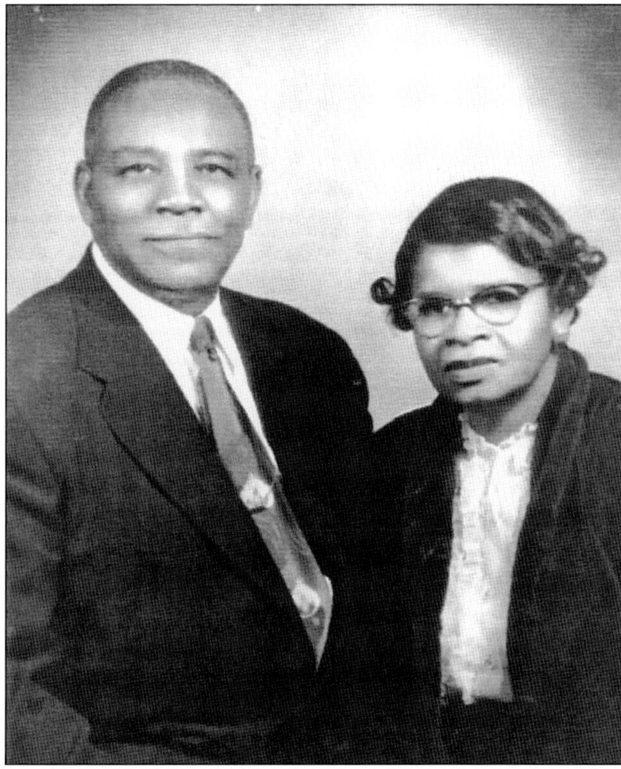

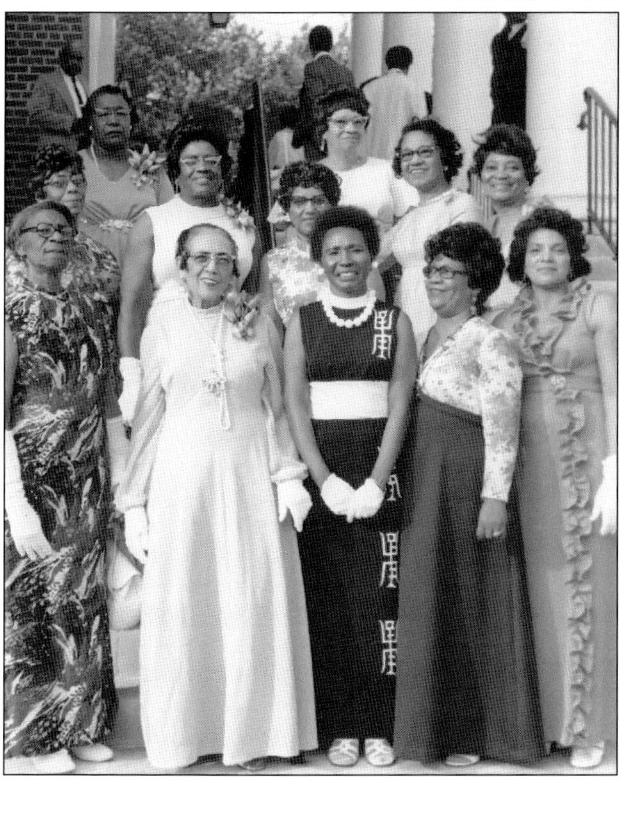

Senior Ushers, 1960s. Not only did the First Baptist ushers show off their beautiful gowns at their own church, but they often wore them to other churches for special events. Shown here celebrating an usher anniversary are, from left to right, (first row) Eva Brewer, Eva Warren, Naomi Boyd, Elizabeth King, and Thelma Prather; (second row) three unidentified, Annie Broadus, Lillian Satterfield, unidentified, and Mozelle Sarders. (EKB.)

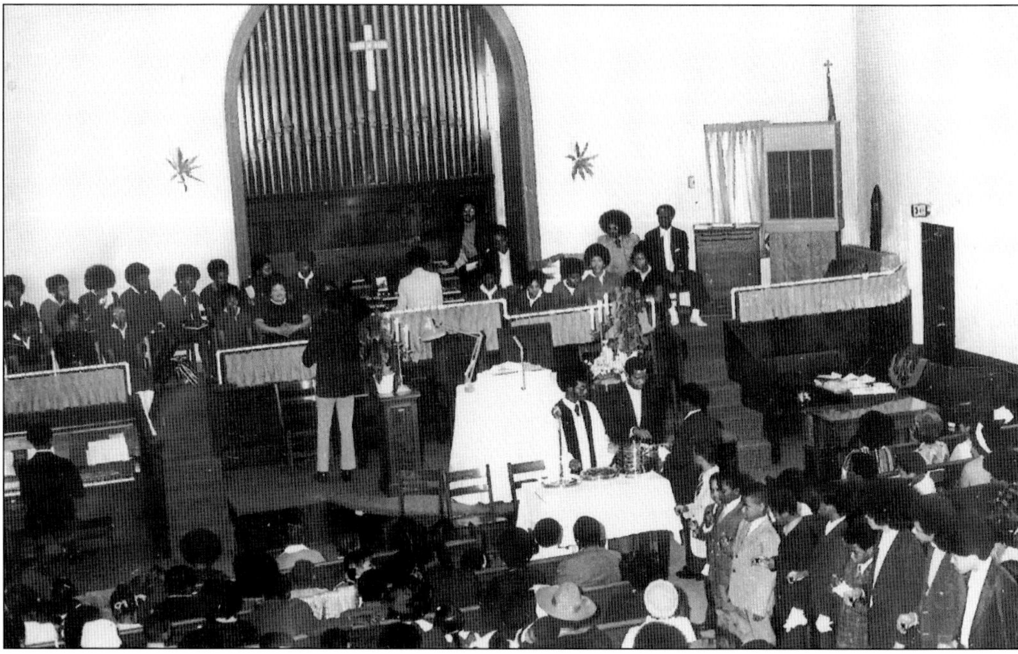

JUNIOR CHURCH COMMUNION, LATE 1960S. All Junior Church services were held in the sanctuary of the Brent Memorial Chapel, the 1929 building of the First Baptist Church of Deanwood on Whittingham Place. Youth administered all aspects of the service, from offering the prayer to preparing the communion wafers. Here junior deacons wait to receive their communion from Rev. Vincent Allen after they have served the congregation. (AM.)

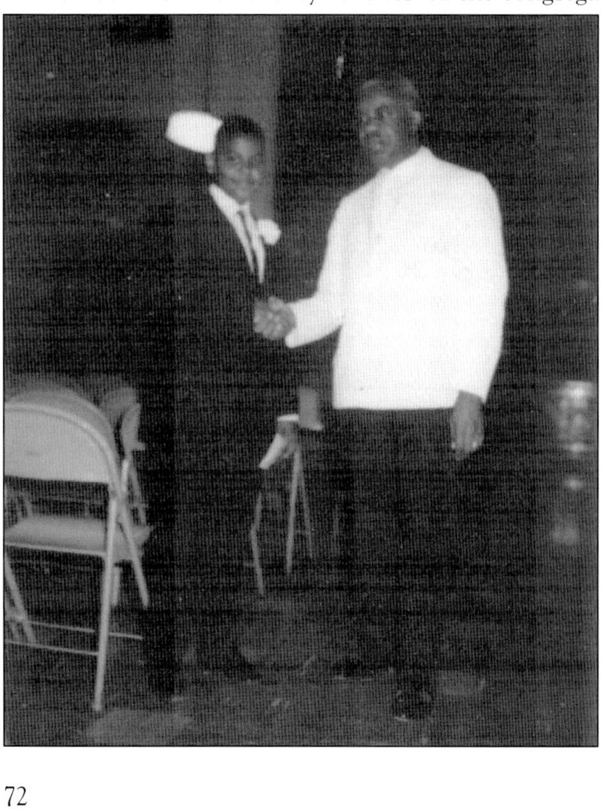

JUAN H. GADDIS AND REVEREND ALLEN, 1969. The late Rev. Andrew J. Allen, pastor of the First Baptist Church of Deanwood, made it a point to attend school graduation ceremonies of all students who were a part of the Junior Church. Here Reverend Allen congratulates Juan H. Gaddis on his successful completion of the sixth grade. (Barbara J. Moore.)

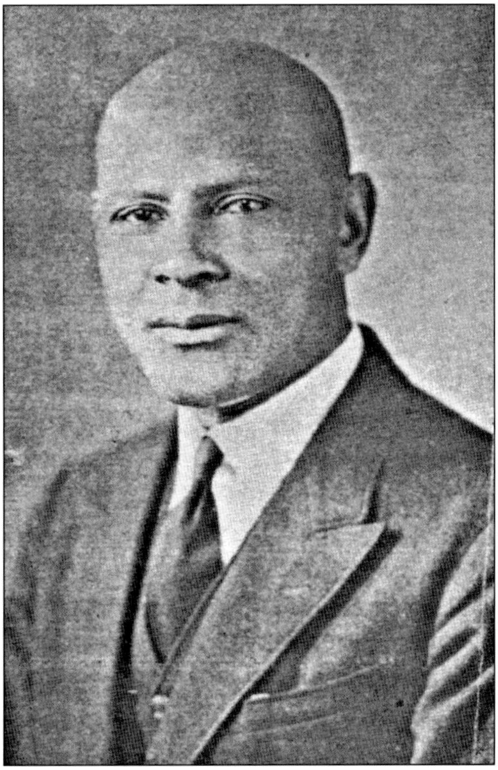

REV. T. S. TILDEN. Reverend Tilden was the sixth pastor to serve Randall Memorial United Methodist Church. The church was established in 1910, after Rev. Armstead Randall and Rev. John H. Snowden moved to the Deanwood neighborhood and realized there were no Methodist churches. Members held their original services in Moses Hall, located on Lane Place between Forty-fourth Street and Whittingham Place. (Randall Memorial United Methodist Church.)

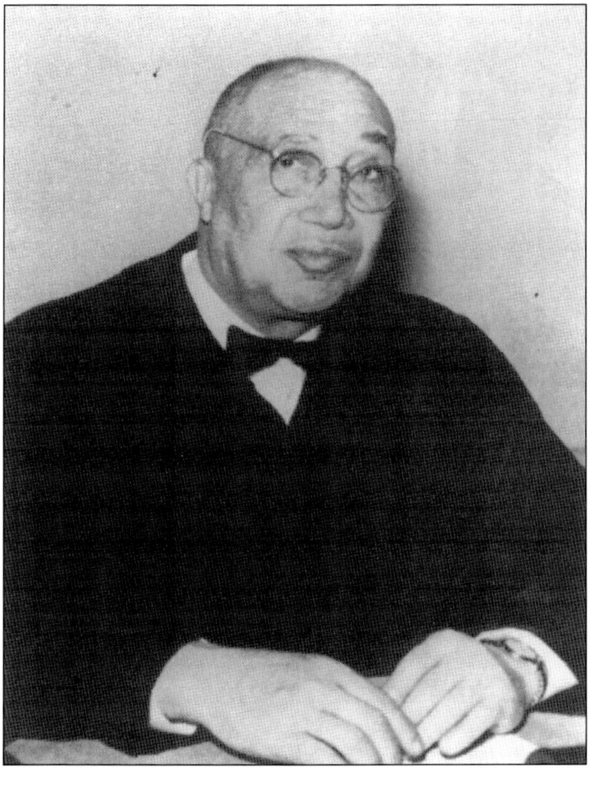

REV. DAVID PLEASANT, C. 1935. The cornerstone of Randall Memorial United Methodist Church's first building was laid on August 4, 1912, by the King Solomon Lodge No. 1, (Free and Accepted Masons). The dedication service and sermon were given by District superintendent W. A. C. Hughes on July 12, 1914. Rev. David Pleasant served as the seventh pastor of the church from 1935 to 1937. (Randall Memorial United Methodist Church.)

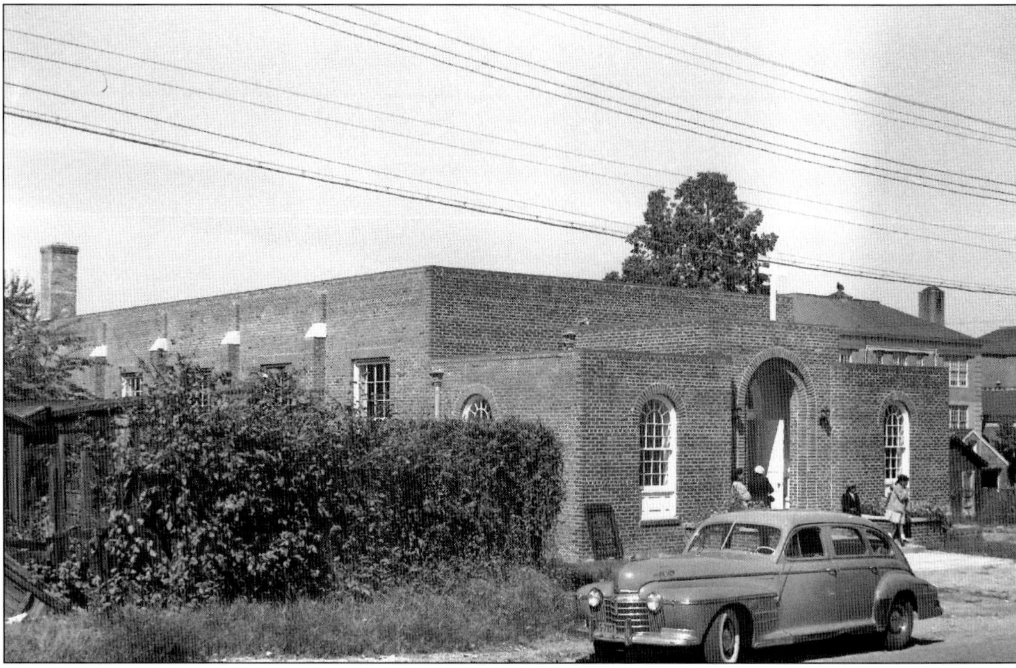

RANDALL CHURCH, SEPTEMBER 25, 1949. A building drive was launched in 1941 by the church's pastor, Rev. J. Lloyd Garrison. Members worked day and night to erect the edifice, which was completed in 1949. The church's new building was designed by African American architect Robert Lionel Fields and was built adjacent to the old one. (Randall Memorial United Methodist Church.)

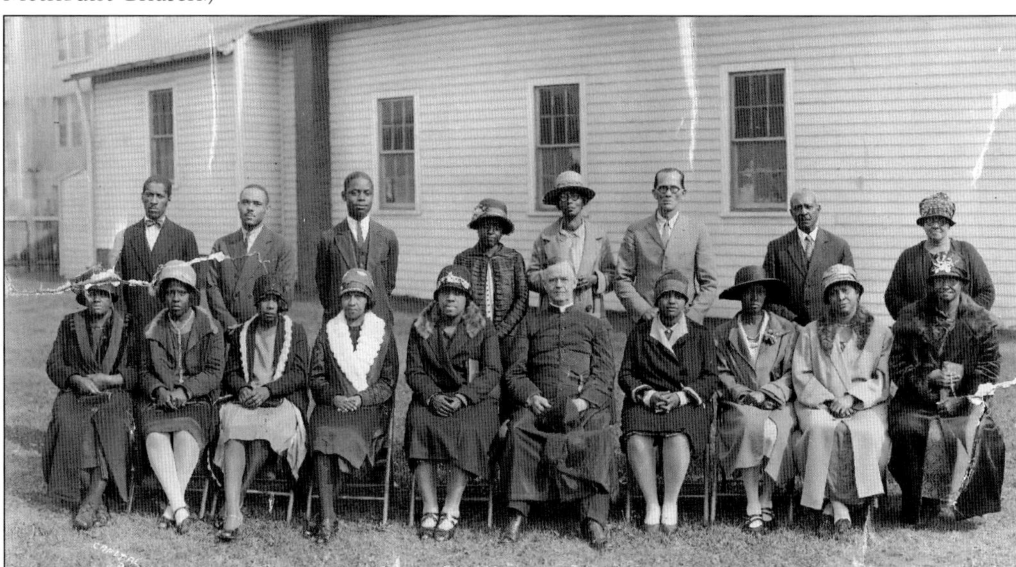

FIRST COMMUNION CLASS, JUNE 5, 1927. The Church of the Incarnation was established in Deanwood in 1912. This picture shows the priest along with his First Communion class in the yard of the Church of the Incarnation. The First Communion is the reception of the Blessed Sacrament and is conducted by a priest during Holy Mass. George Washington Carver Elementary School is seen in the background. (Junius P. Aikers.)

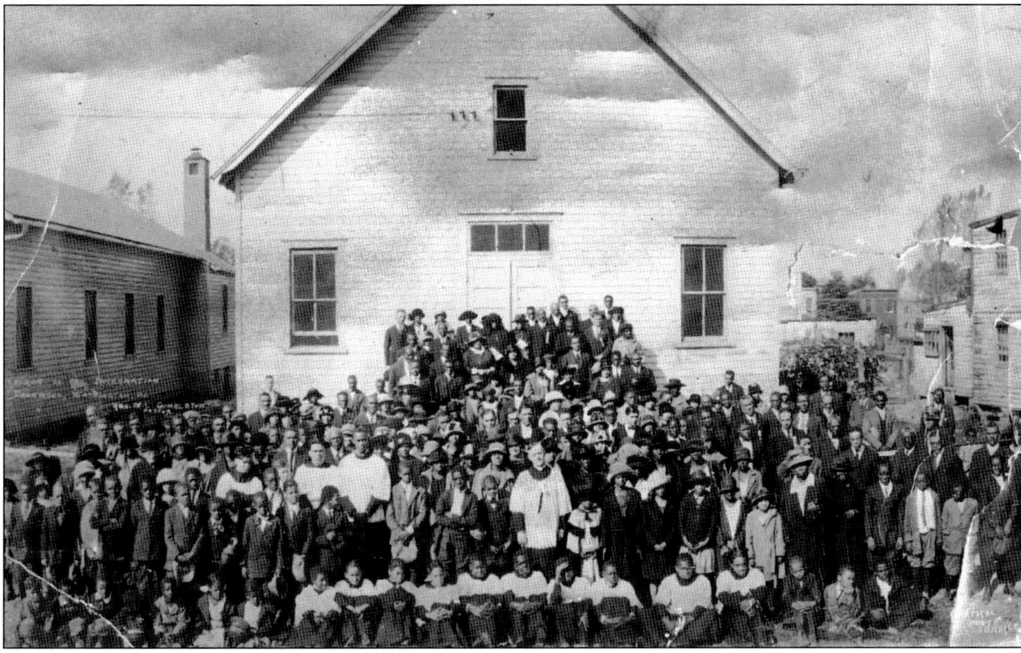

Church of the Incarnation Activity Hall, c. 1928. The church activity hall was located on Browning Place (now Forty-sixth Street) next to the church. Although the Church of the Incarnation was Catholic, it was open to all members of the community, no matter their affiliation. The church's activity hall was used for classes and social activities for the community. (Junius P. Aikers.)

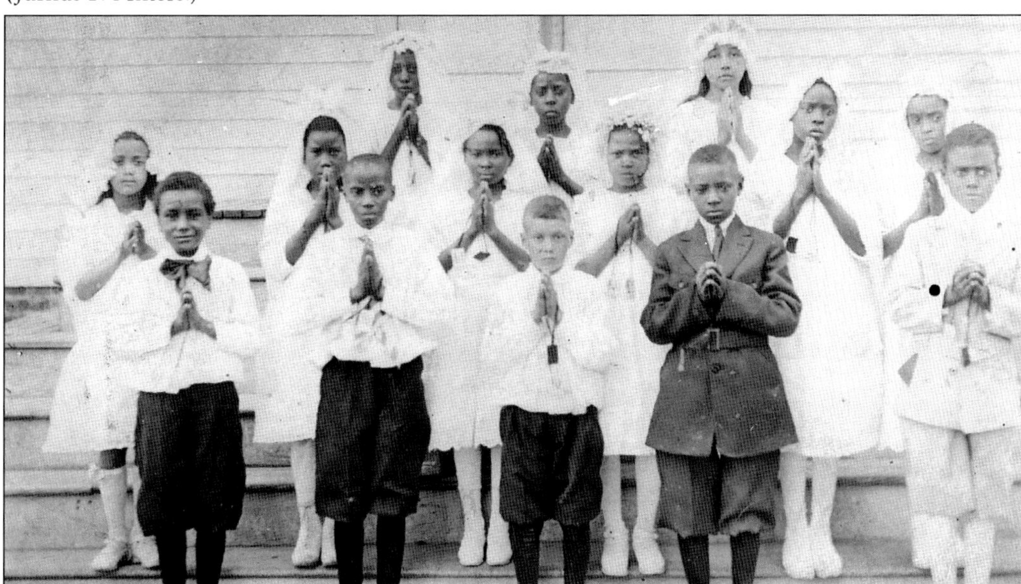

Confirmation Class, May 27, 1928. This picture shows the students of a confirmation class at the Church of the Incarnation. In the 1880s, Pope Pius IX directed the St. Joseph's Society of the Sacred Heart Order (the Josephite fathers) to work among black Americans. By the 1890s, there were several parishes in Baltimore and Washington. Deanwood borders Maryland, which began as a Catholic colony. (Junius P. Aikers.)

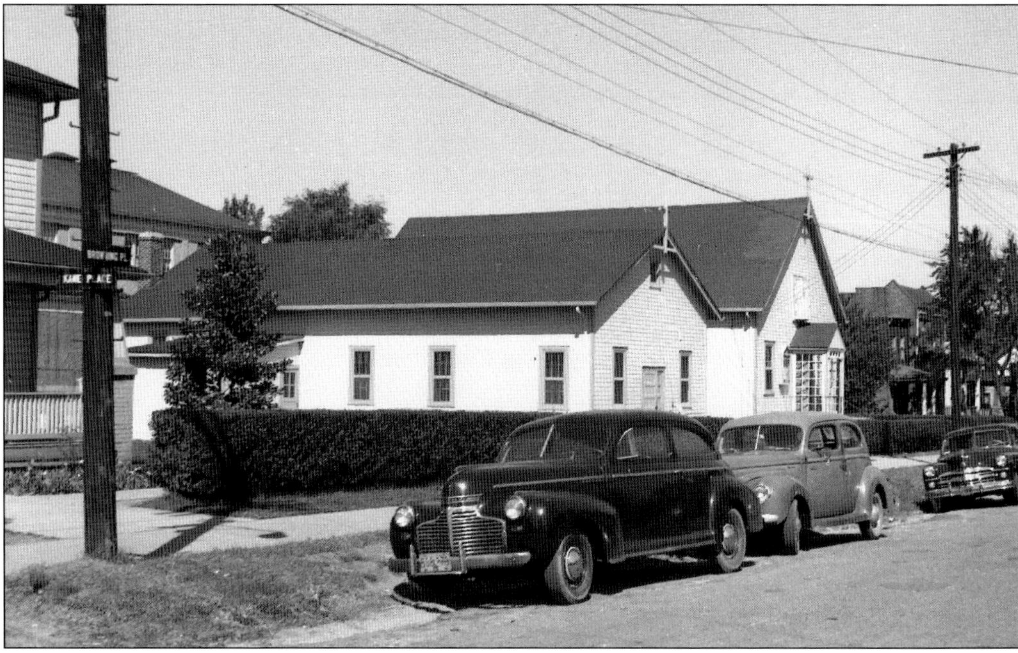

CHURCH OF THE INCARNATION, SEPTEMBER 25, 1949. A portion of the rectory, where the priest lived, can be seen to the far left of the church. It was important to residents that the priests lived in the community. The church later moved to Eastern Avenue, on the border of Deanwood and Burrville. (JTWC, HSWDC.)

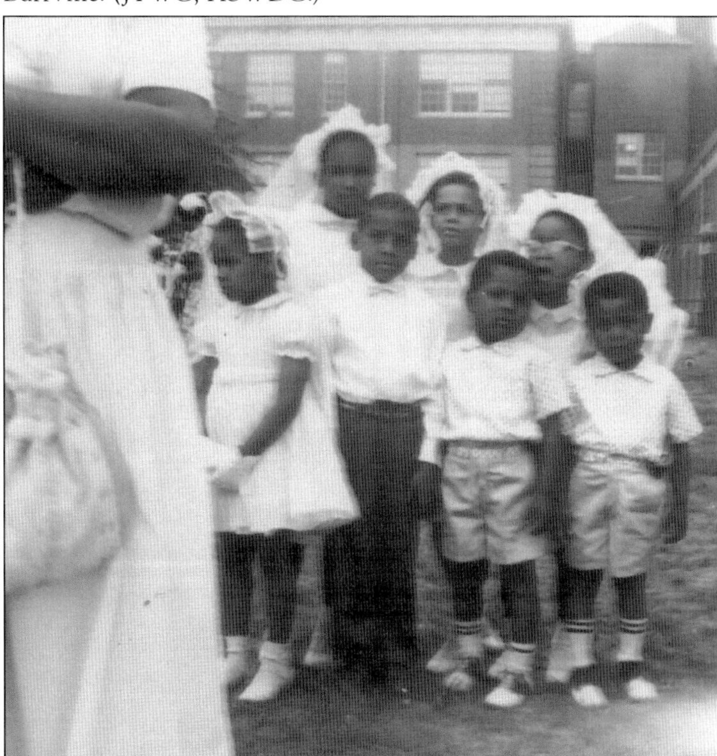

AFTER FIRST COMMUNION, C. 1961. After the First Communion of James Brown, members of the Brown family pose in the yard of the Church of the Incarnation. From left to right are (first row) Marjorie Harris, Theodore Jackson, Celester Brown, and James Brown. Three unidentified girls stand behind them. George Washington Carver Elementary can be seen in the background. (Sandra Brown.)

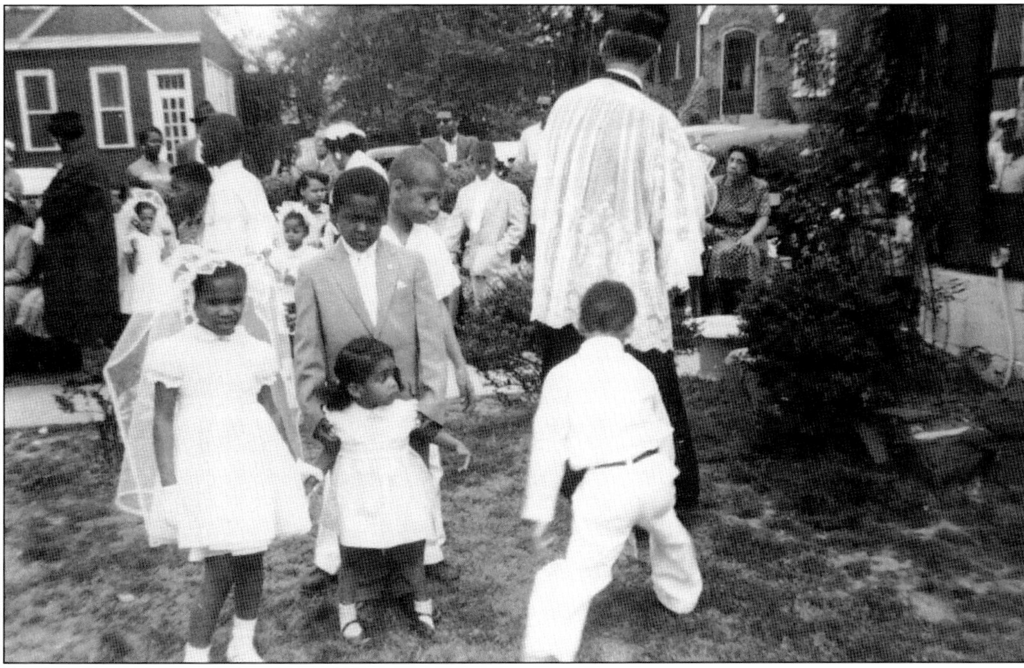

BROWN CHILDREN, C. 1961. Members of the Church of the Incarnation partake in fellowship outside the church after First Communion. The church, regardless of denomination, played an active role in teaching positive values to the neighborhood youngsters. As the priest mixes with the congregants, from left to right, Marjorie Harris, Theodore Brown, and Deborah Jackson pose for the camera. Celester Brown playfully follows behind the priest. (Sandra Brown.)

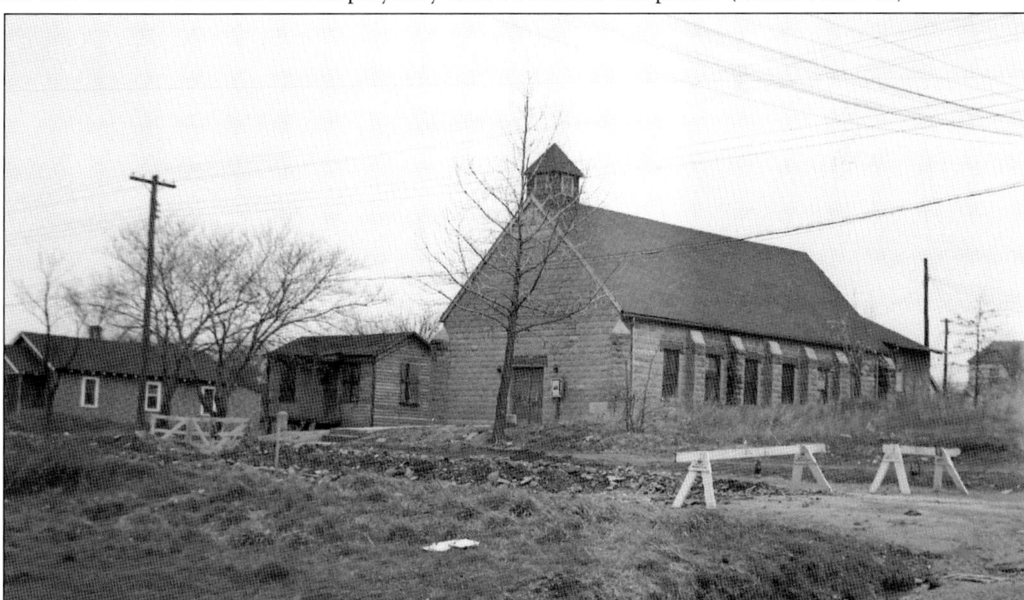

ANTIOCH BAPTIST CHURCH, MARCH 27, 1949. Antioch Baptist Church was born on October 11, 1923. Rev. Julius Wheeler and his devoted visionaries were able to acquire the church property and construct three buildings by tithing, selling chitterling dinners, holding fish fries, and sponsoring musical concerts. (JTWC, HSWDC.)

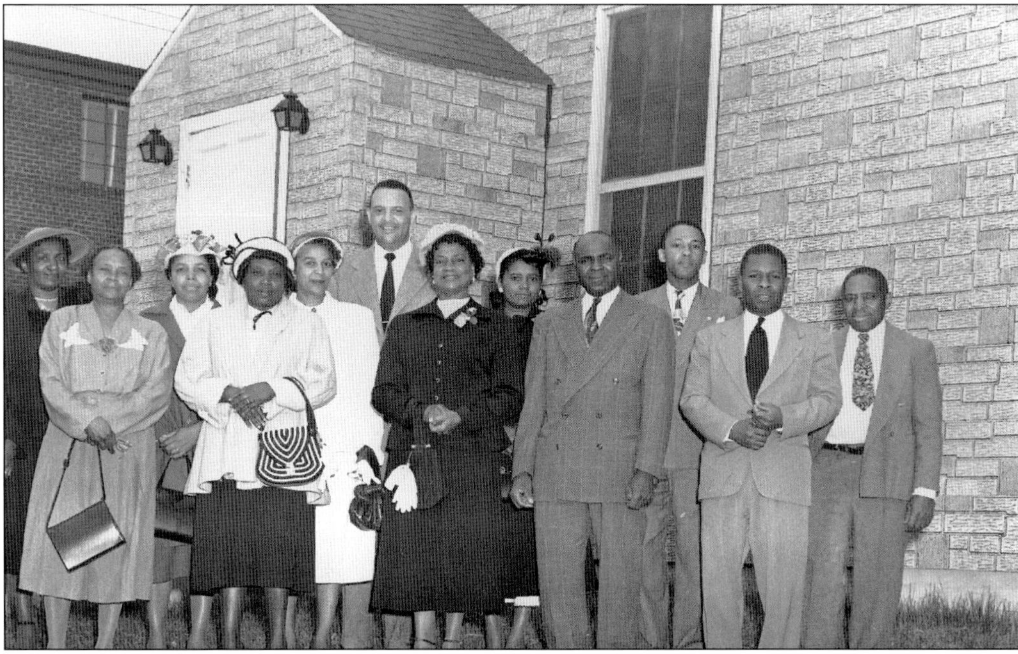

CHURCH LEADERS, LATE 1940S. Leaders of Contee AME Zion Church pose from left to right: (first row) Rev. Estelle Jeffries, Mary J. Simmons, Aris Williams, Charles Steward, and William Turner; (second row) Hattie Lucille Veney, Ethel Butler, Ethel Gibson, Pastor Charles E. Bourne, Dorothy Simms, Joseph Brown, and Harry Hill. (Contee AME Zion Church.)

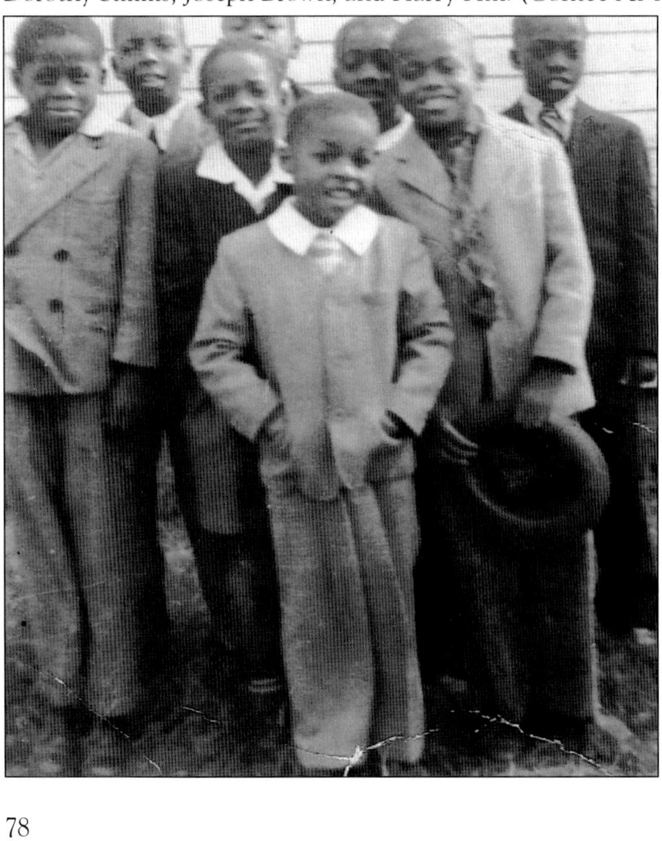

SUNDAY SCHOOL, C. 1945. On Sundays, everyone dressed up and attended the church. Residents were welcome at any church in the community, regardless of their faith. Some of the youngsters pictured in front of Contee AME Zion Church include Guy Tillman (front), Billy Butler (with hat), Clyde Davis (far right, rear), Randall Davis (far left, rear), and Paul Johnson to Randall's immediate right. (Joan Slade Gray.)

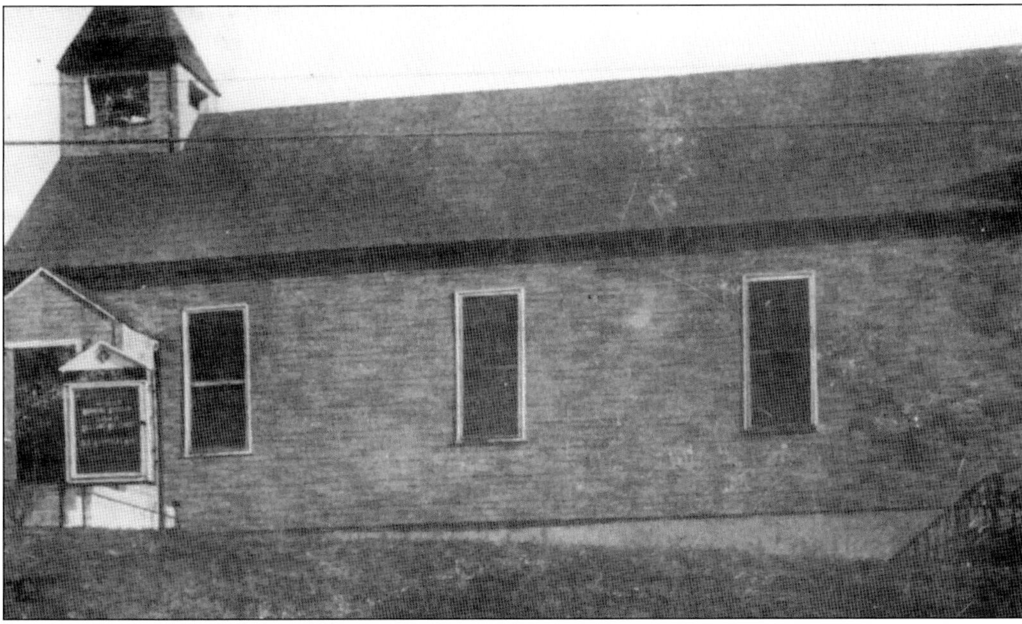

CONTEE CHAPEL AME ZION, 1940S. Contee Church began as a Sunday school in 1884 in the home of Daniel Contee on Eastern Avenue near Bell Place. He was joined by Rev. Albert C. Washington and Rev. Logan Johnson. When it was established as a church, Reverend Johnson became the first pastor. Construction of the first building began in 1885 at 903 Division Avenue. (Contee AME Zion Church.)

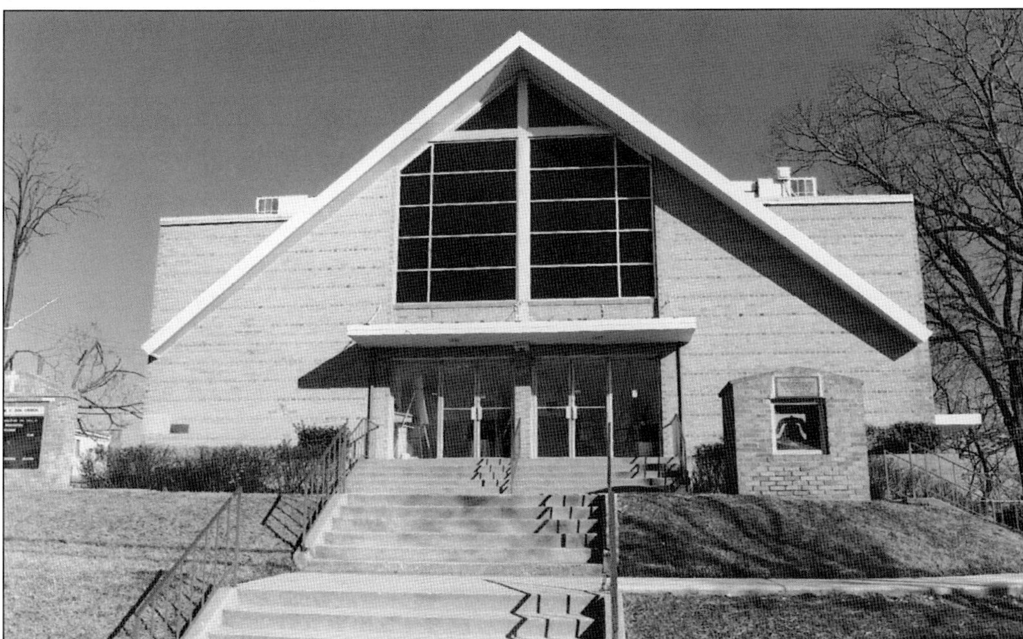

CONTEE AME ZION CHURCH, 1960S. The Contee Chapel AME Zion Church building, as it was originally called, was erected on a tract of land donated by the Deane estate. Under the leadership of Rev. Frederick W. Barnes, the church constructed a new building (above) on the same site in 1963. Soon after, the church opened the Contee day care center. (Contee AME Zion Church.)

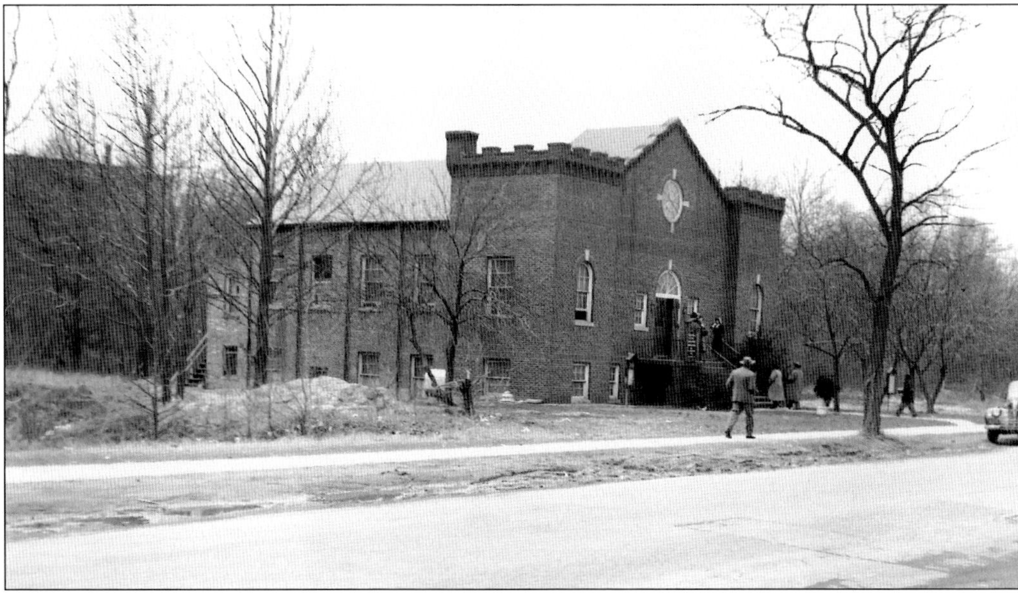

SARGENT MEMORIAL PRESBYTERIAN CHURCH, MARCH 27, 1949. The church was established by Rev. McCraig Lewistall and his faithful followers in Fairmount Heights, Maryland. Under the leadership of H. W. Campbell and with generous contributions from the Sargent family and faithful parishioners, the church was able to build an edifice at 5109 Grant Street (now Nannie Helen Burroughs Avenue) in 1930. (JTWC, HSWDC.)

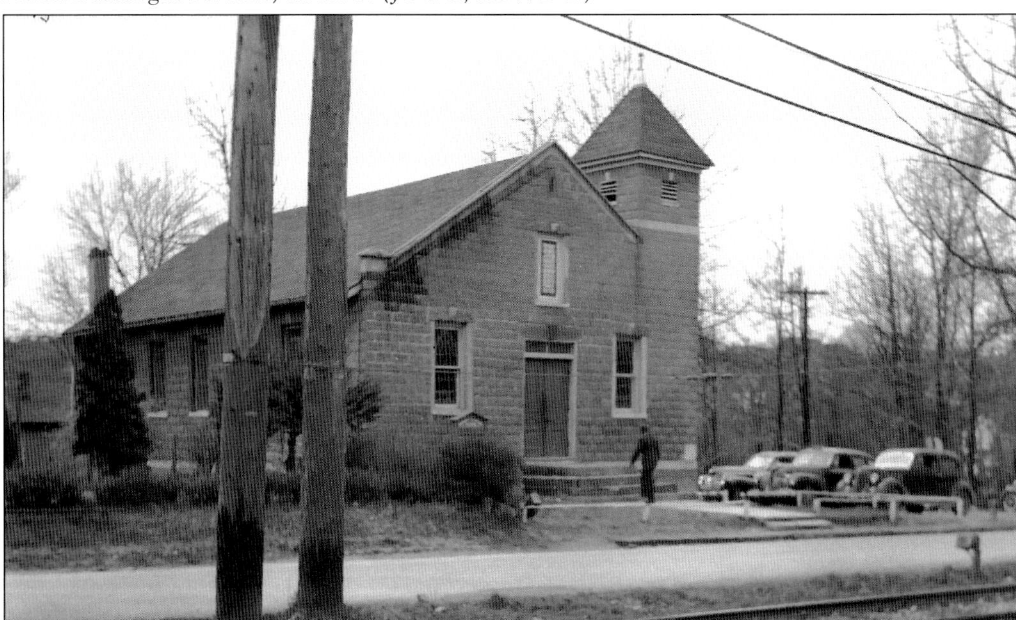

BEULAH BAPTIST CHURCH, MARCH 27, 1949. Beulah Baptist began as a Sunday school organized by Rev. James Cobb. Parishioners originally worshipped in a tin-covered building they called the "tin cup." In 1910, Reverend Cobb and his steering committee created a financial plan for a permanent church. Later Rev. Oliver W. Evans cleared the church debt with his "pay-as-we-build strategy." (JTWC, HSWDC.)

Five

Developing Strong Minds

Recognizing the need to formally educate neighborhood children, Contee AME Zion Church organized a school in its basement in 1886. By 1888, the church successfully erected Burrville Elementary School on a tract of land bounded by Grant Street, Eastern Avenue, Division Avenue, and Fifty-sixth Street.

In 1909, the children of Deanwood had the choice to attend one of two schools when Deanwood Elementary School was erected. Located at Whittingham and Lane Place (now Lee Street), it became an anchor of the community and the alma mater of generations of residents.

Emma F. G. Merritt Elementary School was established in a building constructed in 1943 on the site of the former Suburban Gardens Amusement Park at Hayes Street and Lowrie Place. Merritt was originally to function as a combination elementary and junior high school. However, when it opened, Merritt served only elementary-aged children. It was named in honor of Emma F. G. Merritt, a longtime educator and civic leader who served as president of the local NAACP, a member of the executive board of the Southwest Settlement House, and chairman of the Committee on Finance of the Phyllis Wheatley YWCA.

Deanwood did not get its first junior high school until Kelly Miller opened its doors in September 1949. Up until that time, Deanwood junior high school students traveled outside of the community to attend Browne, Blose, Thomas, or Webb Schools. In 1966, almost 20 years later, the neighborhood got its second junior high school, Roper, which was built at 4800 Meade Street. It was named for Daniel C. Roper, who served as the first assistant postmaster general, U.S. tariff commissioner, commissioner of the internal revenue, and secretary of commerce. It was later renamed Ronald H. Brown Middle School.

Until the *Brown* decision in 1954, youth attended one of the District's three senior high schools for "colored" children: Armstrong, Dunbar, or Cardozo Senior High School. Deanwood did not get its first public high school, H. D. Woodson Senior High, until 1972.

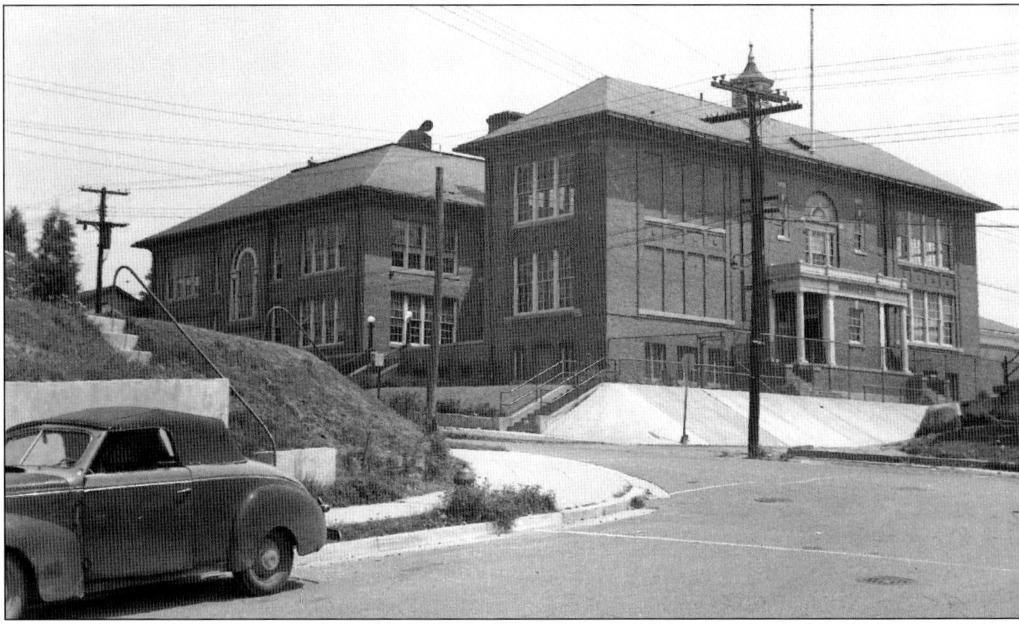

BURRVILLE ELEMENTARY SCHOOL, AUGUST 8, 1948. Burrville Elementary School started in the basement of Contee AME Zion Church in 1886. Both the school and community in which it was located were named Burrville after the Burr family, which donated the land. The original building was razed and replaced in 1912. The building underwent additional restructuring in 1929 and 1930. (JTWC, HSWDC.)

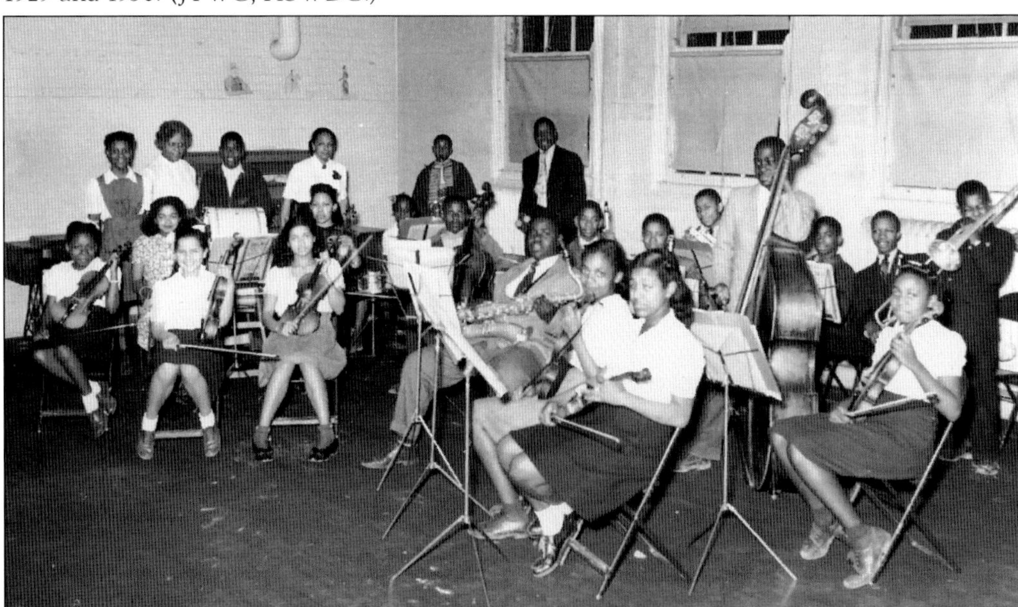

BURRVILLE RECREATION ORCHESTRA, 1940S. The Burrville Recreation Center, located in the Burrville School, formed an orchestra in 1943 under the direction of Wilhelmina Patterson, a local musician of note. The PTA raised $1,500 to purchase instruments. The orchestra appeared in concerts all over Washington, but the players were denied the opportunity to play in Washington's Junior Symphony because of their race. (Dianne Dale.)

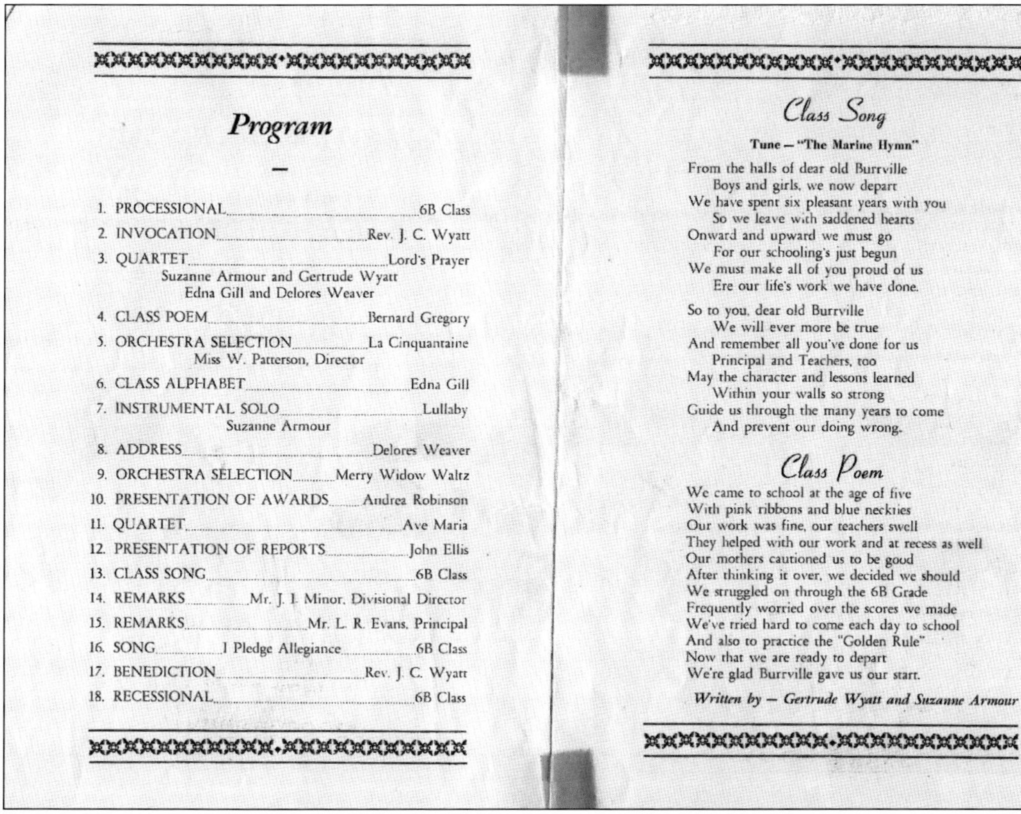

Program

1. PROCESSIONAL .... 6B Class
2. INVOCATION .... Rev. J. C. Wyatt
3. QUARTET .... Lord's Prayer
   Suzanne Armour and Gertrude Wyatt
   Edna Gill and Delores Weaver
4. CLASS POEM .... Bernard Gregory
5. ORCHESTRA SELECTION .... La Cinquantaine
   Miss W. Patterson, Director
6. CLASS ALPHABET .... Edna Gill
7. INSTRUMENTAL SOLO .... Lullaby
   Suzanne Armour
8. ADDRESS .... Delores Weaver
9. ORCHESTRA SELECTION .... Merry Widow Waltz
10. PRESENTATION OF AWARDS .... Andrea Robinson
11. QUARTET .... Ave Maria
12. PRESENTATION OF REPORTS .... John Ellis
13. CLASS SONG .... 6B Class
14. REMARKS .... Mr. J. I. Minor, Divisional Director
15. REMARKS .... Mr. L. R. Evans, Principal
16. SONG .... I Pledge Allegiance .... 6B Class
17. BENEDICTION .... Rev. J. C. Wyatt
18. RECESSIONAL .... 6B Class

Class Song

Tune — "The Marine Hymn"

From the halls of dear old Burrville
Boys and girls, we now depart
We have spent six pleasant years with you
So we leave with saddened hearts
Onward and upward we must go
For our schooling's just begun
We must make all of you proud of us
Ere our life's work we have done.

So to you, dear old Burrville
We will ever more be true
And remember all you've done for us
Principal and Teachers, too
May the character and lessons learned
Within your walls so strong
Guide us through the many years to come
And prevent our doing wrong.

Class Poem

We came to school at the age of five
With pink ribbons and blue neckties
Our work was fine, our teachers swell
They helped with our work and at recess as well
Our mothers cautioned us to be good
After thinking it over, we decided we should
We struggled on through the 6B Grade
Frequently worried over the scores we made
We've tried hard to come each day to school
And also to practice the "Golden Rule"
Now that we are ready to depart
We're glad Burrville gave us our start.

Written by — Gertrude Wyatt and Suzanne Armour

Burrville Promotion Exercises, 1946. When it was originally founded, Burrville Elementary School served students in grades one through six. Later it extended through eighth grade and added kindergarten. In 1946, the school ended in the sixth grade. The promotion exercises for Class 6B occurred on Tuesday, June 18, 1946, and included a performance of the "Merry Widow Waltz" by the Burrville Recreation Orchestra. (Dianne Dale.)

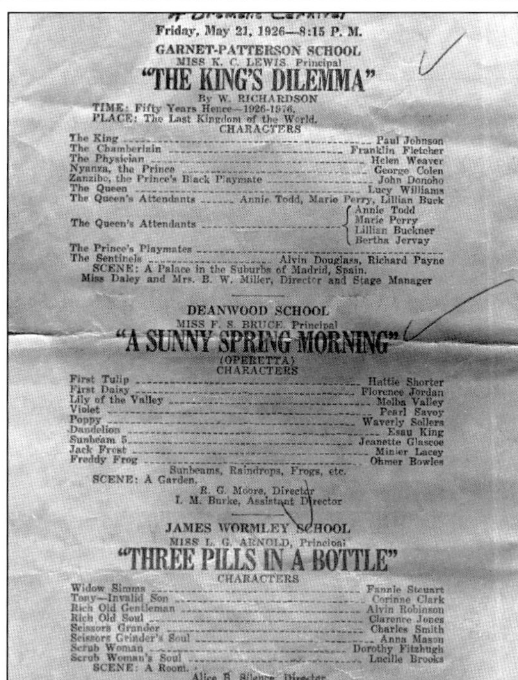

Friday, May 21, 1926—8:15 P. M.

GARNET-PATTERSON SCHOOL
MISS K. C. LEWIS, Principal

"THE KING'S DILEMMA"

By W. RICHARDSON
TIME: Fifty Years Hence—1926-1976.
PLACE: The Last Kingdom of the World.

CHARACTERS

The King .... Paul Johnson
The Chamberlain .... Franklin Fletcher
The Physician .... Helen Weaver
Nyanza, the Prince .... George Colen
Zanzibo, the Prince's Black Playmate .... John Donoho
The Queen .... Lucy Williams
The Queen's Attendants .... Annie Todd, Marie Perry, Lillian Buck
The Queen's Attendants .... Annie Todd, Marie Perry, Lillian Buckner, Bertha Jervay
The Prince's Playmates ....
The Sentinels .... Alvin Douglass, Richard Payne
SCENE: A Palace in the Suburbs of Madrid, Spain.
Miss Daley and Mrs. B. W. Miller, Director and Stage Manager

DEANWOOD SCHOOL
MISS F. S. BRUCE, Principal

"A SUNNY SPRING MORNING"

(OPERETTA)

CHARACTERS

First Tulip .... Hattie Shorter
First Daisy .... Florence Jordan
Lily of the Valley .... Melba Valley
Violet .... Pearl Savoy
Poppy .... Waverly Sollers
Dandelion .... Esau King
Sunbeam 5 .... Jeanette Glascoe
Jack Frost .... Minier Lacey
Freddy Frog .... Ohmer Bowles
Sunbeams, Raindrops, Frogs, etc.
SCENE: A Garden.
R. G. Moore, Director
I. M. Burke, Assistant Director

JAMES WORMLEY SCHOOL
MISS L. G. ARNOLD, Principal

"THREE PILLS IN A BOTTLE"

CHARACTERS

Widow Simms .... Fannie Steuart
Tony—Invalid Son .... Corinne Clark
Rich Old Gentleman .... Alvin Robinson
Rich Old Soul .... Clarence Jones
Scissors Grander .... Charles Smith
Scissors Grinder's Soul .... Anna Mason
Scrub Woman .... Dorothy Fitzhugh
Scrub Woman's Soul .... Lucille Brooks
SCENE: A Room.
Alice B. Silence, Director
B. B. Jackson, Stage Manager

Dramatic Carnival, May 21, 1926. From May 17 through May 22, 1926, D.C. Public Schools held a "Dramatic Carnival," a play competition among 21 schools in Divisions 10 through 13. Deanwood competed against Garnet-Patterson, Wormley, and Sumner-Magruder Schools among other black schools by performing an operetta called *A Sunny Spring Morning.* (DCPL, WD, Curtis Collection.)

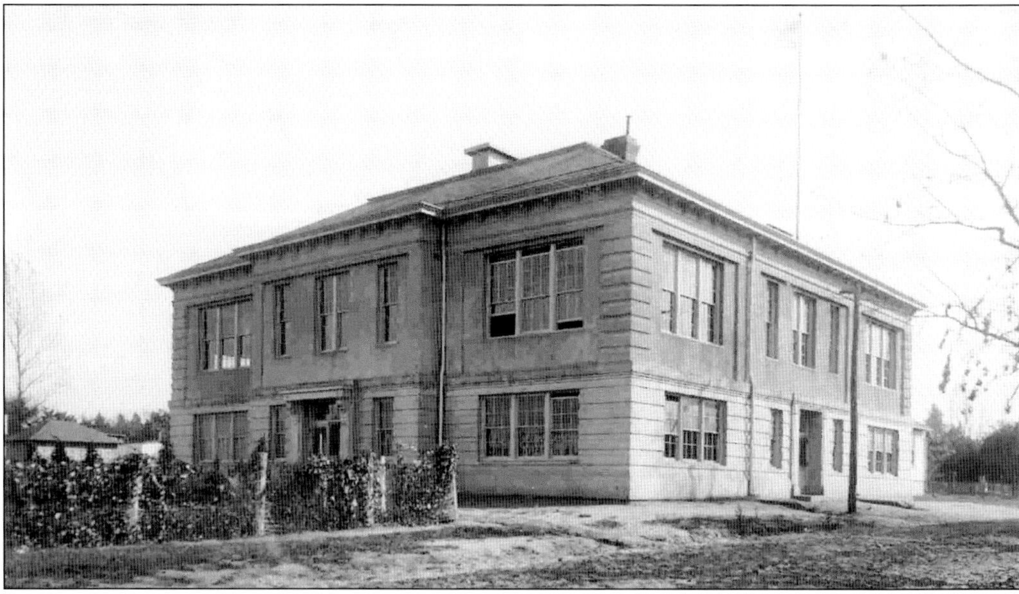

DEANWOOD SCHOOL, 1940S. On May 21, 1862, Congress passed an act to "establish and maintain a system of free schools for the benefit of Colored people of the District of Columbia." Finally Deanwood Elementary School, designed by architect Snowden Ashford, was built in 1909 to serve as the first public school for the African American children in the community. (Charles Sumner School Museum and Archives.)

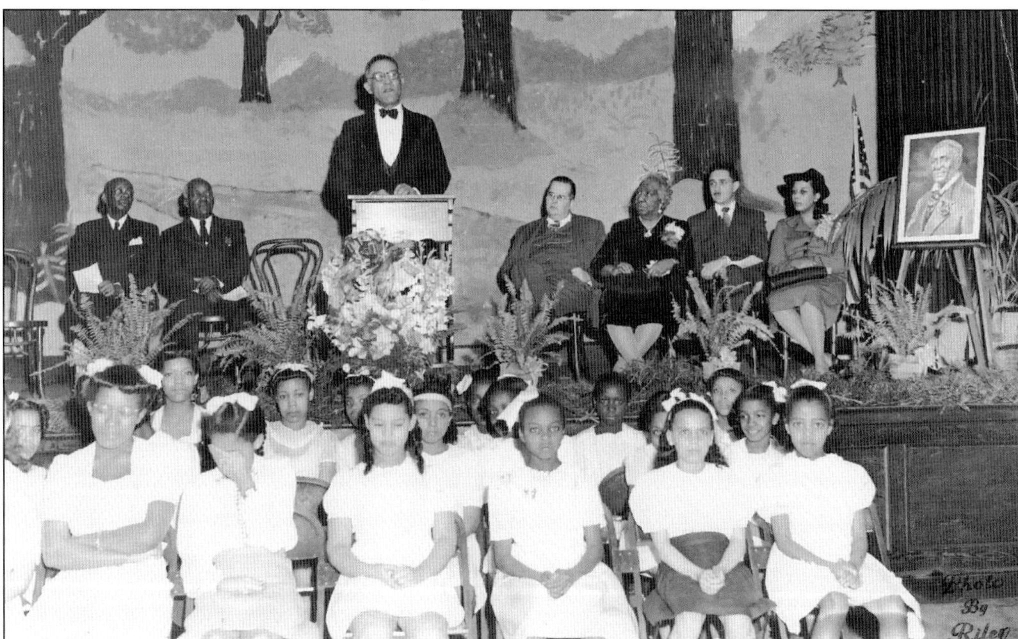

RENAMING DEANWOOD SCHOOL, 1946. Principal Beatrice B. Brown (third from right) and PTA president Dorothy Dixon (right) grace the stage as a shy glee club waits patiently to sing for the standing-room-only crowd. At the ceremony, a large photograph and bust of George Washington Carver were presented, and children later enjoyed a party as their beloved school was renamed George Washington Carver Elementary School. (Bettie Staley Littlejohn.)

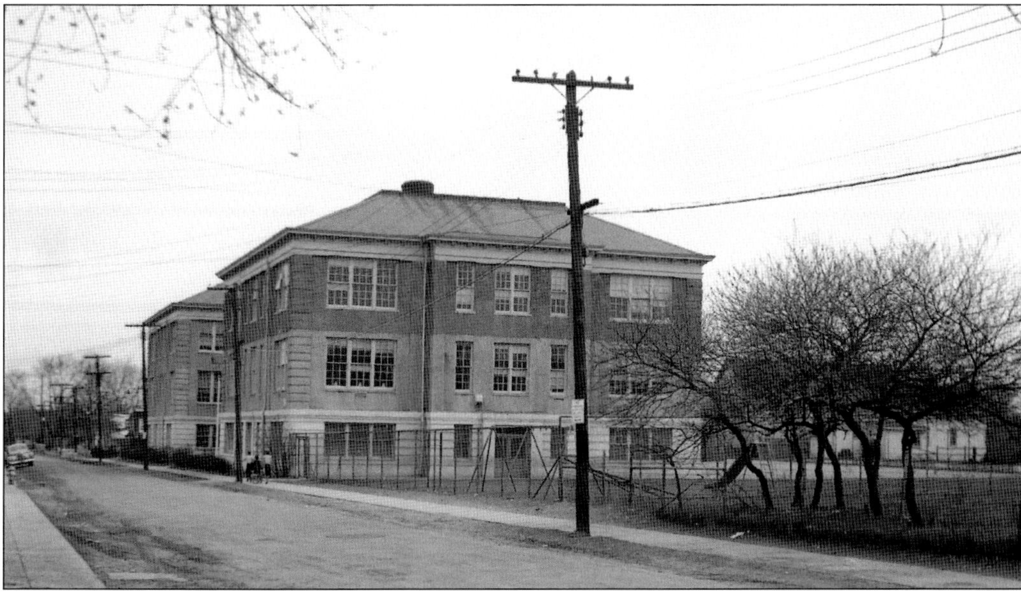

GEORGE WASHINGTON CARVER ELEMENTARY SCHOOL, 1949. George Washington Carver Elementary School (formerly Deanwood School) was built in sections between 1909 and 1930. The school was damaged by fire in 1961. The original section was razed in 1969 and rebuilt in 1970. Carver formally closed its doors in 1988 before reopening as IDEA Public Charter School in 1999. The Church of the Incarnation is seen behind the school. (JTWC, HSWDC.)

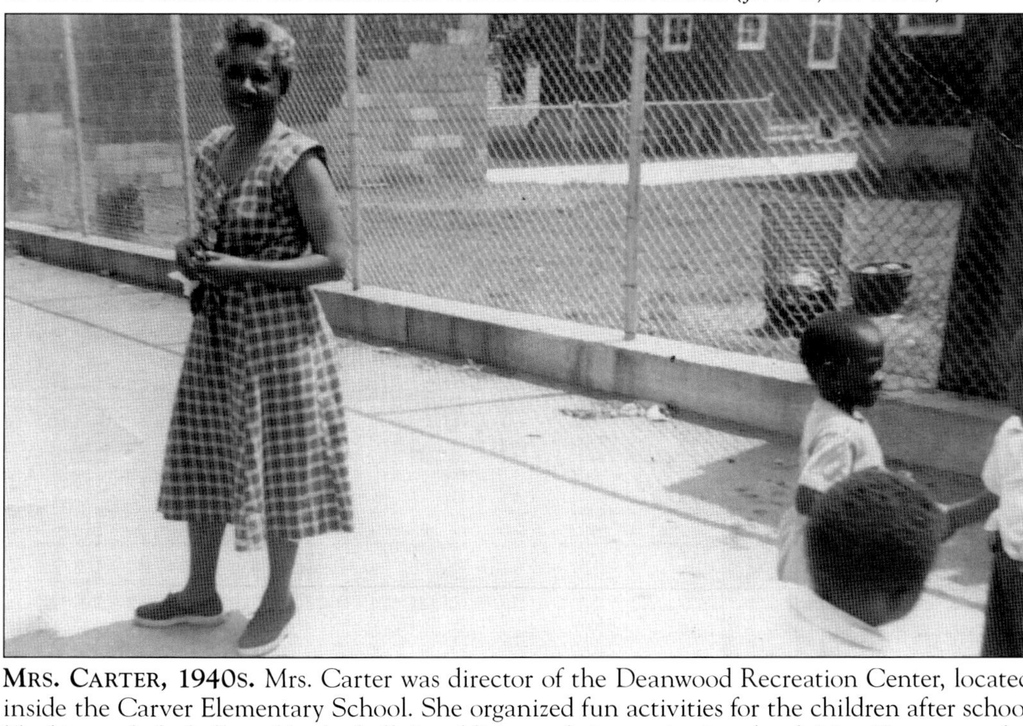

MRS. CARTER, 1940S. Mrs. Carter was director of the Deanwood Recreation Center, located inside the Carver Elementary School. She organized fun activities for the children after school like bingo, dodgeball, and basketball. In addition to being active in school, Mrs. Carter was also an advisor to the Deanwood Junior Civic Association. In that role, she helped the youth of the neighborhood develop their community leadership skills. (Sandra Brown.)

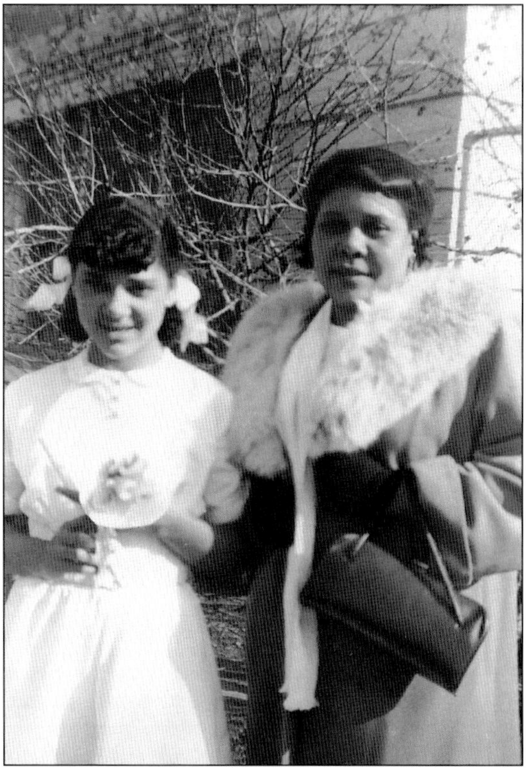

SIXTH GRADE GRADUATION DAY, C. 1951. Goldie King (left) and her mother, Sarah King, enjoy sixth-grade graduation, a very special event in the Deanwood neighborhood. Everyone turned out to honor Carver Elementary School graduates as they made their transition into junior high school. (Sylvia Brown.)

GLADYS WALLACE AND JACKIE KING, 1969. Even after it became George Washington Carver Elementary School, sixth-grade graduation continued to be a time of celebration in the Deanwood community. Here teacher Gladys Wallace stands with her student Jackie King outside of the school after the ceremony. (Jackie Washington.)

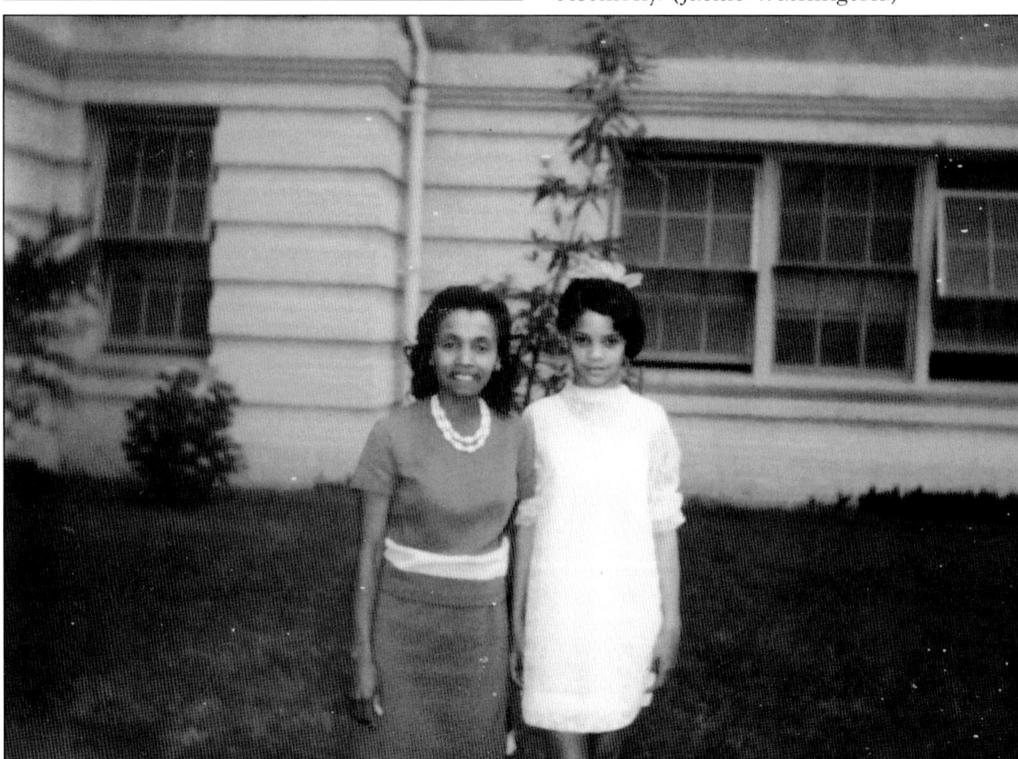

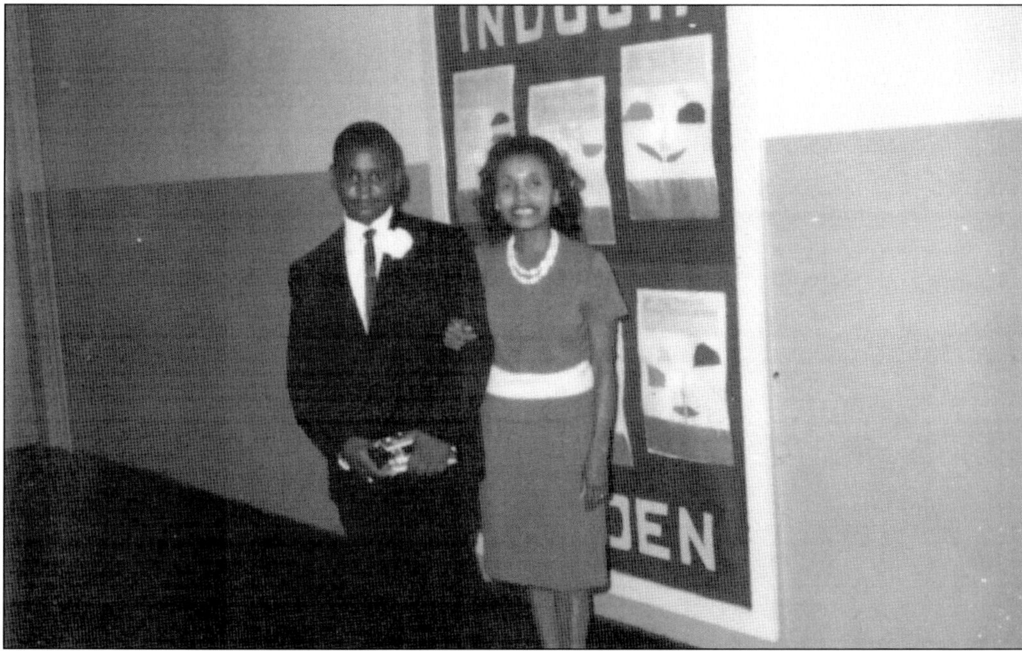

JUAN H. GADDIS AND GLADYS WALLACE, 1969. Many parents made it a point to mark this milestone in their children's lives. Here Gladys Wallace takes another photograph, this time on the inside of the school, with Juan H. Gaddis, another member of George Washington Carver Elementary School's class of 1969. (Barbara J. Moore.)

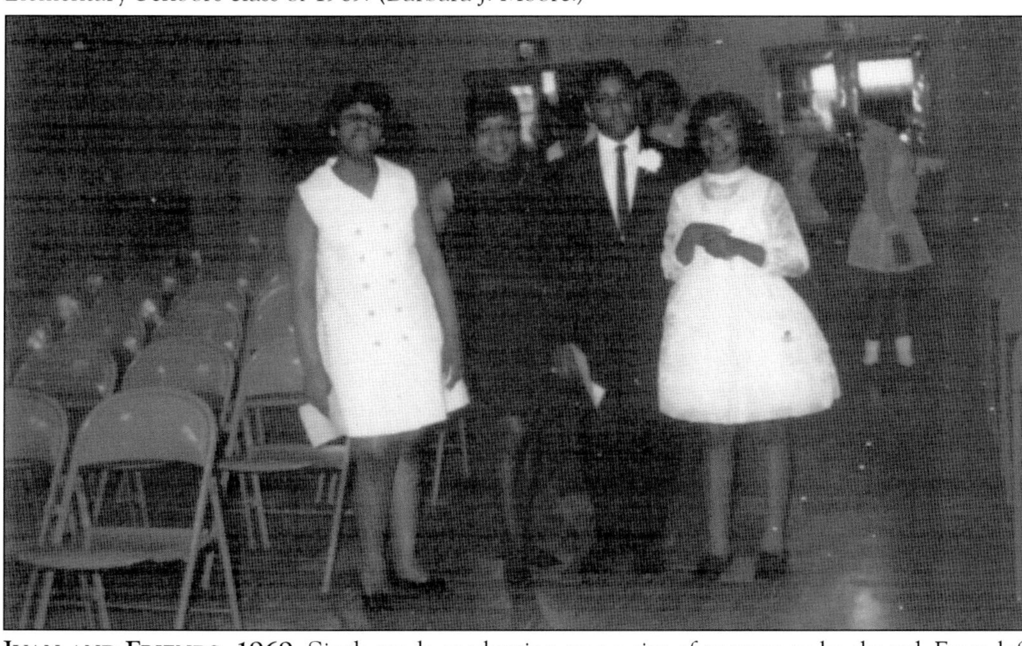

JUAN AND FRIENDS, 1969. Sixth-grade graduation was a rite of passage to be shared. From left to right, Denise Howard; Rachel Stokes; their church musician, Juan H. Gaddis; and Tawanda Hackley celebrate together. The three friends not only attended elementary school together but also worshipped together, as all were members of the First Baptist Church of Deanwood. (Barbara J. Moore.)

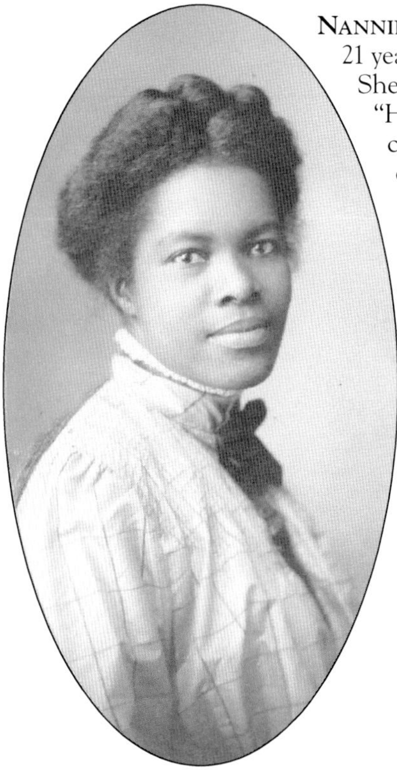

NANNIE HELEN BURROUGHS, C. 1910. Nannie Helen Burroughs was 21 years old when she rose to prominence in the black community. She became a national leader after she gave a speech entitled "How the Sisters are Hindered from Helping" at the annual conference of the National Baptist Convention in 1900. She opened the National Training School for Women and Girls in Deanwood nine years later. (NHBS.)

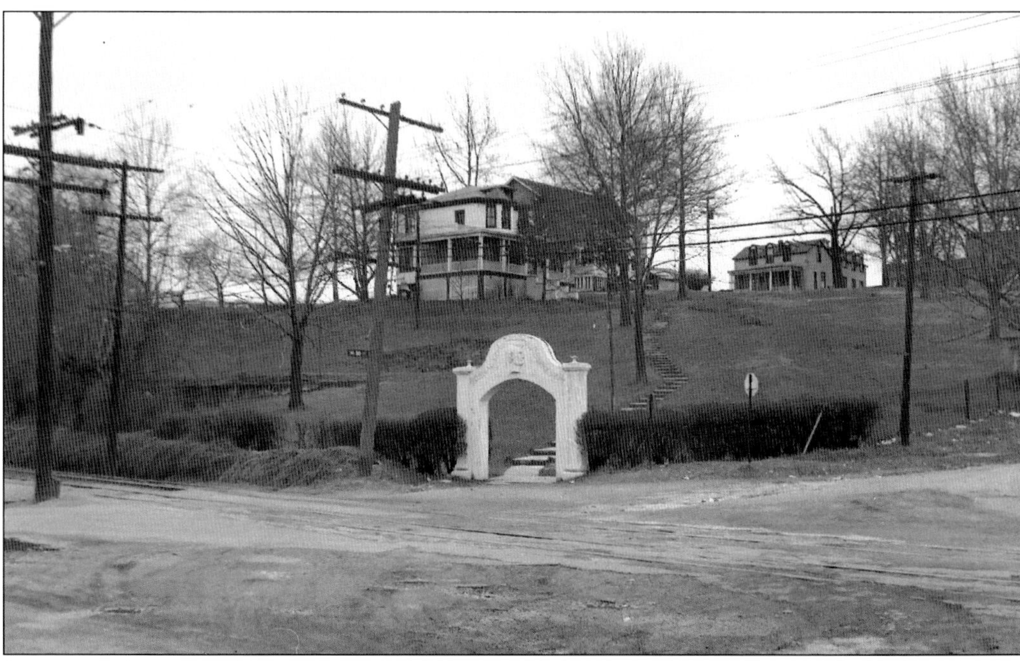

NATIONAL TRAINING SCHOOL, MARCH 27, 1949. Nannie Helen Burroughs purchased the site for the National Training School for Women and Girls in 1907 for the establishment of a school to train young African American women. Dubbed the "Holy Hill," it consisted of six acres of land and an eight-room home at Fiftieth and Grant Streets. (JTWC, HSWDC.)

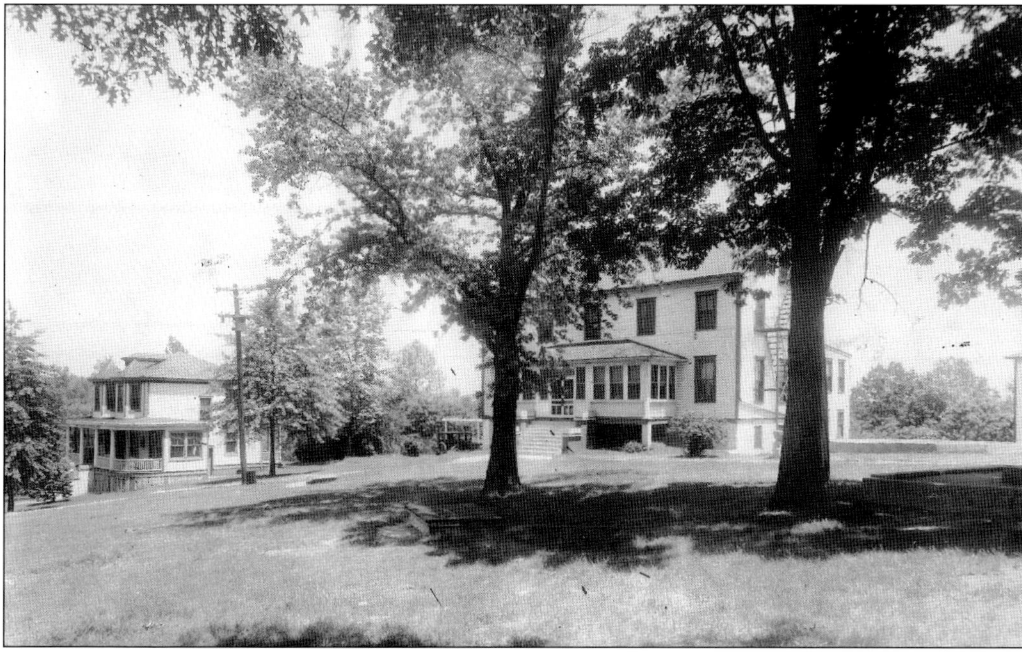

Holy Hill, c. 1910. Burroughs traveled the city to find the hill on which to build her school. Above are two of her school buildings, Burdette Hall (left) and Pioneer Hall (right). Dr. Burroughs died in 1961 after serving as the school's president for 52 years. In 1964, it was renamed in her honor and continues to operate as an elementary school. (NHBS.)

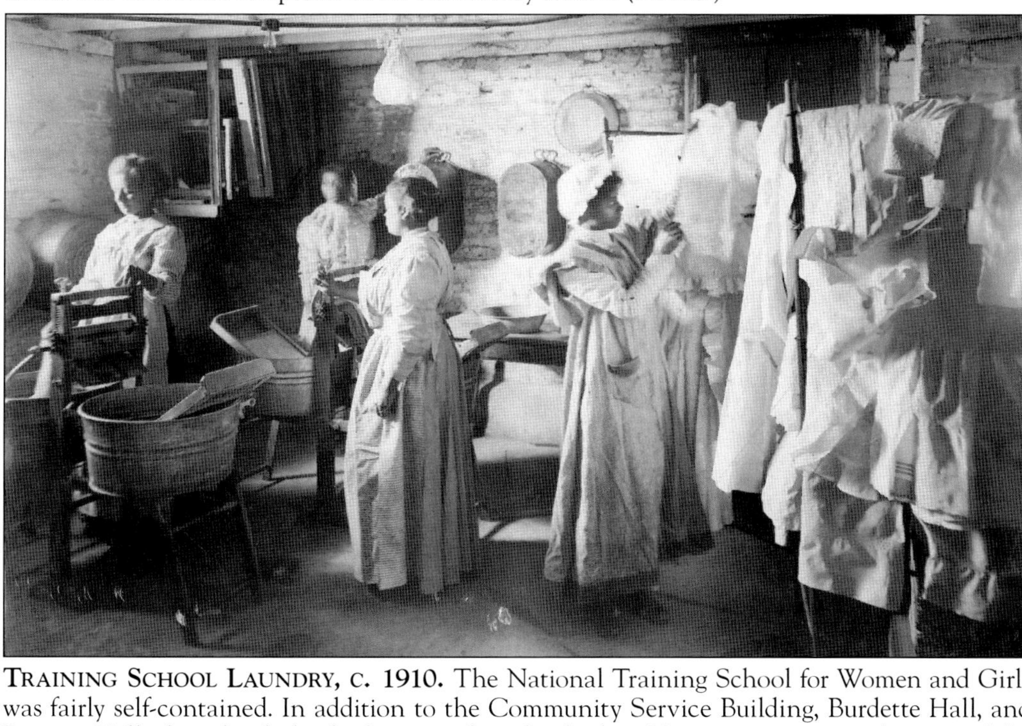

Training School Laundry, c. 1910. The National Training School for Women and Girls was fairly self-contained. In addition to the Community Service Building, Burdette Hall, and Pioneer Hall, the school also had its own laundry facility. Here some women take care of the students' cleaning needs. (NHBS.)

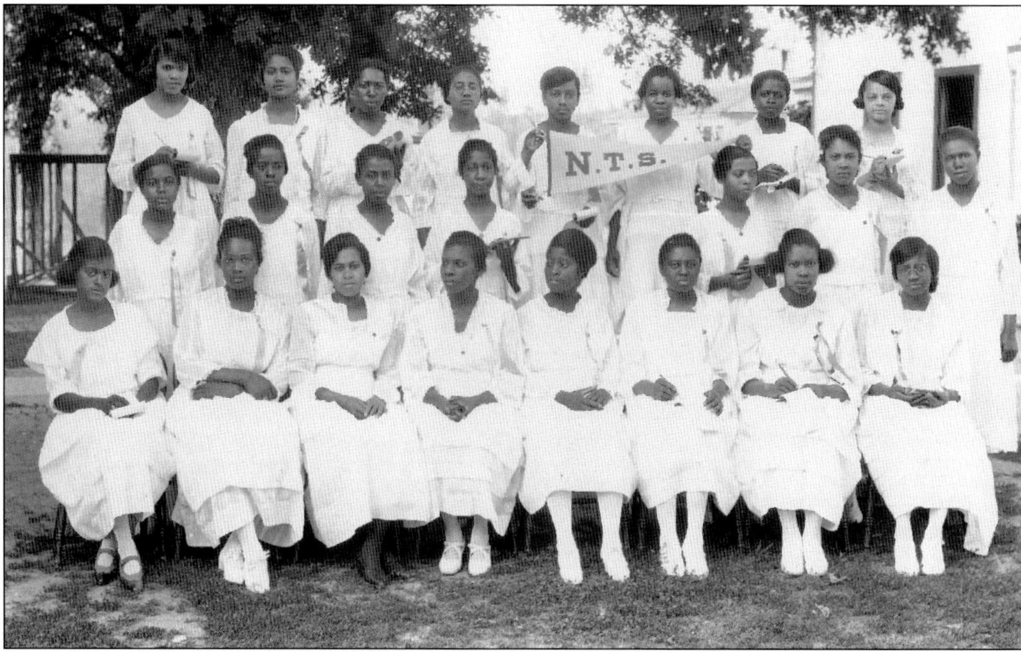

TRAINING SCHOOL CLASS PORTRAIT, 1930S. In addition to attracting students from across the United States, the National Training School for Women and Girls also drew girls from Africa and the Caribbean. In its first 25 years, more than 2,000 women from these areas matriculated at the school. (NHBS.)

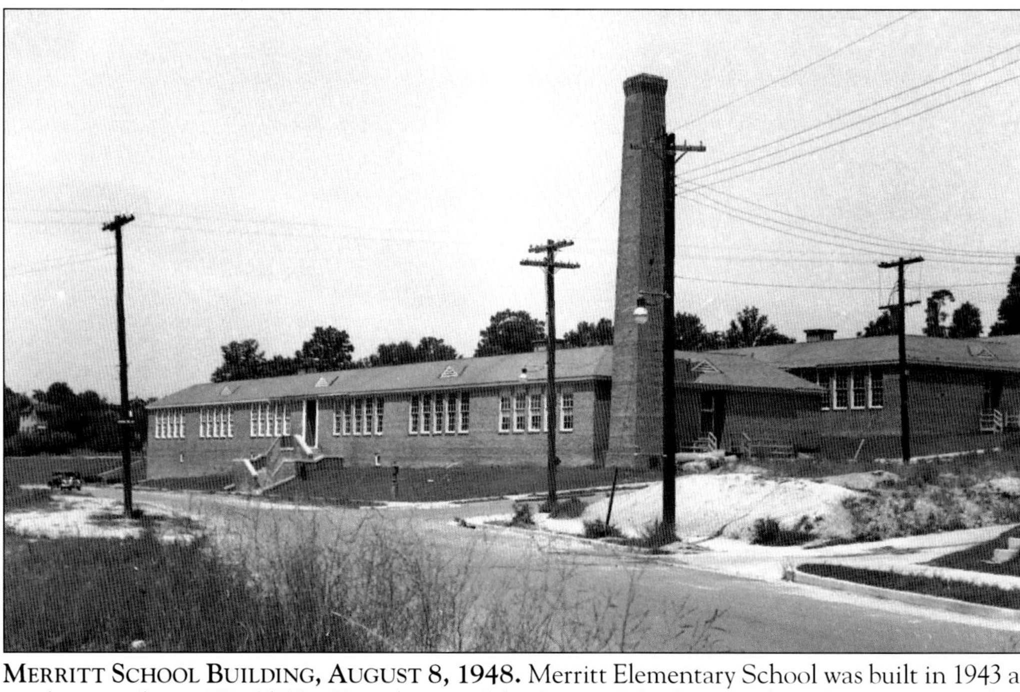

MERRITT SCHOOL BUILDING, AUGUST 8, 1948. Merritt Elementary School was built in 1943 as war housing during World War II on the site of the former Suburban Gardens Amusement Park. It was located down the street from the Suburban Heights housing development and represented a third elementary school choice for children of the Deanwood community. (JTWC, HSWDC.)

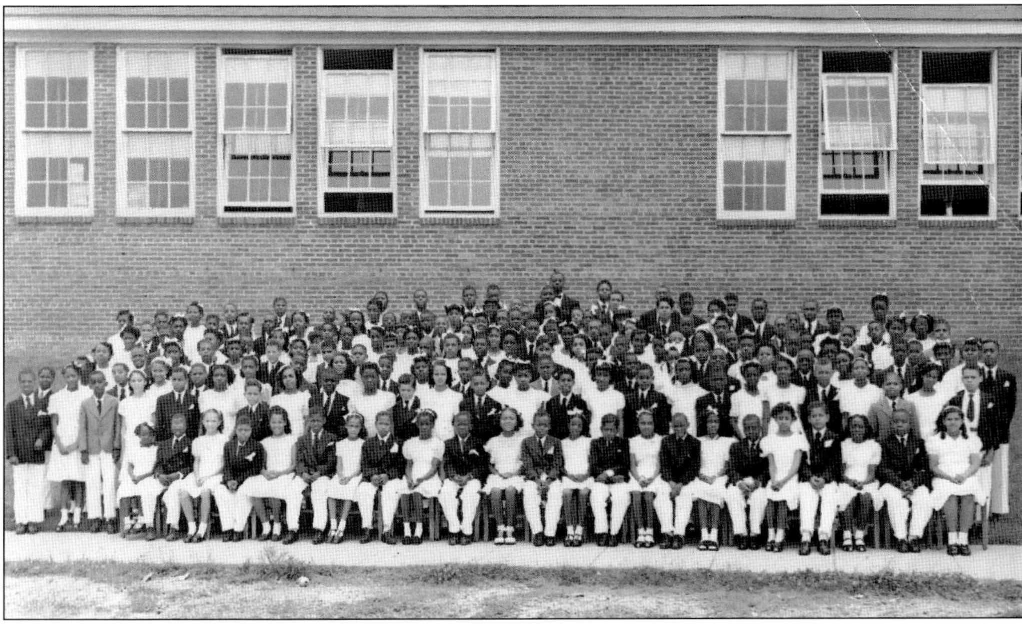

MERRITT GRADUATION, 1948. Bertha J. McMurdock served as the principal of Merritt School in the late 1940s and early 1950s. She led the school during segregation and was known as a stickler for etiquette. She reportedly insisted that her teachers keep classroom window blinds at the same length to present a uniform appearance to passersby. (Joan Slade Gray.)

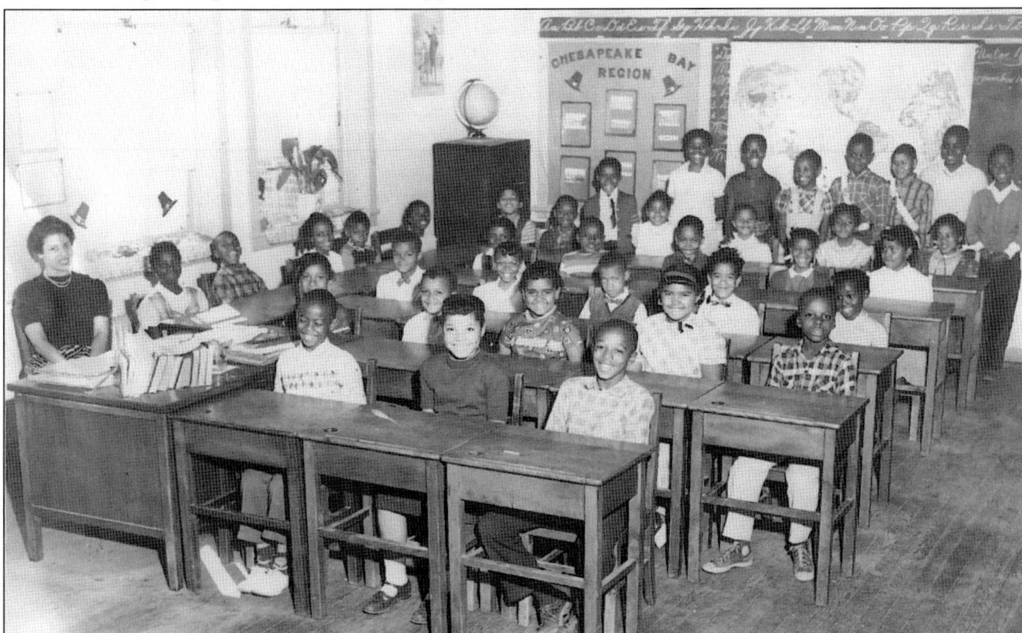

MERRITT SCHOOL CLASSROOM, C. 1956. Mildred Greene was Merritt's fourth-grade teacher. She enjoyed teaching her students about the Chesapeake Bay region. One of her students, Alice Chandler, fondly remembers being treated to a class trip across the Chesapeake Bay Bridge to experience eating oysters. Greene taught in the D.C. public school system for over 40 years, serving at both Merritt and George Washington Carver Elementary Schools. (Alice Chandler.)

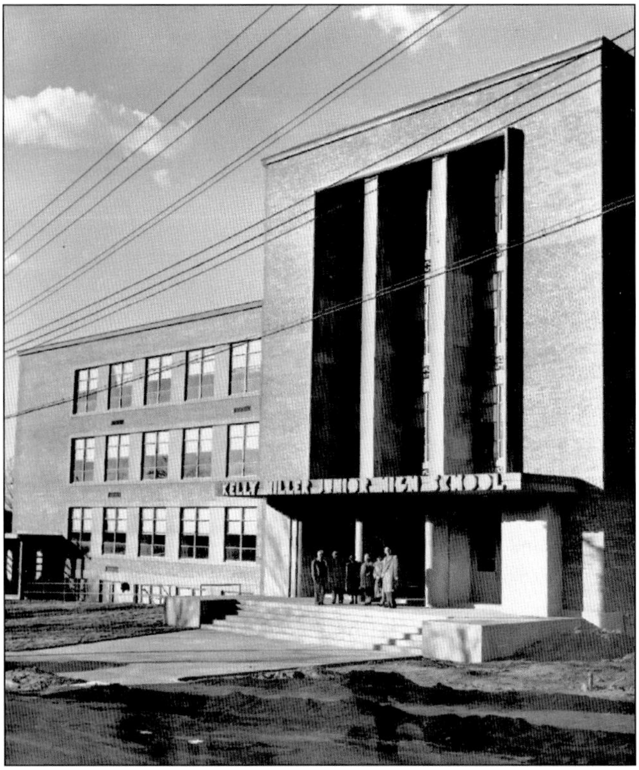

KELLY MILLER JUNIOR HIGH SCHOOL, 1949. Opening the school represented a victory for the parents and civic leaders in the community. It was the first junior high school in the neighborhood and had the capacity to serve 1,200 students. The school was named for an esteemed educator and an outspoken leader in Washington's black community. The building was demolished and subsequently rebuilt. (DCPL, WD, *Washington Star* Collection.)

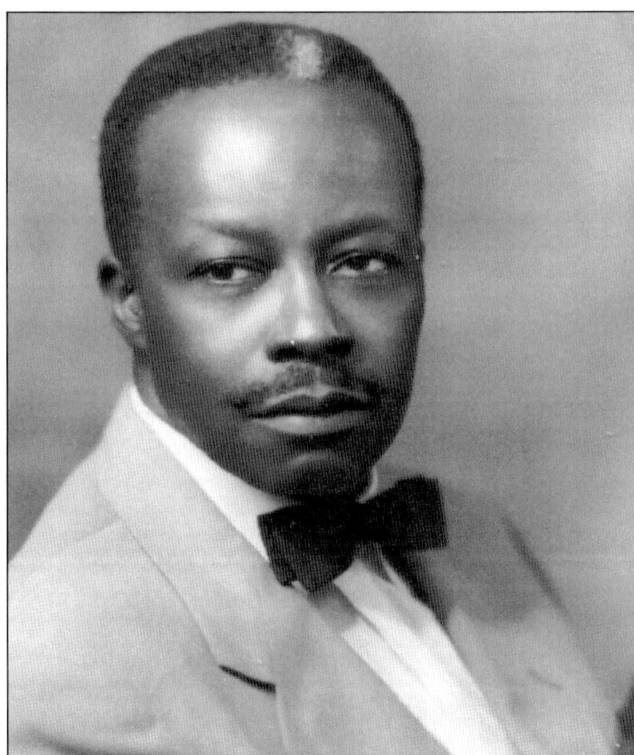

DR. CHANCELLOR WILLIAMS, 1950S. Dr. Williams, renowned African American historian and admired Howard University professor, resided at 5000 Sheriff Road. The Deanwood resident received his master of arts degree in history from Howard in 1935 and in 1949 earned his doctorate from American University. Dr. Williams published numerous books, lectures, and articles, including *The Raven*, *The Rebirth of African Civilization*, and *Destruction of the Black Civilization*. (Aressa V. Williams.)

Six

A Sense of Civic Pride

Deanwood residents have a long history of civic participation. The Deanwood Civic Association, established in 1893, was one of the first in Washington, D.C. When residents saw a community need, they were quick to organize themselves and find a solution to the problem. Official minutes from the D.C. Board of Education meetings show that the association was very active in seeking improved conditions in the school as well as holding government officials accountable for the education of their children. Adult leaders understood the importance of passing the torch to the next generation and did this through the Deanwood Junior Civic Association. In the Junior Civic Association, Deanwood youngsters were trained to be advocates for the community. Their activities included distributing community meeting fliers, decorating the community Christmas tree, and helping prepare for the outdoor neighborhood family movie, which was held on the Deanwood School playground every other Saturday in the summer.

In addition to being active in the civic life of their local community, Deanwood residents of all ages actively served their country. They did this through their chosen professions, military service, and by volunteering their time and skills. Two Deanwood men, Andrew D. Turner and Alfred Q. Carroll Jr., proudly served in World War II as Tuskegee airmen. The Nurses Unit of the First Baptist Church of Deanwood supported the war effort by serving as community volunteers at the Freedman's and Veterans Hospitals and as air raid wardens during the blackouts after completing their first aid training with the American Red Cross. Community volunteers such as Geraldine Haywood were recruited by the government and taught life-skills classes, such as canning, at the Deanwood School to women in the community who were on "relief." Children even joined in the effort, as the entire Deanwood Elementary School participated in the war bond efforts by raising money to purchase jeeps to support the U.S. military fighting abroad. This continued with later residents, such as Earl S. Simpson, who acted as the Deanwood archivist/historian. His research and knowledge preserved the neighborhood's history and, many times, was instrumental in supporting Deanwood citizens' lobbying efforts.

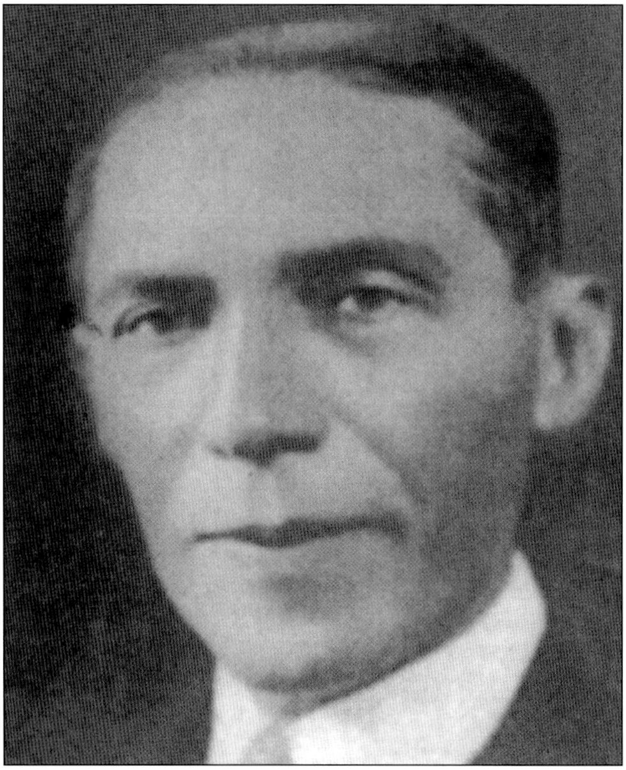

HOWARD DILWORTH WOODSON, 1955. In the early 1940s, Woodson and his wife, Pauline, raised their four boys (John, Harold, Paul, and Granville) on Fitch Place. In addition to being an accomplished architectural engineer, Woodson also helped establish many civic organizations in the community, including the Northeast Boundary Civic Association, the Far Northeast Council, the Far Northeast Business and Professional Association, and the National Technical Association. (Harris and Ewing.)

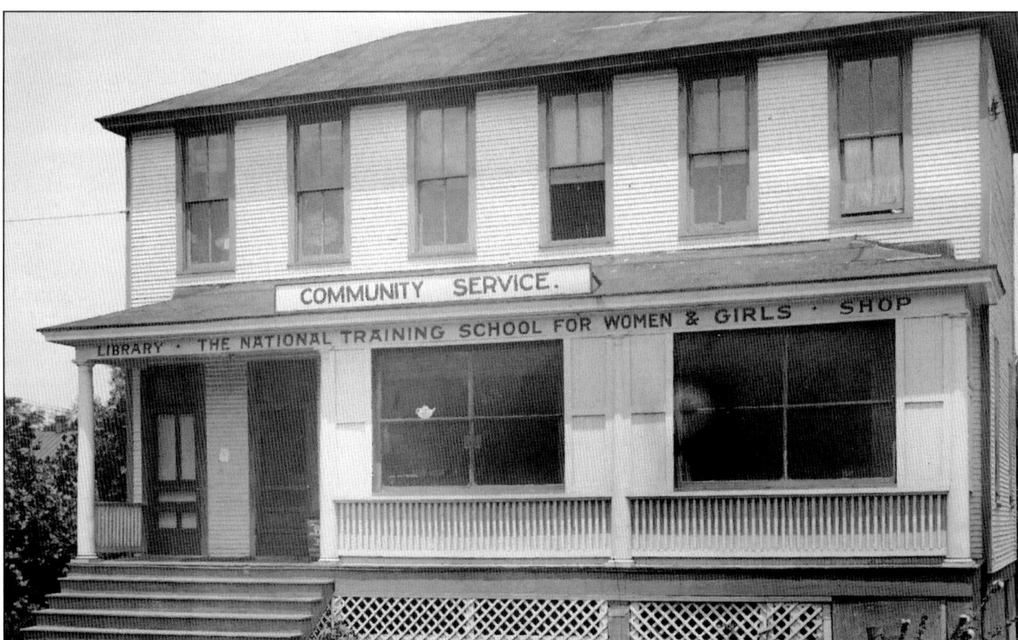

NATIONAL TRAINING SCHOOL, C. 1910. In the spirit of its founder, educator, political organizer, and civil rights activist Nannie Helen Burroughs, the National Training School for Women and Girls also emphasized the importance of civic responsibility. One of the buildings on the campus was the Community Service Building. (NHBS.)

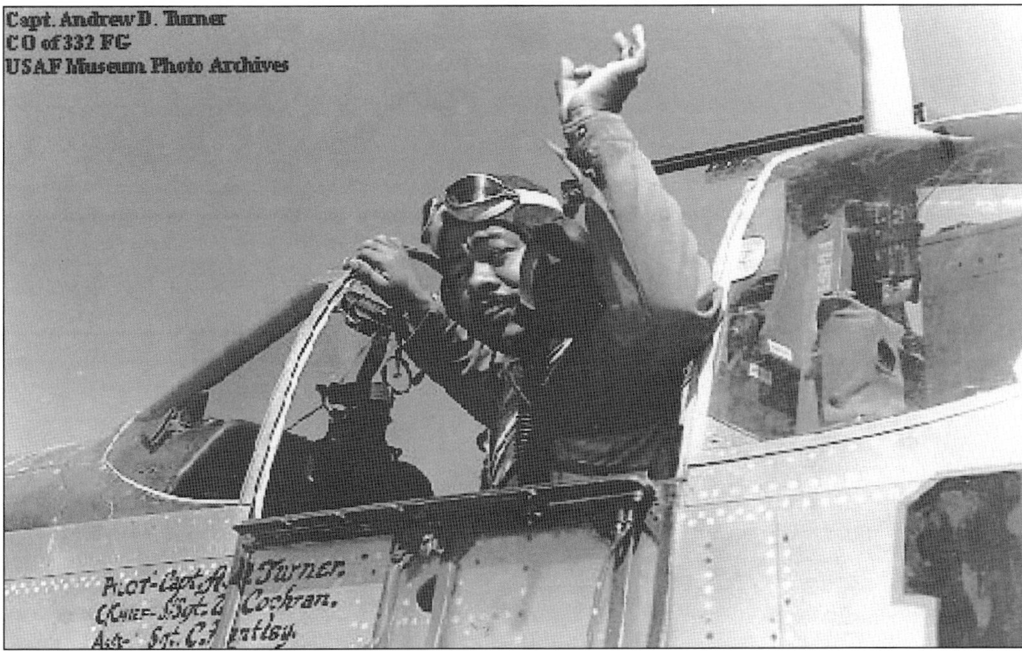

ANDREW D. TURNER, EARLY 1940S. Andrew Turner was commissioned at Tuskegee Army Air Field on October 9, 1942. He was appointed commanding officer of the 100th Fighter Squadron in 1944 and promoted to the rank of major in 1945. At the time of this photograph, Turner was a captain, seen in his jet, the "Skipper's Darlin'." (U.S. Air Force Museum Photograph Archives.)

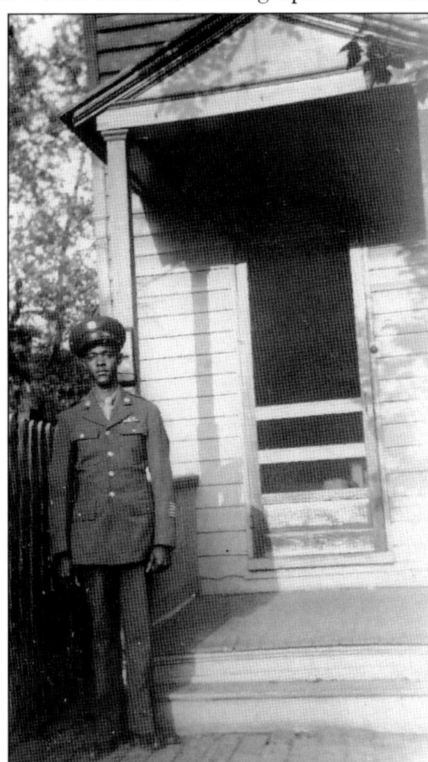

SERVICE TO OUR COUNTRY, C. 1945. Here Willie Bobo stands proudly in his uniform in front of his house at Forty-ninth Street and Sheriff Road, showing that Deanwood residents were faithful to their community as well as to their country. The community also provided housing for many black soldiers returning from their terms of service during World War II. (Doris Taylor-Collins.)

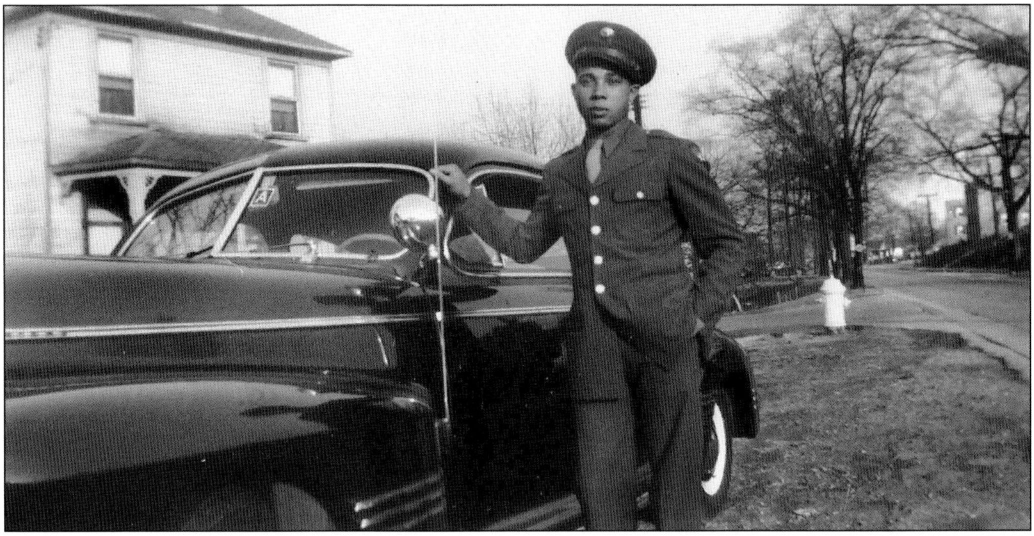

HIRAM HAYWOOD, MID-1940S. Deanwood was home to many military men. Hiram Haywood, whose family lived on Sheriff Road, served in the U.S. Air Force. He received his basic training at Keesler Field in Biloxi, Mississippi, before being stationed to Tuskegee, Alabama. Other returning military men and their families were able to move into new housing built in Deanwood during and after World War II. (WF.)

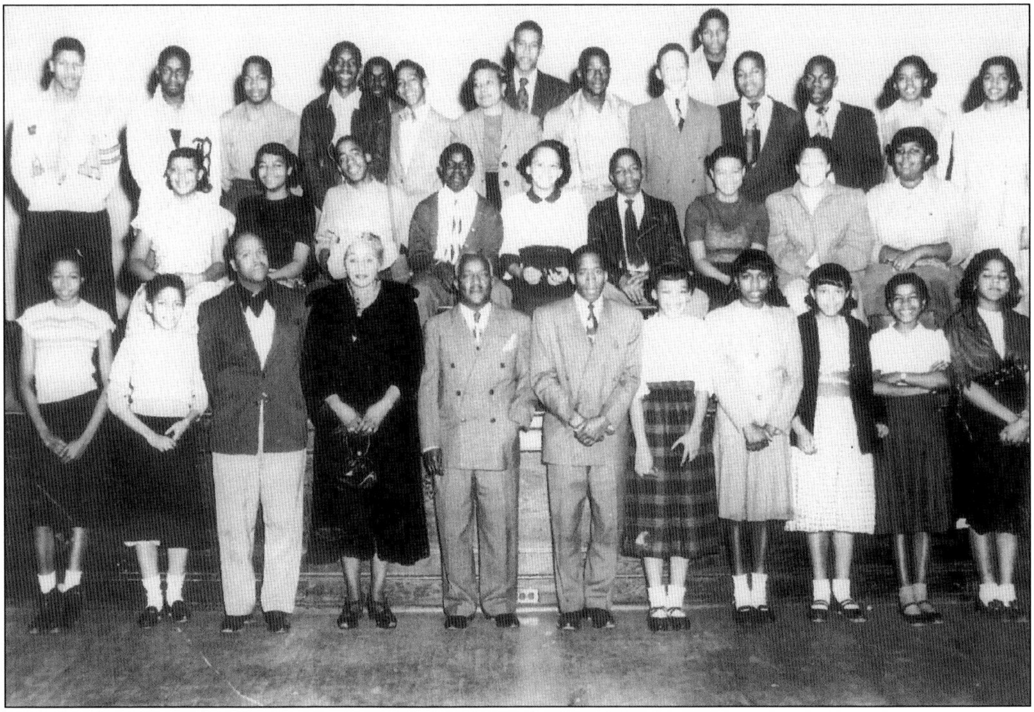

JUNIOR CIVIC ASSOCIATION, 1948. The Deanwood Junior Civic Association, established in 1948, was the first chartered junior association in the city. It was established by Mrs. King, Mrs. Carter, and Arena Leppard under the leadership of their president, Maurice Banks, and adult advisors, Mrs. Kane and Patrick Tolliver. Energetic teens worked with their parents and advisors to keep their neighborhood clean and free from crime. (Maurice Banks.)

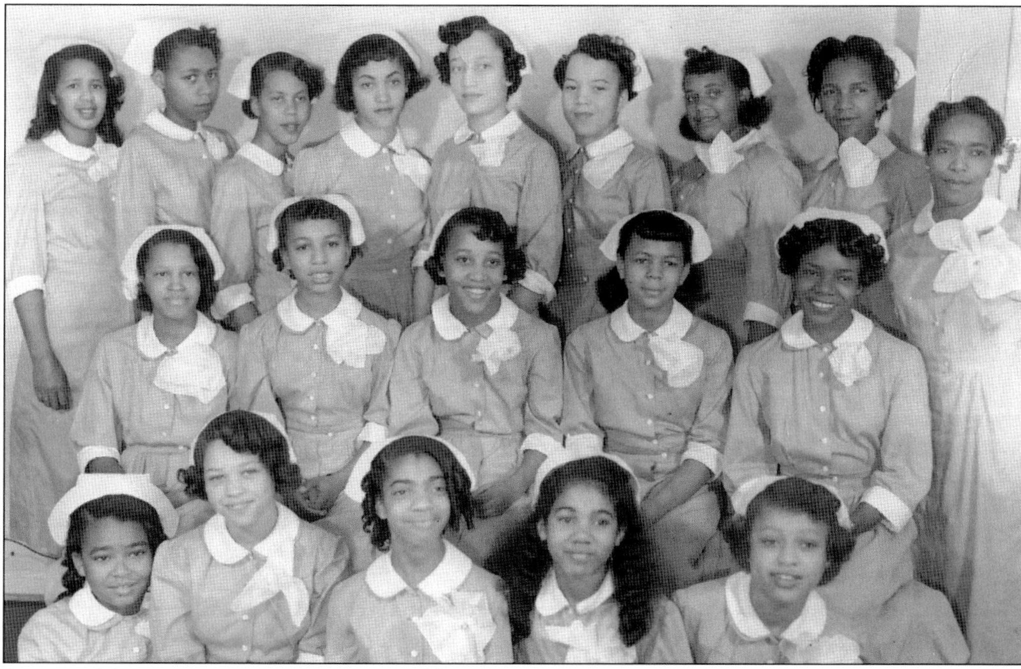

JUNIOR NURSES, C. 1950. Supervised by their advisor, Arena Leppard (far right), the Junior Nurses carried out their duties in a professional way. Like their counterparts in the main church, the Junior Nurses cared for the members during service. They were always dressed in freshly starched uniforms and known for their beautifully starched white handkerchiefs, which marked them as nurses. (EKB.)

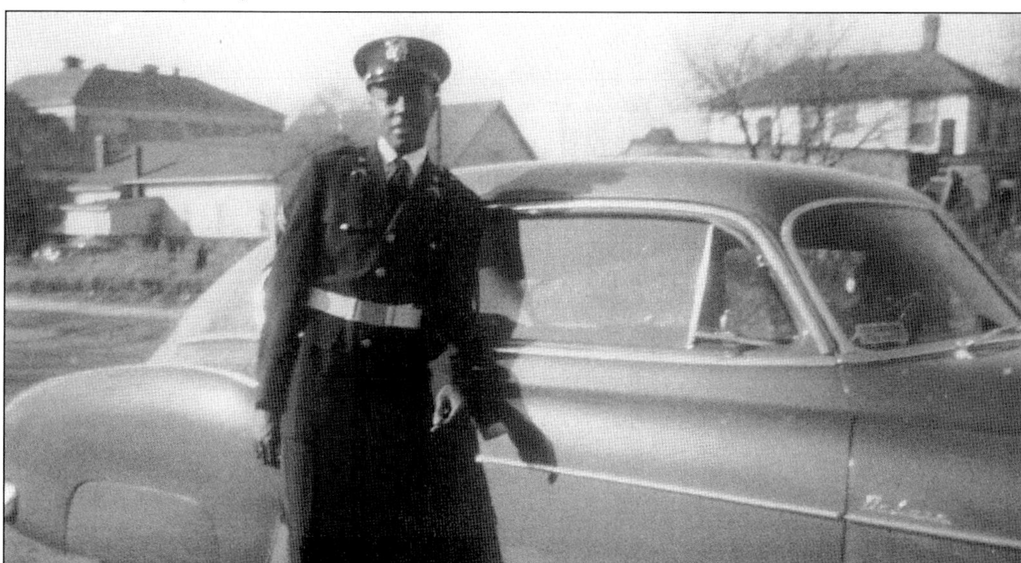

ARMSTRONG CADET CORPS, C. 1951. Dedication to community and country started early among Deanwood residents. Henry Miller poses next to his aunt's car in his sergeant's uniform. He was a member of Armstrong High School's Cadet Corps. The school was named for Samuel C. Armstrong, who commanded a black regiment in the Civil War and was the founder and first president of the Hampton Institute. (AM.)

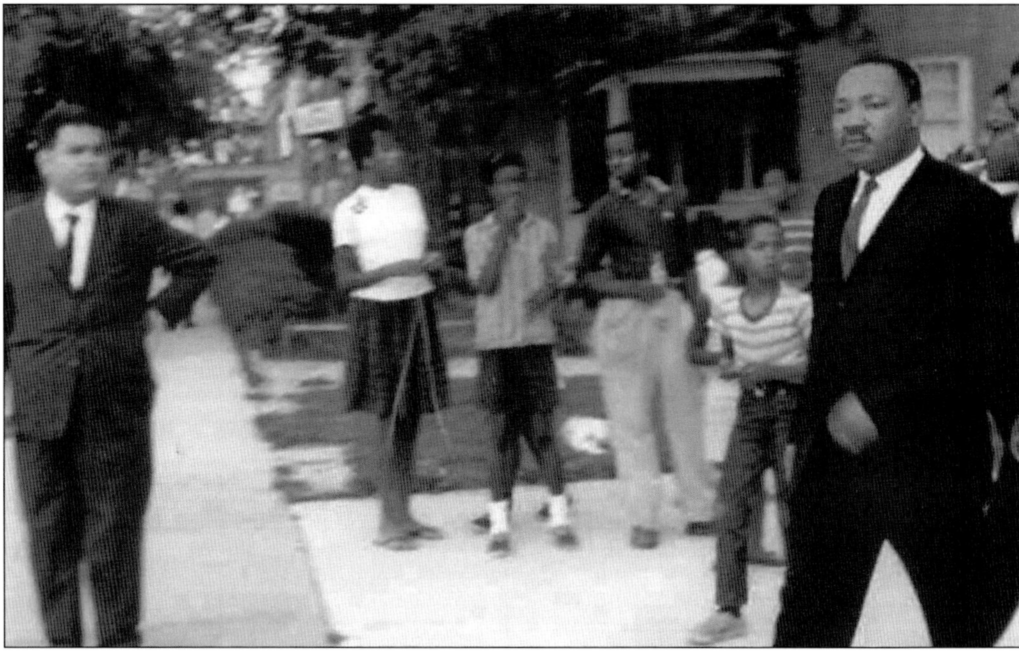

Dr. Martin Luther King, 1965. In 1965, Martin Luther King Jr., escorted by Walter Fauntroy, came to Deanwood to speak to the community about the importance of civil rights. A group of young people looks on as he leaves Sargent Memorial Presbyterian Church on Grant Street, the site of his speech. (Rev. Eugene James.)

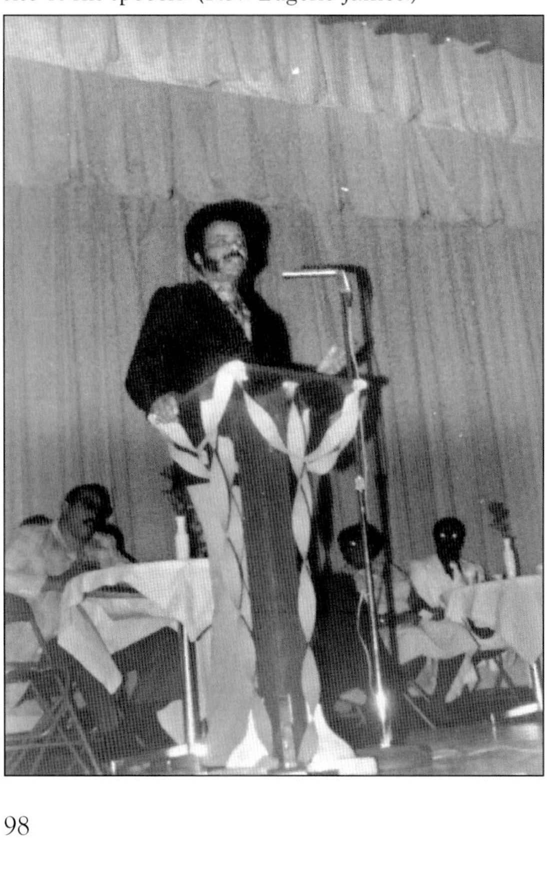

Petey Greene, 1970s. Local radio personality and community activist Petey Greene moderated James "Sleepy" Harrison's testimonial dinner, which was attended by hundreds of Deanwood residents. Harrison made an impact on the lives of many young men in the community by volunteering his time to teach them basketball. He gained the lifelong friendship and admiration of men, and prominent athletes, such as Dave Bing and John Thompson Jr. (Sleepy Harrison.)

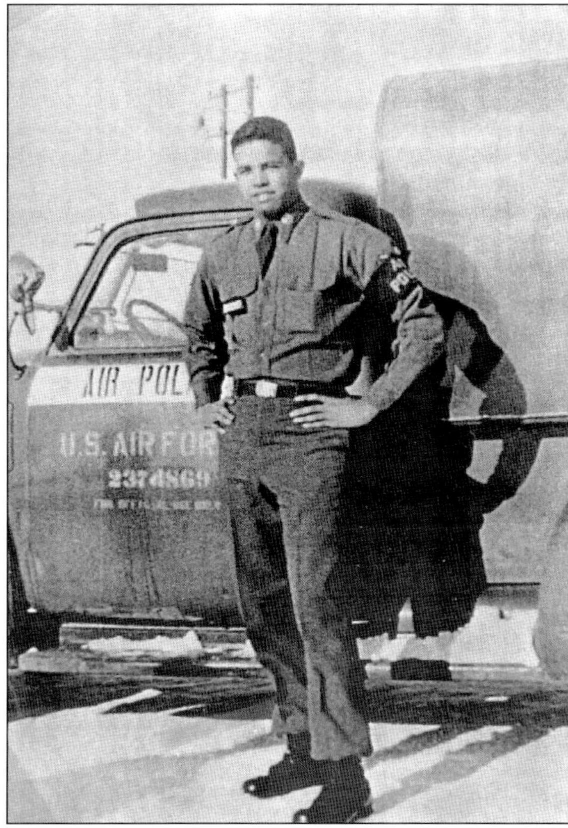

JOHN TURNER JR., EARLY 1950S. John Reginald Turner Jr., one of Deanwood's finest, joined the Air Force after graduation from high school. While in the service, he was a member of the military police. After receiving an honorable discharge, he returned to Deanwood and joined the District of Columbia Fire Department. (Earlyne K. Turner.)

CIVIL SERVANT, 1964. After graduation from Howard University's dental hygiene program, Katherine Chatmon (Stokes), right foreground, worked with Deanwood dentist Dr. William K. Collins. In 1954, she went to work for the Bureau of Dental Health with the D.C. Department of Health. In the position, she traveled through the city and taught schoolchildren about the importance of good dental health practices and how to take care of their teeth. (Katherine Chatmon.)

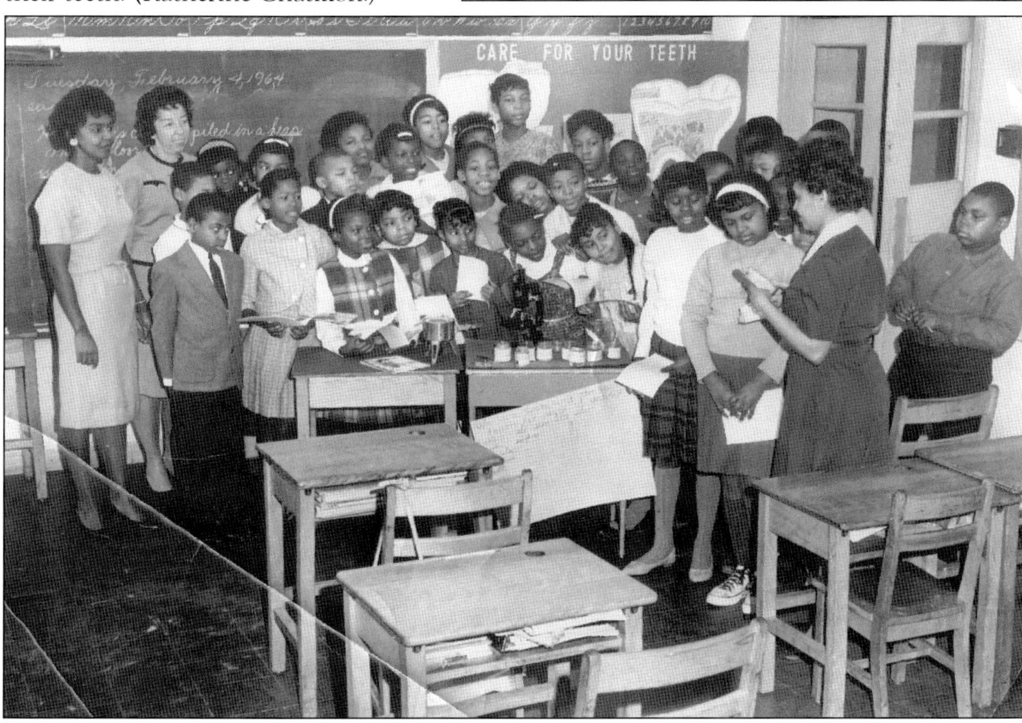

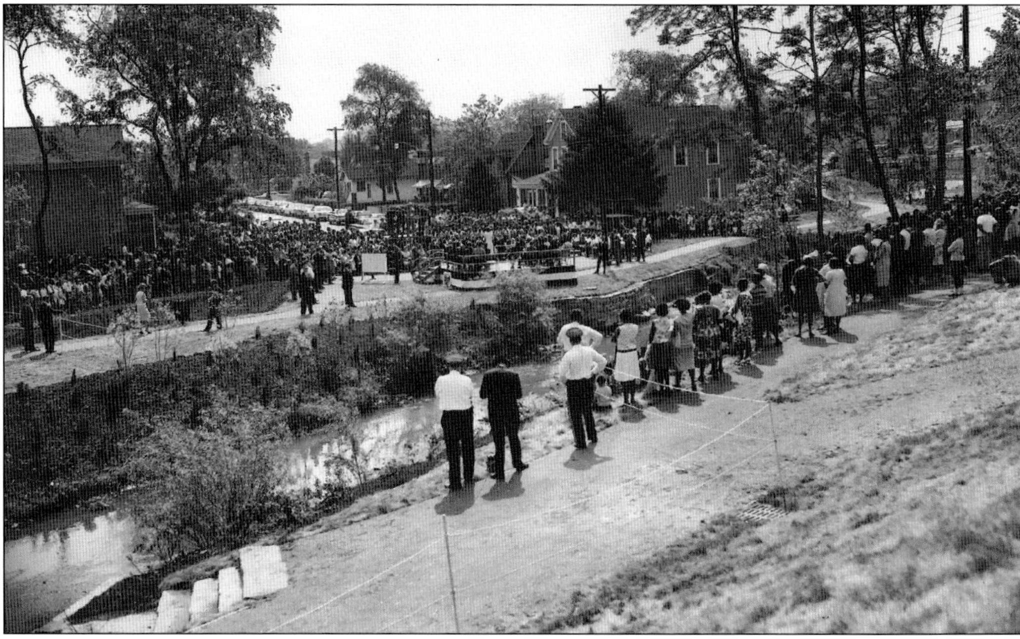

Community Support, May 18, 1966. Here we see the hundreds of Deanwood residents who came out to celebrate the dedication of the Watts Branch Parkway Project. Longtime residents of the neighborhood have always had a special connection to the Anacostia River and Watts Branch. A visit by Lady Bird Johnson brought national attention and appreciation to a local community treasure. (NCPE, NPS.)

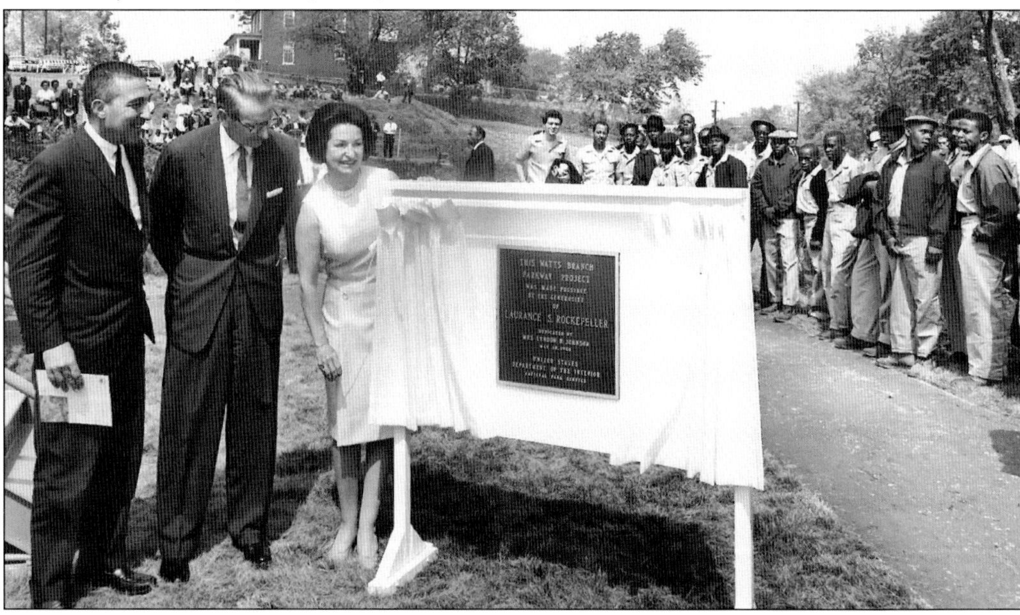

Watts Branch Dedication, May 18, 1966. During Lyndon B. Johnson's presidency, his wife, Lady Bird Johnson, championed conservation. During her days as first lady, she promoted the growth and protection of the country's national parks and the planting of wildflowers on the nation's highways. The Deanwood community turned out en masse when the first lady came to dedicate the Watts Branch Parkway Project. (NCPE, NPS.)

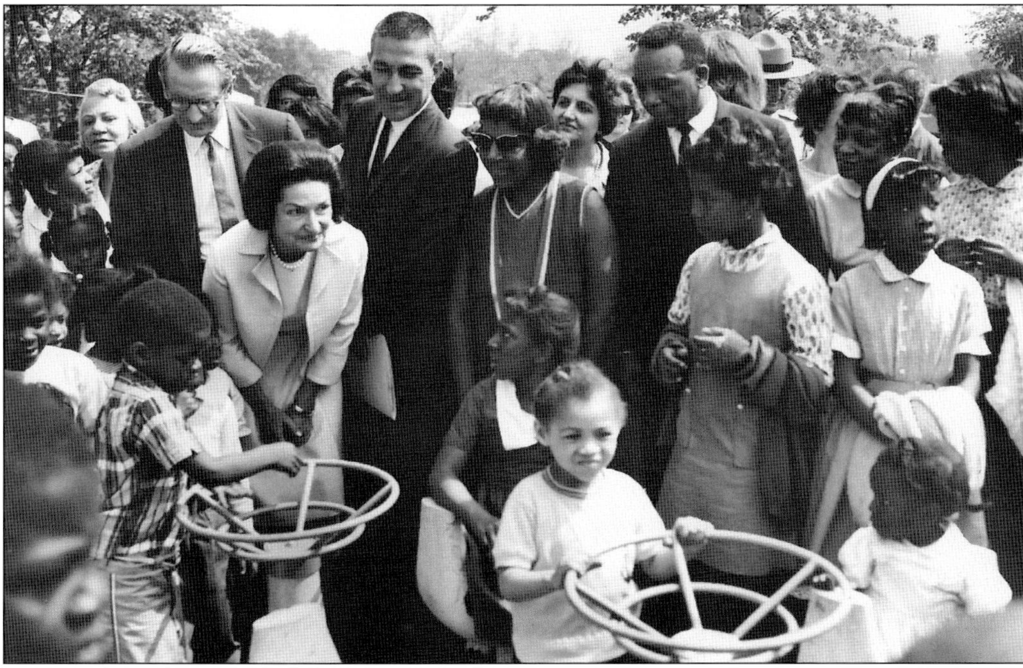

AFTER THE DEDICATION, MAY 18, 1966. After the dedication ceremony, the first lady took time to talk with some of the residents. U.S. secretary of the interior Stewart Udall (to the right of Johnson) and D.C. mayor Walter Washington (right of center) were among the notable figures who joined her on her trip to the Deanwood community. (NCPE, NPS.)

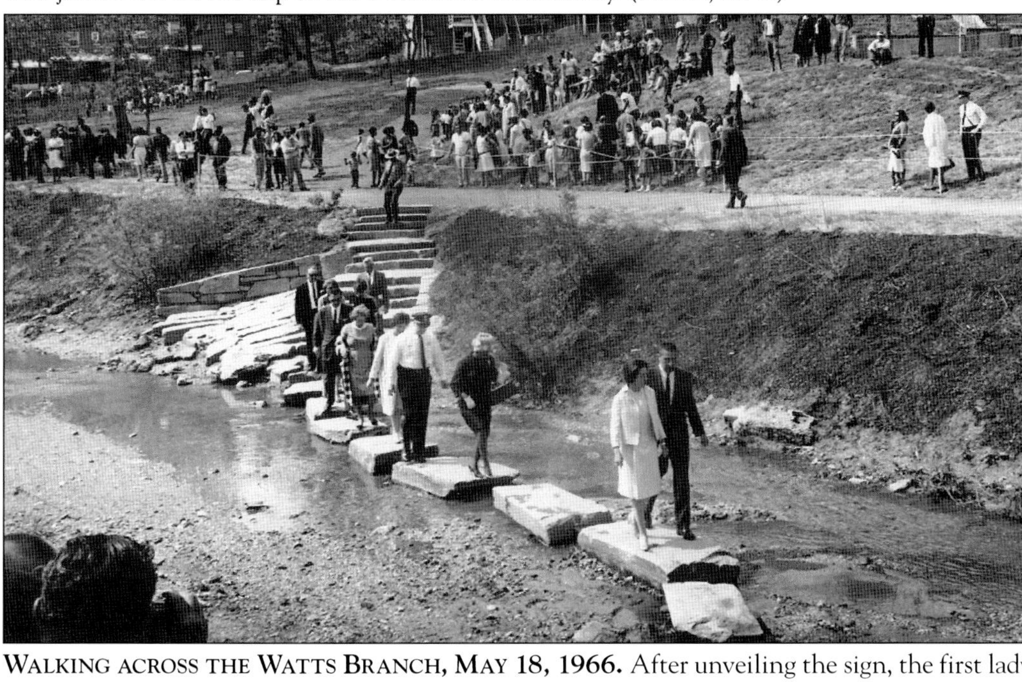

WALKING ACROSS THE WATTS BRANCH, MAY 18, 1966. After unveiling the sign, the first lady and her entourage decided to cross the branch. The houses that line Gault Place can be seen in the background. The Gault Place Bridge, which allowed traffic to cross the branch between Forty-second and Forty-fourth Street, was built some 10 years earlier. (NCPE, NPS.)

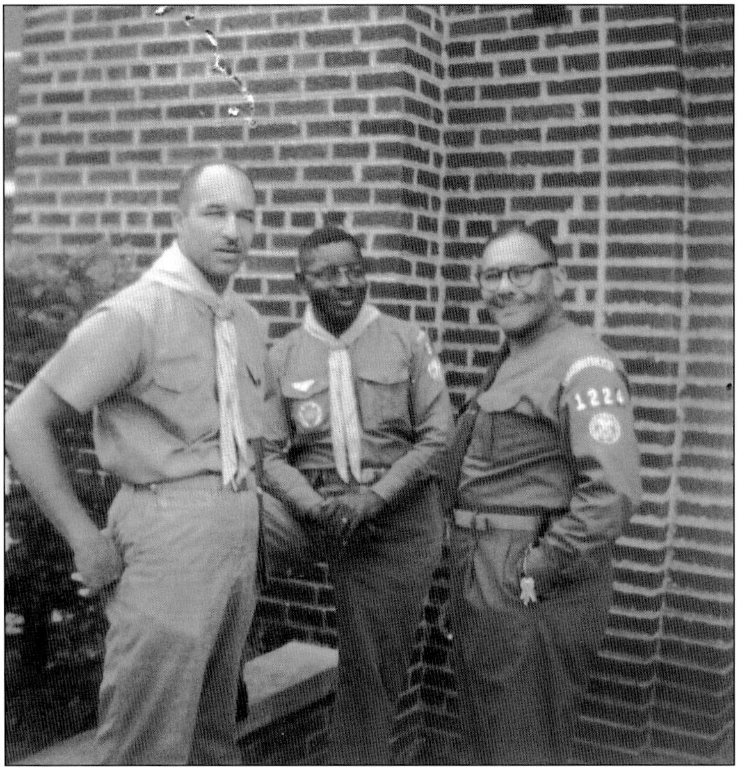

Boy Scout Troop Leaders, c. 1970. Randall Memorial United Methodist Church and other churches offered a Boy Scouts program to the young people of the community. Scouting prepared young men to make ethical and moral choices over their lifetimes by instilling values in them. The men shown here offered their time and guidance as troop leaders. (Randall Memorial United Methodist Church.)

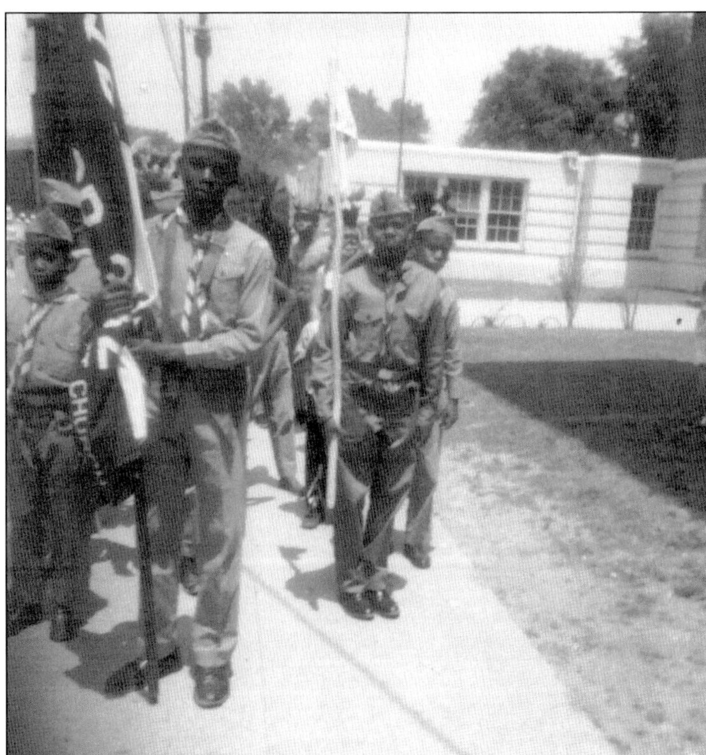

Boy Scout Troop, 1970. The young men of Randall's Boy Scout troop prepare to march in a parade. Scouting was a popular activity among young men and taught them focus and discipline, which they exhibit here as they stand in formation and await instructions from their leaders. George Washington Carver Elementary School can be seen in the background. (Randall Memorial United Methodist Church.)

Seven

Having a Grand Old Time

Although it was located on the outskirts of Washington, two attractions made Deanwood a popular destination for Washingtonians from other parts of the city—Suburban Gardens Amusement Park and the Benning Race Track. The track opened in 1890 in the adjoining community of Kenilworth, along the Anacostia River. Located between Benning Road and Kenilworth Avenue, it operated for nearly 20 years. The grandstand and clubhouse brought "high society" whites to far Northeast by the thousands in the early 1900s. Deanwood residents enjoyed a special relationship with the racetrack and claimed it as their own, as many worked as jockeys, trainers, and stable hands.

Suburban Gardens opened in 1921 at Fiftieth and Hayes Streets. It was originally owned by the Universal Development and Loan Company, Incorporated (UDLC), a black real estate and development company in which H. D. Woodson was the supervising architect. It closed its doors in 1940 and holds the distinction of being the only permanent amusement park ever operated within Washington, D.C., city limits.

Before it closed, Suburban Gardens was sold to Jewish businessman Abe Lichtman. In 1928, Lichtman's Deanwood Amusement Company built the Strand Theater at Grant Street (now Nannie Helen Burroughs Avenue) and Division Avenue to serve black patrons. The two-story, brick, 600-seat theater served Northeast Washington until it closed in 1959. Not only was it an entertainment venue, it also regularly employed Deanwood residents.

Churches were also vital to the social life of the community. Many organized activities like neighborhood picnics, baseball games, and trips to Carr's and Sparrow's Beaches. These were two black beaches located in Anne Arundel County, Maryland, and were so popular that the organized trips there practically shut down the neighborhood.

Residents also formed social clubs as a way to fellowship. The Deanwood Ladies were organized in 1947 and were originally called the Cavaliers. They were known throughout Deanwood for their 25¢ dances, 50¢ hayrides, free picnics, and holiday celebrations. A few other social clubs of the 1940s and 1950s included the Tea Rose Social, Just Us, Inc., the Latonialettes, and the Junior Egyptians.

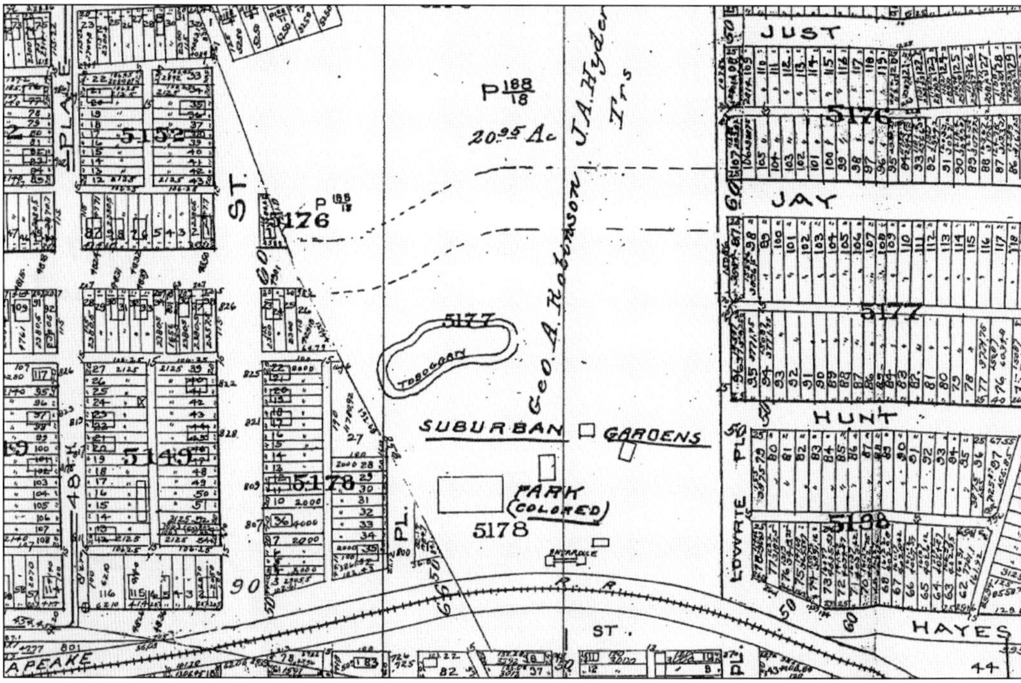

BAIST MAP, C. 1937. This map features the Suburban Gardens Amusement Park, a major attraction in the community. Suburban Gardens employed residents from the neighborhood and drew African American visitors from all across the city and the Mid-Atlantic region. For 10¢, patrons enjoyed a carousel, dance hall, playground, swimming pool, and other amusement park attractions. (DCPL, WD.)

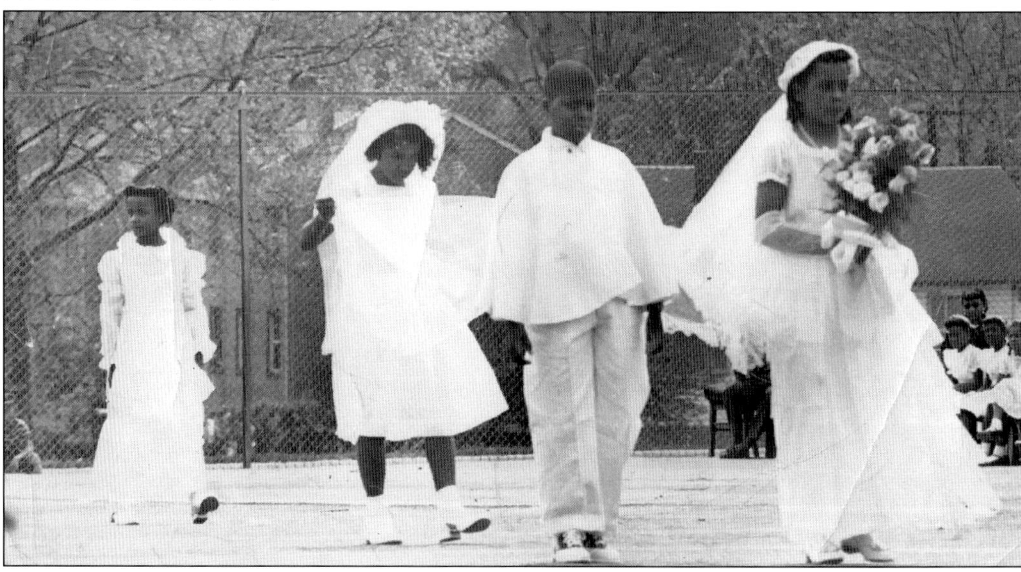

MAY DAY, C. 1953. Many times schools hosted social events. To celebrate the arrival of spring, schools held May Day festivals. Children danced around a maypole, from which streamers hung. They elected a May queen and May king and exchanged May baskets—paper baskets filled with goodies. Here, from left to right, an unidentified young girl, Judy Gordon, Wilson Harrison, and Mimea Patterson celebrate at Merritt School. (Joan Slade Gray.)

QUEEN'S COURT, c. 1953. May Day was also a popular festival for students of the George Washington Carver Elementary School. Here Aressa V. Williams (left) sits next to a fellow member of the queen's court as she holds her May Day basket and sits among the flowers in the school's yard. (Hattie Phillips.)

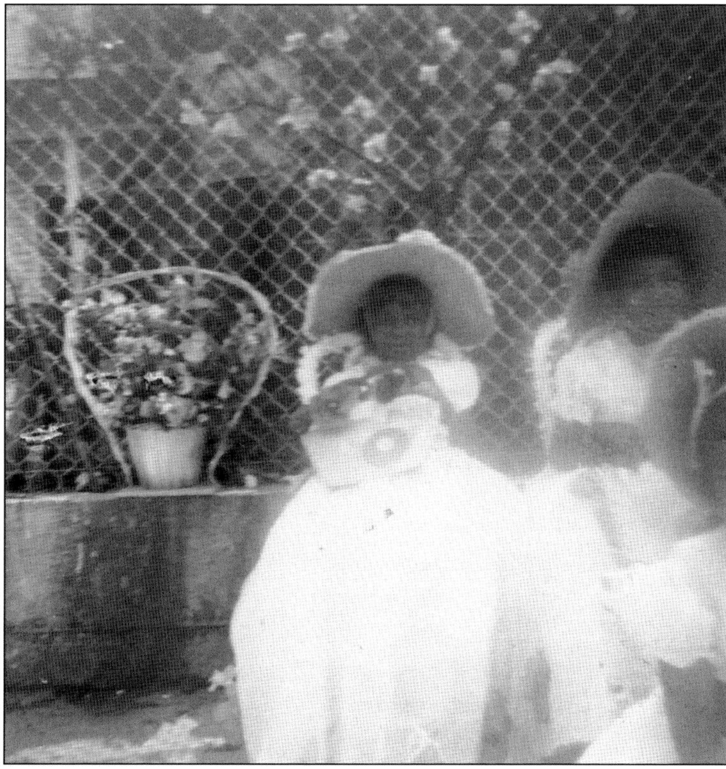

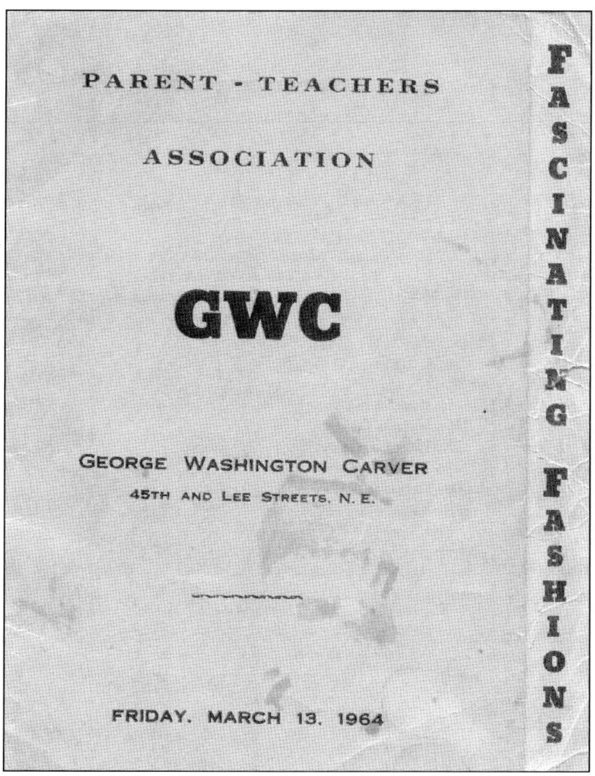

PARENT - TEACHERS

ASSOCIATION

GWC

GEORGE WASHINGTON CARVER

45TH AND LEE STREETS, N. E.

FRIDAY, MARCH 13, 1964

FASCINATING FASHIONS

FASCINATING FASHIONS, 1964. The schools in Deanwood provided many activities for students to socialize and have a good time. They were often used as opportunities to expand their horizons. The fashion show allowed the young ladies and young men of the community to build their self-confidence as they modeled the fashions of the day. (Erin Gantt.)

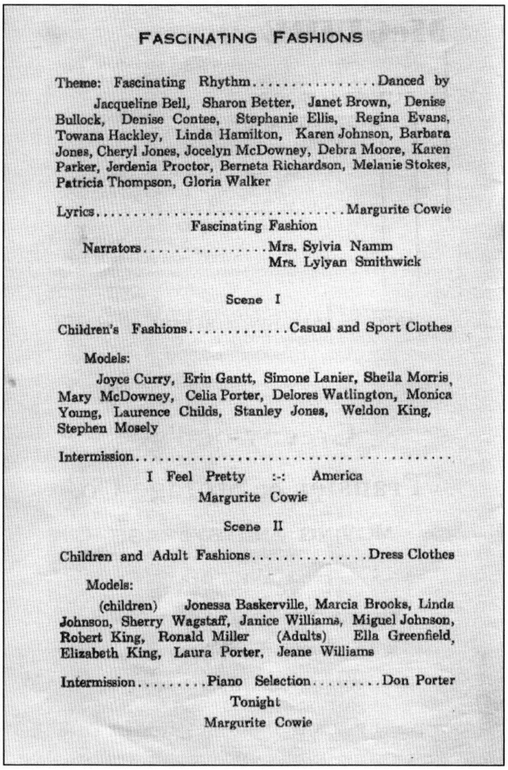

FASCINATING FASHIONS

Theme: Fascinating Rhythm................Danced by
Jacqueline Bell, Sharon Better, Janet Brown, Denise Bullock, Denise Contee, Stephanie Ellis, Regina Evans, Towana Hackley, Linda Hamilton, Karen Johnson, Barbara Jones, Cheryl Jones, Jocelyn McDowney, Debra Moore, Karen Parker, Jerdenia Proctor, Berneta Richardson, Melanie Stokes, Patricia Thompson, Gloria Walker

Lyrics................................Margurite Cowie
Fascinating Fashion

Narrators................Mrs. Sylvia Namm
Mrs. Lylyan Smithwick

Scene I

Children's Fashions.............Casual and Sport Clothes

Models:
Joyce Curry, Erin Gantt, Simone Lanier, Sheila Morris, Mary McDowney, Celia Porter, Delores Watlington, Monica Young, Laurence Childs, Stanley Jones, Weldon King, Stephen Mosely

Intermission...

I Feel Pretty :-: America
Margurite Cowie

Scene II

Children and Adult Fashions...............Dress Clothes

Models:
(children) Jonessa Baskerville, Marcia Brooks, Linda Johnson, Sherry Wagstaff, Janice Williams, Miguel Johnson, Robert King, Ronald Miller (Adults) Ella Greenfield, Elizabeth King, Laura Porter, Jeane Williams

Intermission.........Piano Selection.........Don Porter
Tonight
Margurite Cowie

FASCINATING FASHIONS PROGRAM, 1964. The PTA of George Washington Carver Elementary School sponsored the Fascinating Fashions fashion show on March 13, 1964. The program shows that it was an intergenerational affair, as both children and adult fashions were on display. It provided the opportunity for both students and their parents to strut their stuff on the runway. (Erin Gantt.)

JUNIOR CHURCH MEMBERS, C. 1947. The church was the center of a lot of the social activities for many Deanwood families. From left to right, Earl Jr., Earlyne, and Elaine King enjoyed singing together in the First Baptist Church of Deanwood's Junior Church. Many individuals in the adult choirs began their participation in one of the Junior Church choirs. (EKB.)

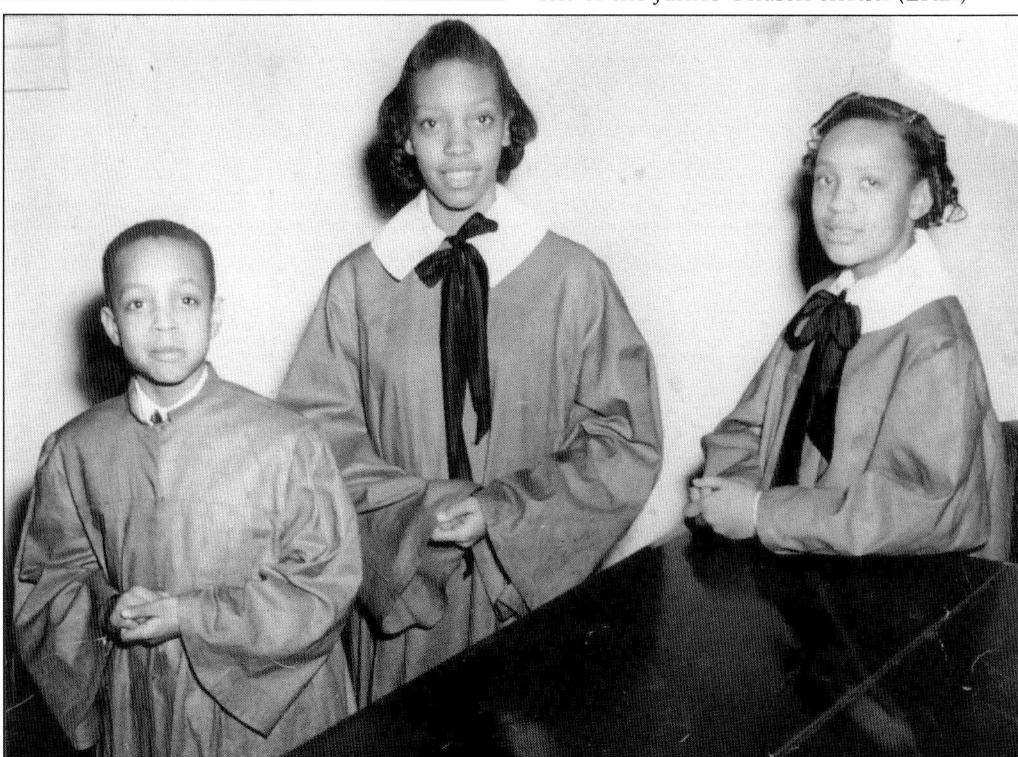

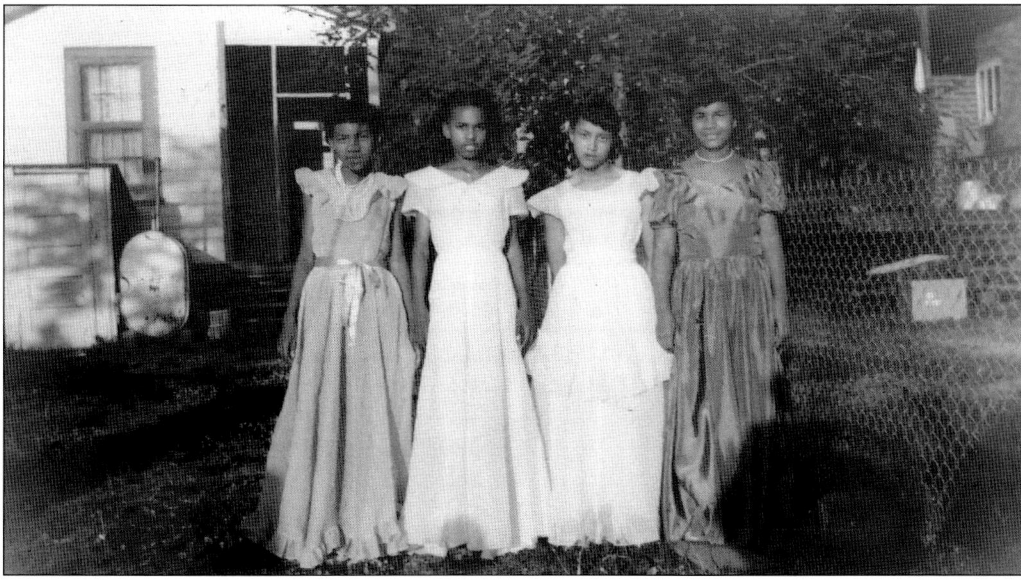

A Springtime Youth Activity, 1948. Churches provided a variety of activities for the youth of the community. From left to right, Audrey Williams Burke, Willie Mae Waring-Harrison, Doris Broadus-McCants, and Jane Coleman-Armstead attend a formal event sponsored by the Junior Church at the First Baptist Church of Deanwood. They are photographed in their beautiful gowns in Doris Broadus's backyard at 908 Forty-fifth Place. (Audrey Williams Burke.)

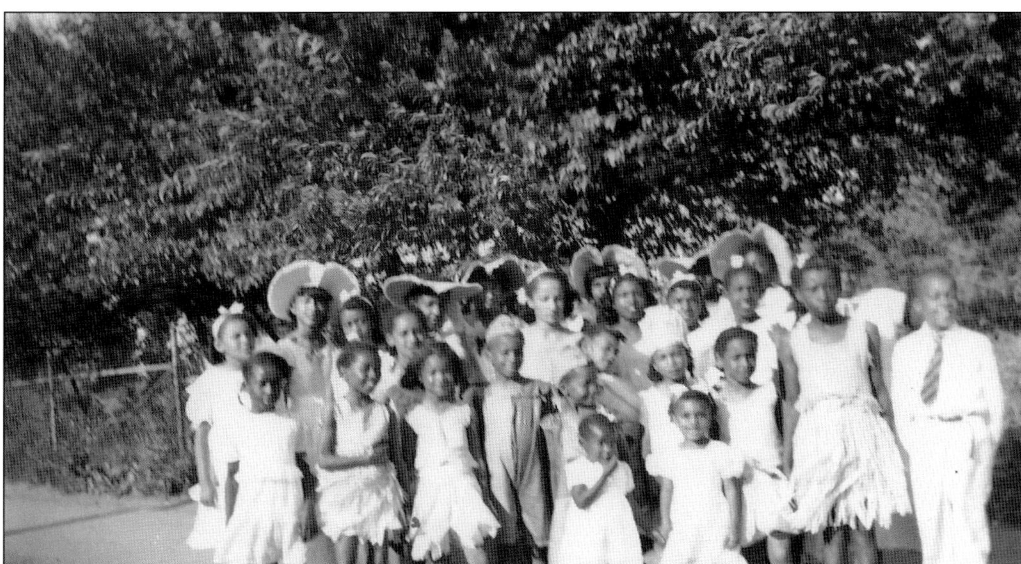

Youth Activity at Church, 1950s. In addition to worshipping together, neighborhood children enjoyed socializing at church. They provided activities year-round to keep youth of the community engaged. This group of Deanwood youth poses together at a springtime activity at the First Baptist Church of Deanwood. (Audrey Williams Burke.)

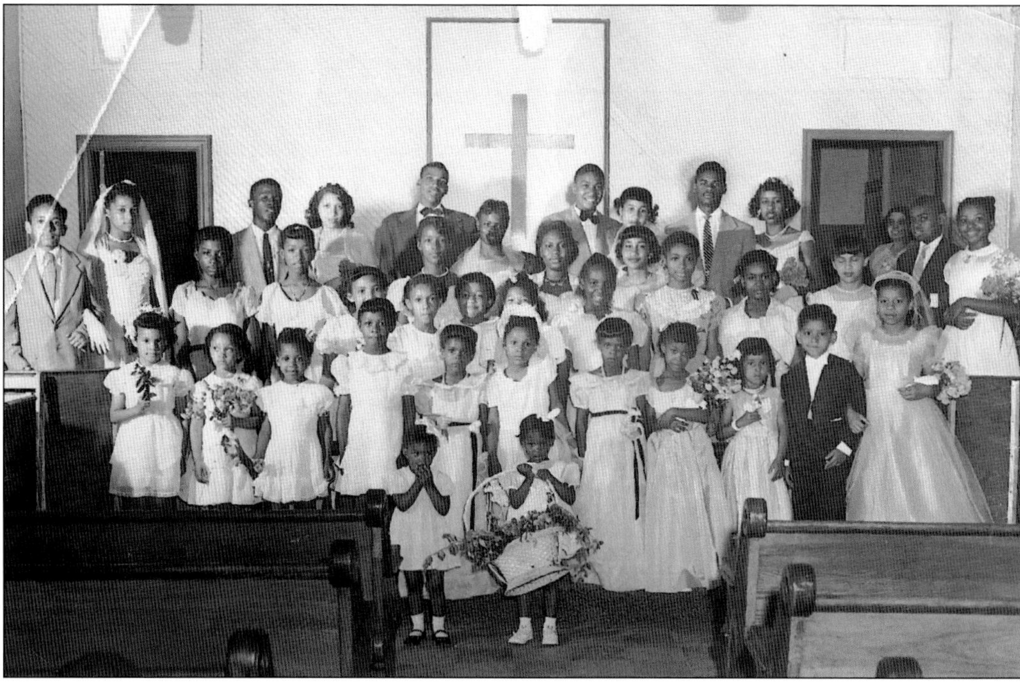

TOM THUMB WEDDING, C. 1951. Tom Thumb weddings were a common way for churches to raise funds for youth activities. The wedding party at Contee AME Zion Church consisted of brides, grooms, bridesmaids, and flower girls. At the conclusion of the presentation, the bride and groom that raised the most money were crowned Master and Miss Tom Thumb. (Joan Slade Gray.)

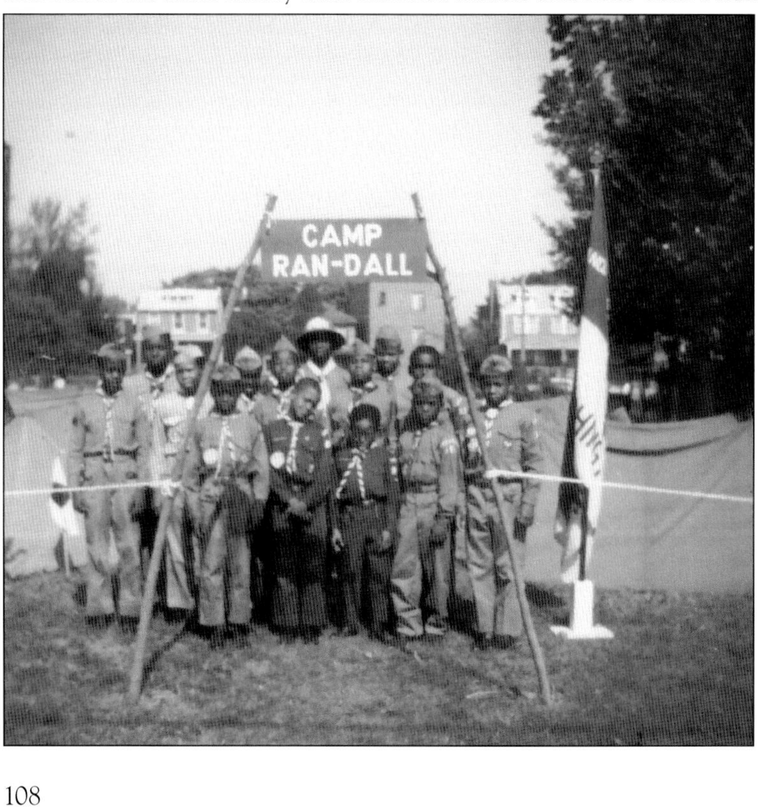

CAMP RAN-DALL, 1963. All churches had programs to engage the young people of the community. Randall Memorial was one of the many churches that had a Cub and Boy Scout troop in which the young men of the neighborhood participated. Camp Ran-Dall exposed them to the joys of camping on the church grounds. (Randall Memorial United Methodist Church.)

CAMP RAN-DALL BRAVE, 1963. Camp Ran-Dall set up its tents on the side of Randall Memorial. This way, neighborhood children did not have to travel too far from home to learn about the joys of camping, Native American culture, and survival skills from the leaders of the church. (Randall Memorial United Methodist Church.)

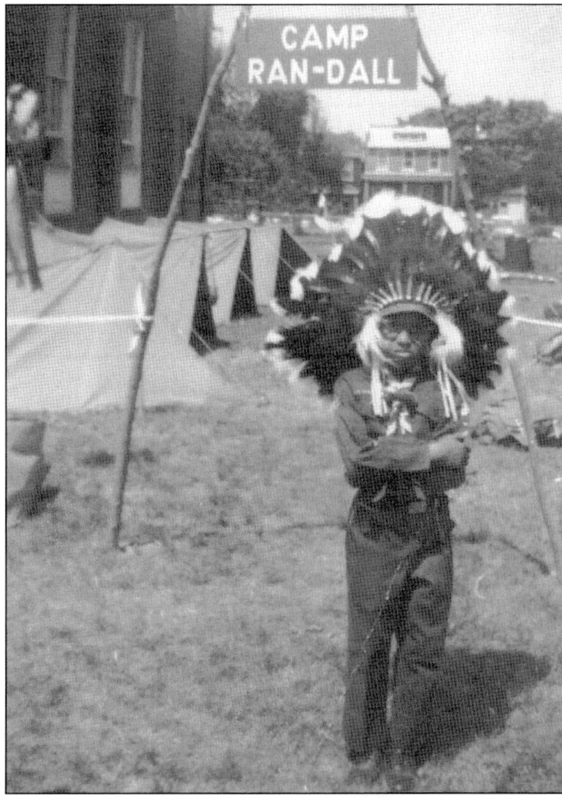

SUB-DEBUTANTES, 1964. Debutante activities included a presentation of the debutantes and "sub-debs" (young ladies who would be debutantes the following year), a musical and literary program, a banquet for debutantes and escorts, and presentations to the debutantes on the last night. Some of the sub-debutantes of 1964 included, from left to right, Betty Moore, Jacqueline Johnson, Marcia Stokes, Diana Taylor, Gwendolyn Johnson, Regina Brewer, and Tonya Talley. (AM.)

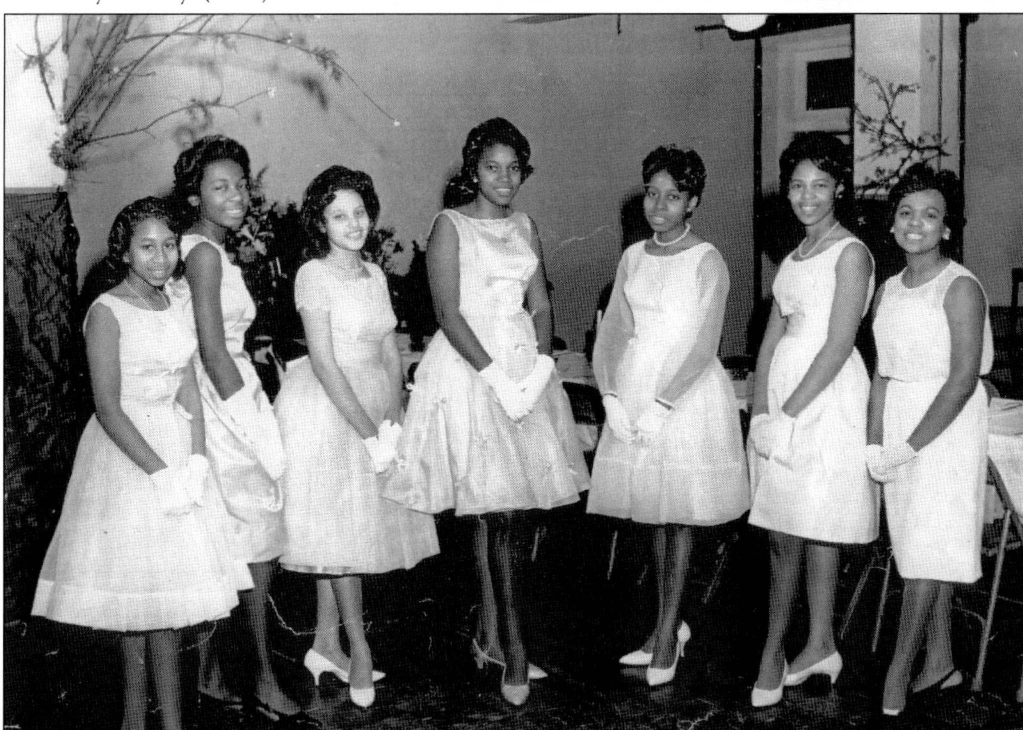

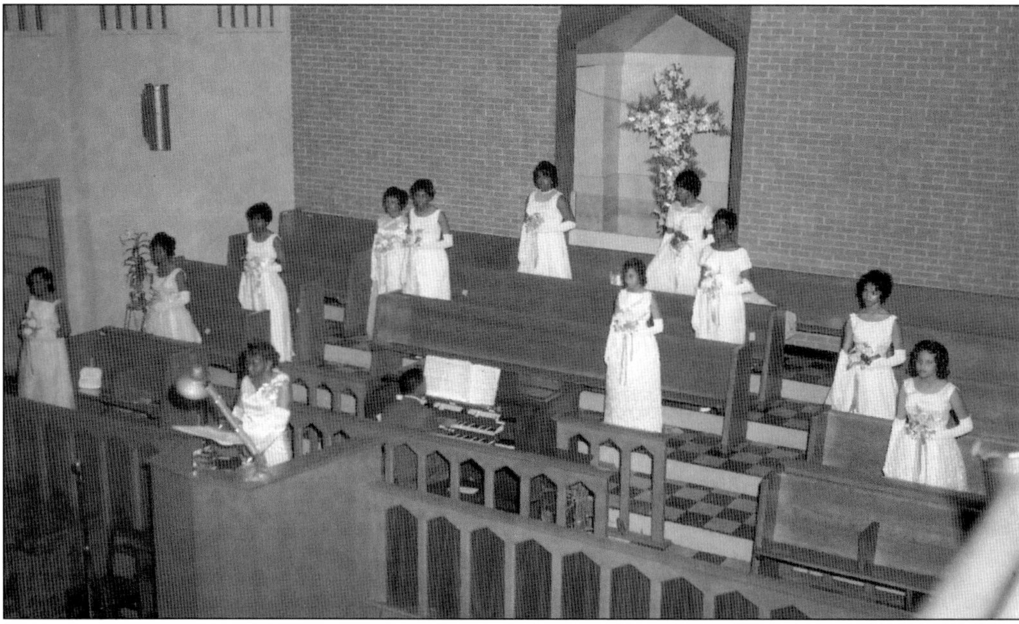

FIRST BAPTIST DEBUTANTES, 1965. To honor the young ladies of the community, Henrietta Silas Greene of the First Baptist Church of Deanwood established the debutante presentations in 1963. Young ladies of the church were presented to society and encouraged to continue their Christian walk into adulthood. To prepare for their coming out, "debs" were coached and groomed by charm-school professionals. (Tonya Talley Smith.)

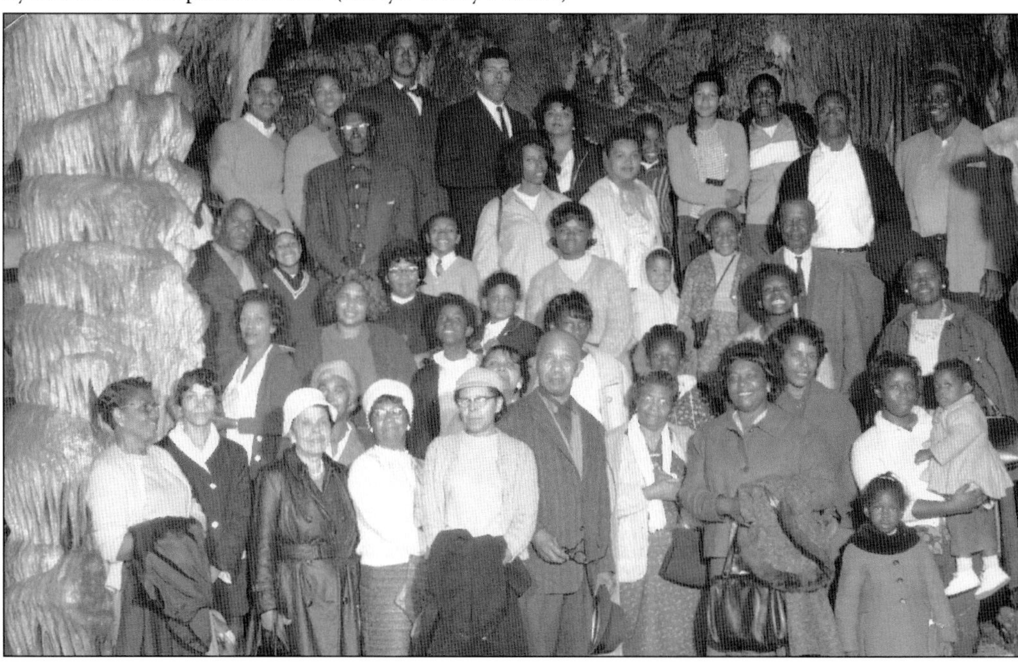

CHURCH EXCURSION, 1960S. Churches coordinated activities for both youth and adult members. It was not unusual to coordinate busloads of people for the more popular trips. Members of Randall Memorial traveled to Luray Caverns to partake in fellowship and enjoy the unique rock formations. (Randall Memorial United Methodist Church.)

BEACH TRIP. Trips to Carr's and Sparrow's Beaches were neighborhood favorites. They were the legacy of Annapolis landowner Fred Carr, who was believed to have been a runaway slave. In addition to allowing families to have fun outside of the neighborhood, trips allowed residents to cool off, celebrate the arts, enjoy the outdoors, and fellowship with their neighbors. Here Mary Hines takes a break from the water to pose for a photograph. (Sandra Brown.)

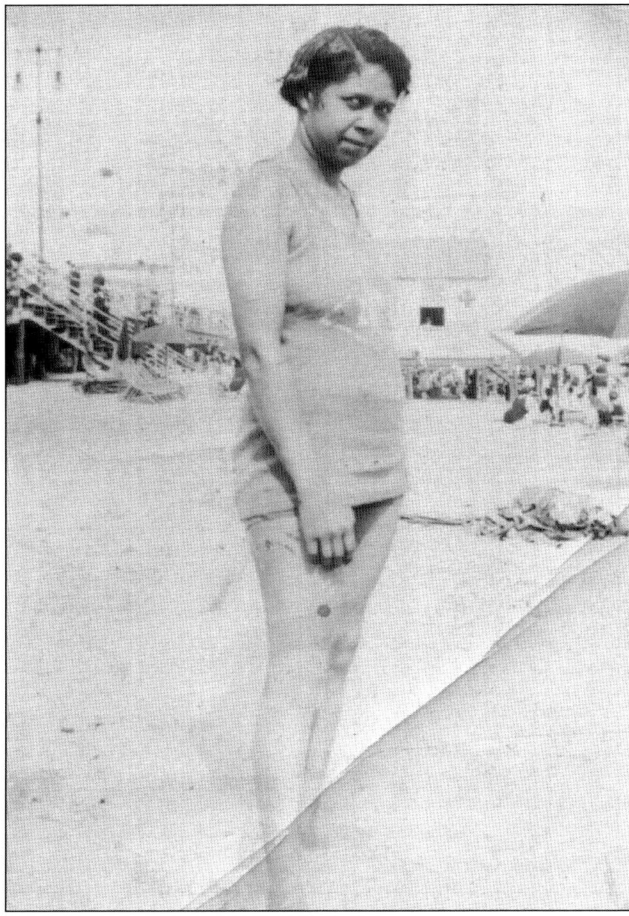

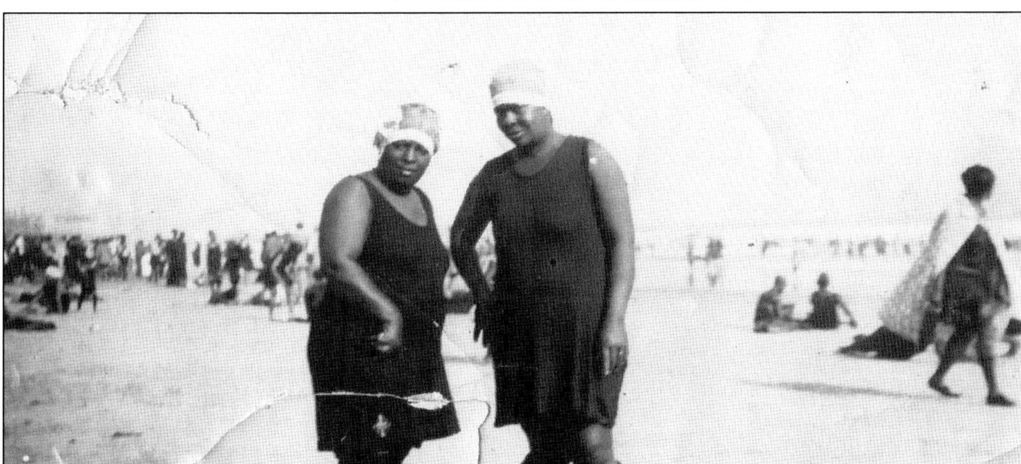

FRIENDS AT SPARROW'S BEACH. At the time of his death in 1927, Fred Carr had amassed 246 acres of farmland fronting the Chesapeake Bay. In his will, Carr requested that his property be equally divided among his four daughters. In 1929, two of his daughters, Elizabeth Carr and Florence Sparrow, bought the land interests of their siblings and established Carr's Beach and Sparrow's Beach. (Sandra Brown.)

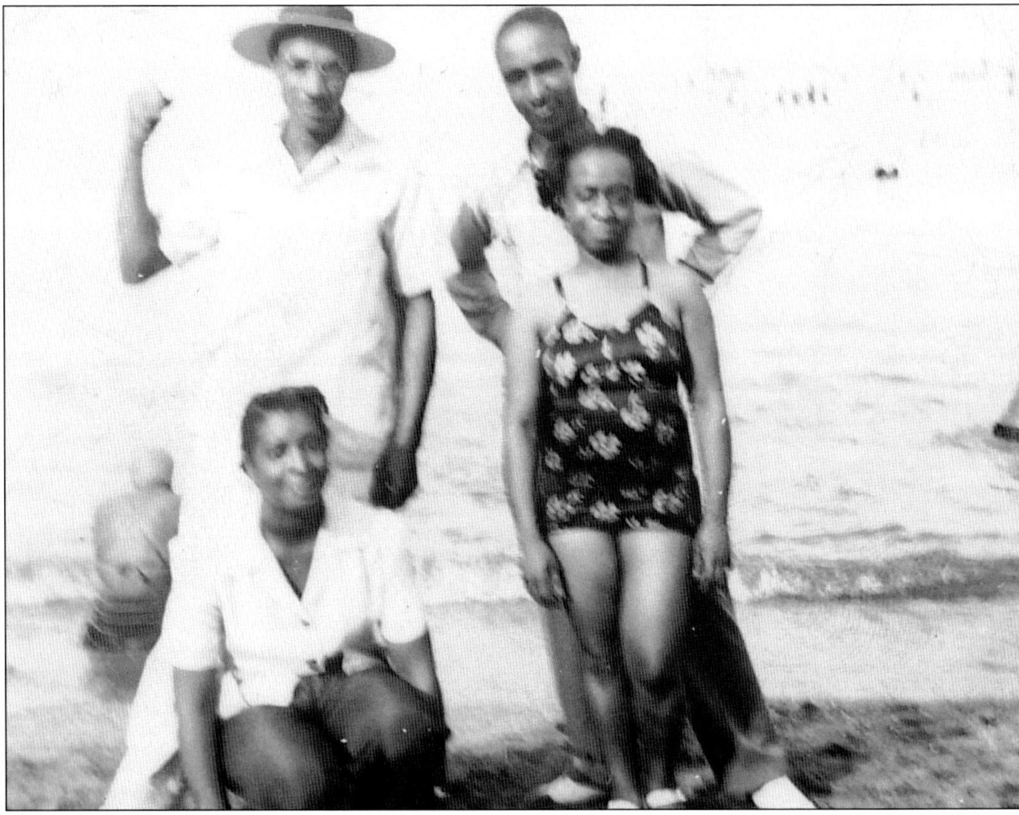

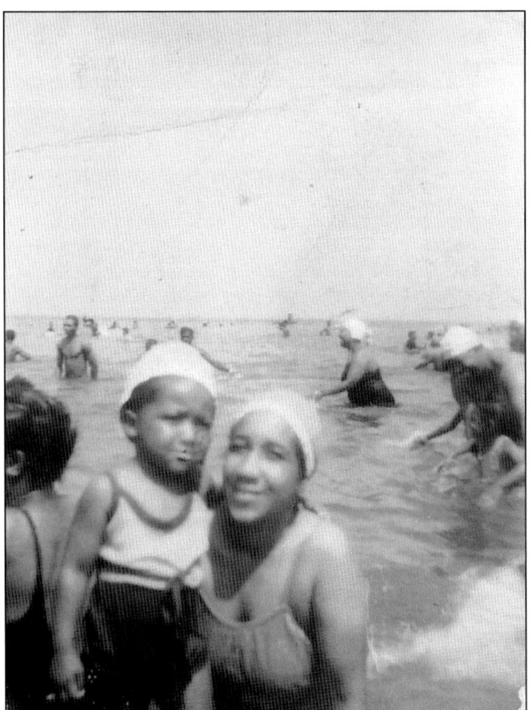

FRIENDS AT THE BEACH, 1940S. Shown here are Deanwood residents Grayce and William Taylor (left) and Agnes and Charles Rodgers (right). An accomplished pilot, William Taylor became a major in the Civil Air Patrol, an auxiliary of the U.S. Air Force. In the 1940s and 1950s, he used his aviation skills in the patrol to conduct domestic search-and-rescue missions. (Doris Taylor-Collins.)

FAMILIES AT THE BEACH, 1945. Ruth B. Slade (right) and Janet Slade Young enjoy a day at Sparrow's Beach. Busloads of Deanwood residents would travel to Annapolis for a day in the sun and water. These church-sponsored trips were so popular that the community practically shut down on these days. (Joan Slade Gray.)

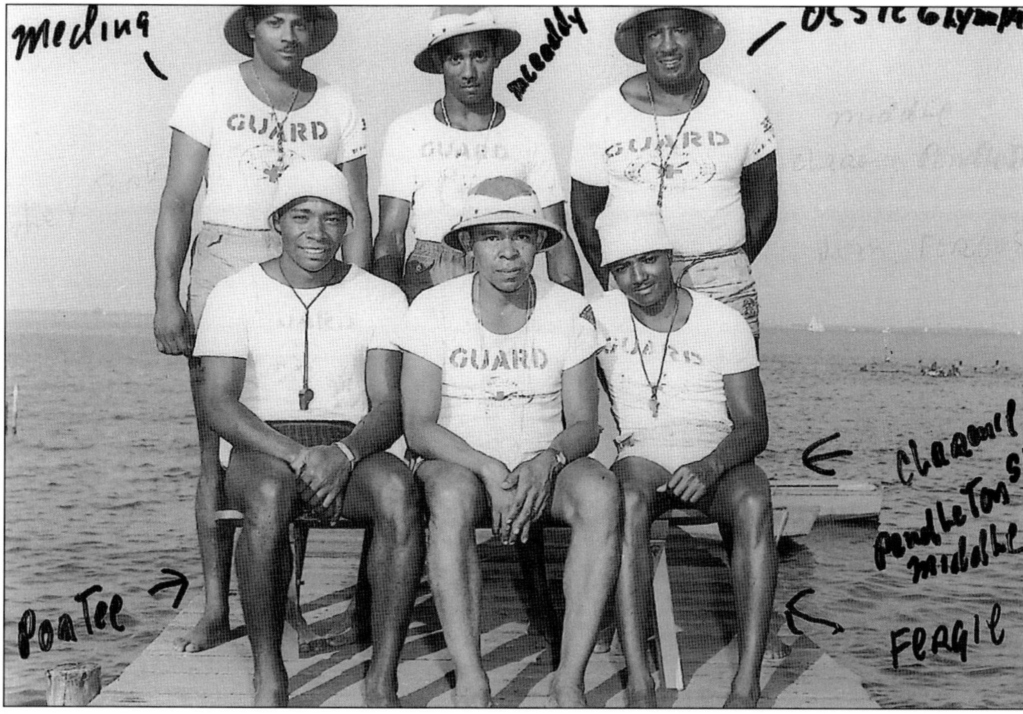

LIFEGUARDS, C. 1950. Lifeguards at Sparrow's Beach pose with the Chesapeake Bay in the background. Clarence Pendleton Sr. (first row, center) went to Howard University. After graduating, he worked extensively with the D.C. Department of Recreation, serving as the first supervisor and later as technical head of the District's roving leader program. His son Clarence Pendleton Jr. became the first black chairman of the U.S. Commission on Civil Rights. (Jim Ferguson.)

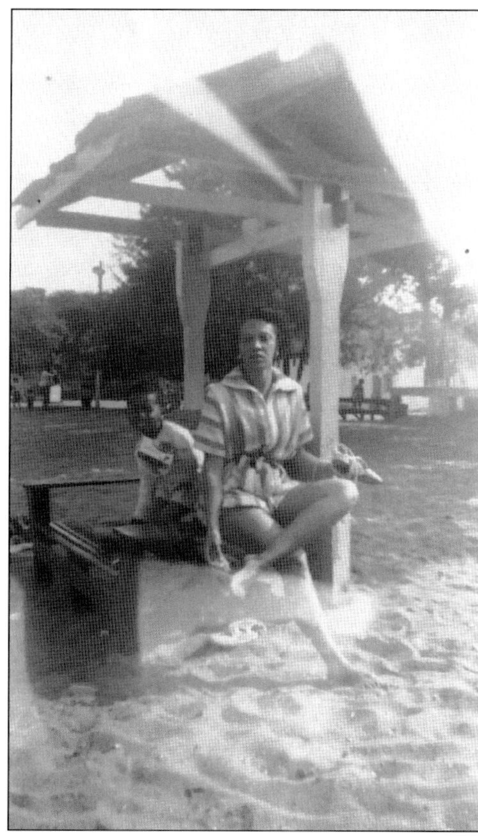

MOTHER AND SON, C. 1950. Geraldine Carroll (right) and her son, Alfred Q. Carroll III, seek some relief in the shade from the hot summer sun on Carr's Beach. Carroll's husband, Alfred Q. Carroll Jr., was a Tuskegee airman and a member of the 99th Fighter Squadron. He received his wings at the Tuskegee Army Air Field on November 3, 1943. (Geraldine Carroll.)

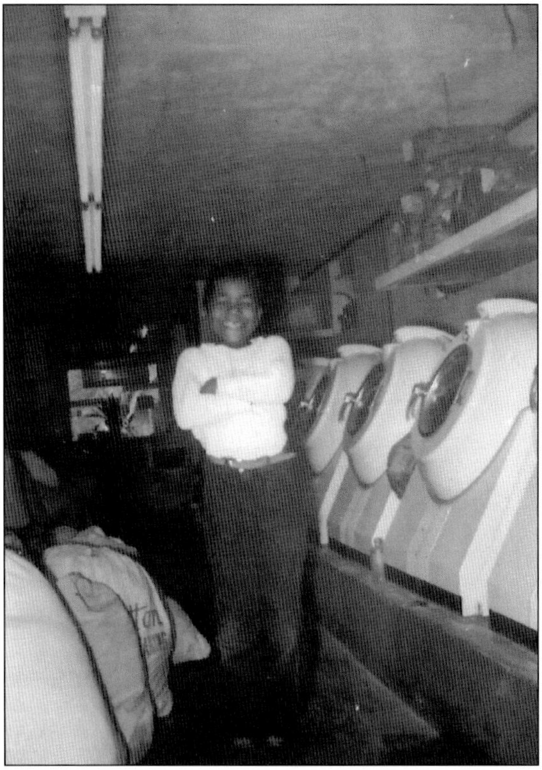

LOUIS TURNER, 1950S. Youngsters sometimes found unconventional ways to have a good time. Here Reginald Turner's son, Louis, spends time at his father's Laundromat at Forty-seventh and Sheriff Road. Many of the businesses in the community were family owned and operated, so it was not unusual for children to spend time hanging around the family business. (EKB.)

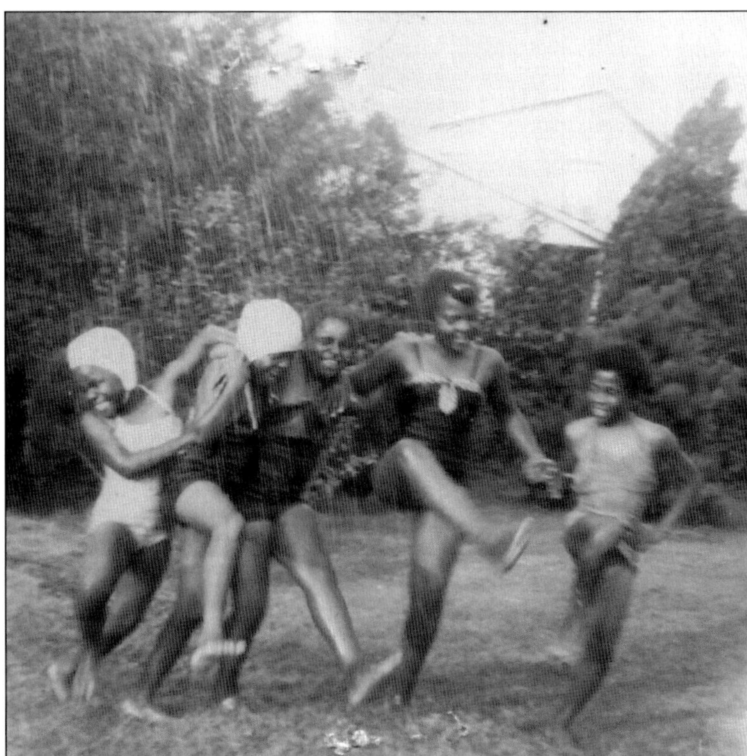

COOLING OFF IN SUMMER, 1960S. Residents were not always able to make it to the beach to cool off. Children often played in a shower of water from a neighbor's hose or soaked themselves with an open fire hydrant. From left to right, Yvette Springs, Verdell Williams, Carolyn Springs, Barbara Bullock, and Barbara Jennifer play in Chancellor and Mattie Williams's front yard at 5000 Sheriff Road. (Hattie Phillips.)

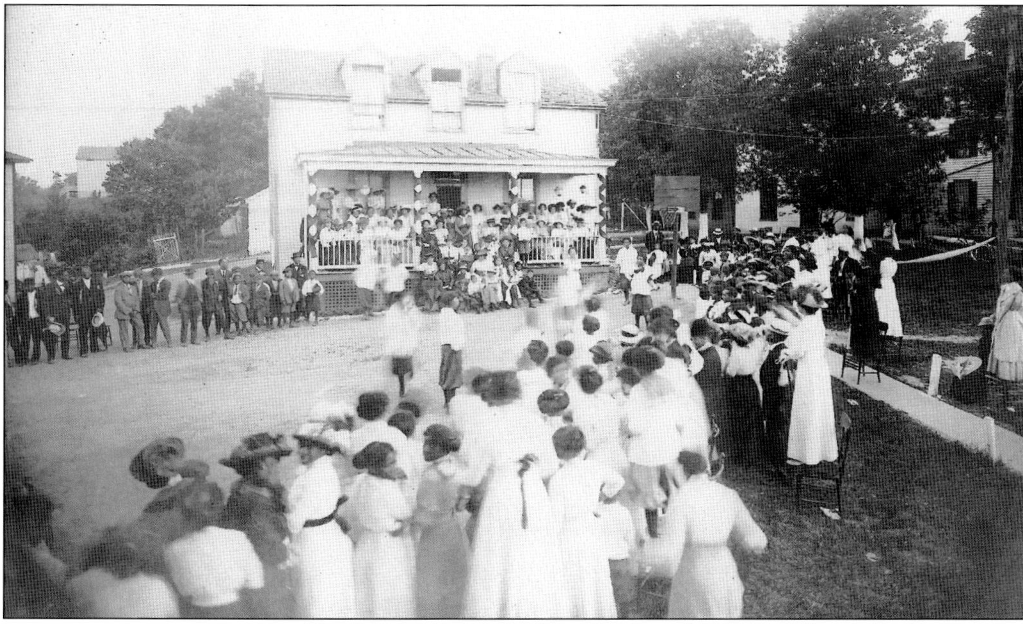

BASKETBALL GAME, C. 1910. The curriculum of the National Training School for Women and Girls focused on developing the entire person. In addition to teaching missionary training, an industrial curriculum, and challenging academic subjects, the school also fostered the development of the physical body and encouraged the students to have fun. Here students enjoy a friendly game of basketball on the school grounds. (NHBS.)

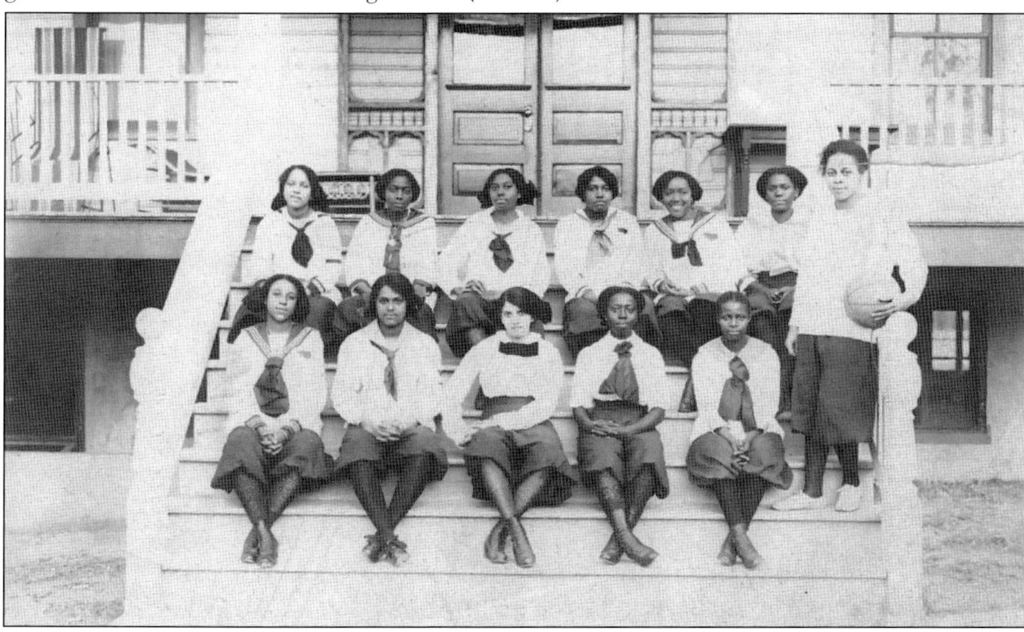

BASKETBALL TEAM, C. 1910. In later years, the school's motto became "We Specialize in the Wholly Impossible." Nannie Helen Burroughs believed in the need for black women to become self-sufficient wage earners and provided a range of classes and activities to help prepare them for this future. Here the school's basketball team poses in uniform on the steps of one of the school buildings. (NHBS.)

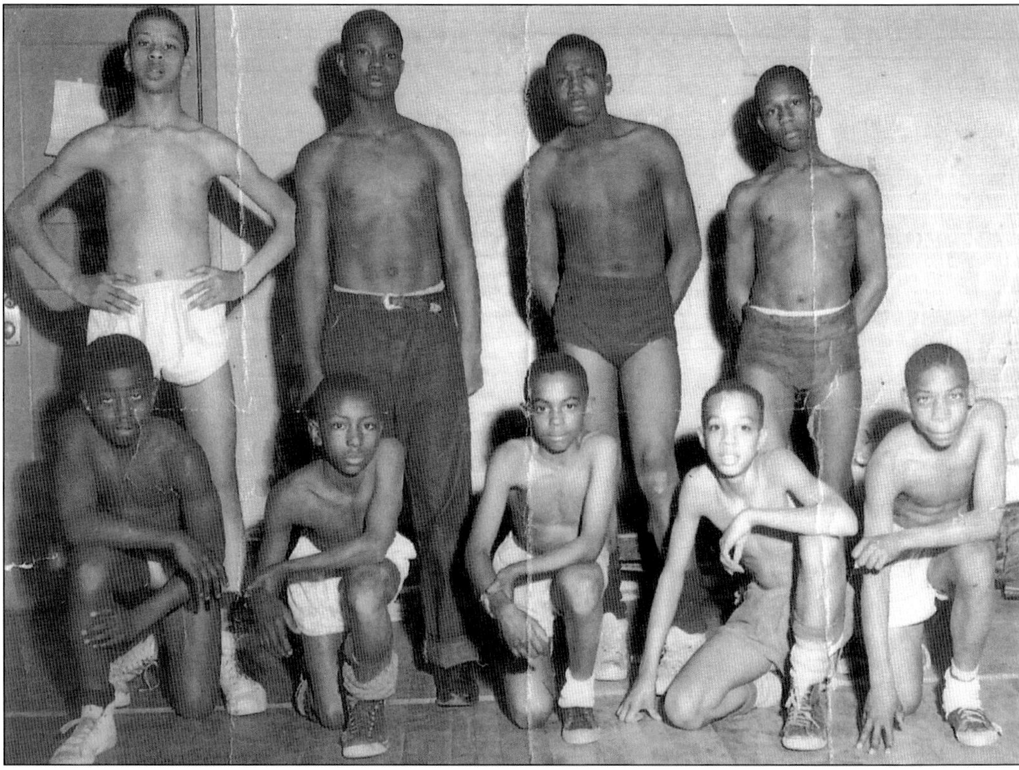

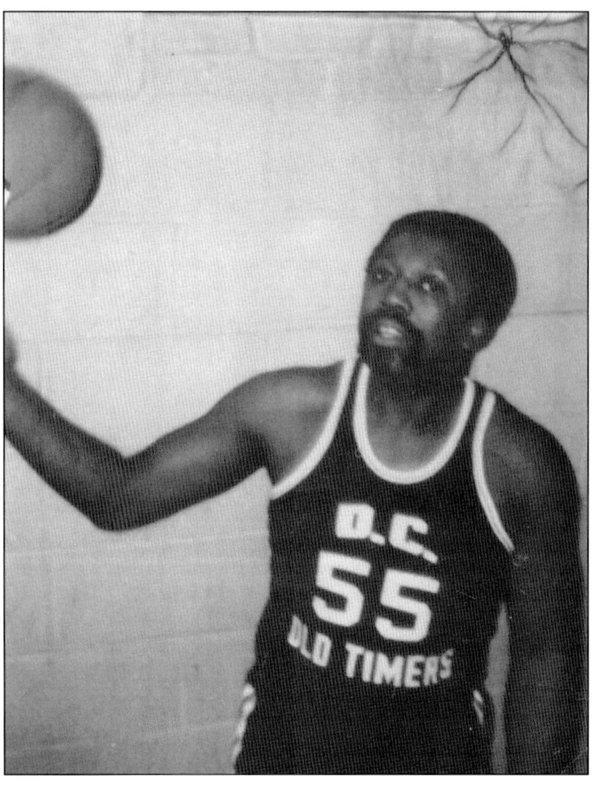

DEANWOOD BASKETBALL TEAM, 1949. Neighborhood games were also a large part of recreation in Deanwood. Eager to play basketball, these boys wore whatever they owned to play the game. Two years later, they got uniforms. Team members are, from left to right, (first row) Ezra "Chop Chop" Cummings, Robert Makel, Thomas Bolden, Earl King Jr., and Sylvester Smith; (back row) Richard Childs, James Hall, James "Sleepy" Harrison, and Herbert Bradley. (Sleepy Harrison.)

JAMES "SLEEPY" HARRISON, 1970s. After playing basketball as a young man in Deanwood, "Sleepy" Harrison grew up to coach and mentor other Deanwood athletes. He helped to produce many talented basketball players for various high schools around the city. After a successful high school coaching career, he returned to the neighborhood to play for the Washington, D.C., Old Timers League. (Sleepy Harrison.)

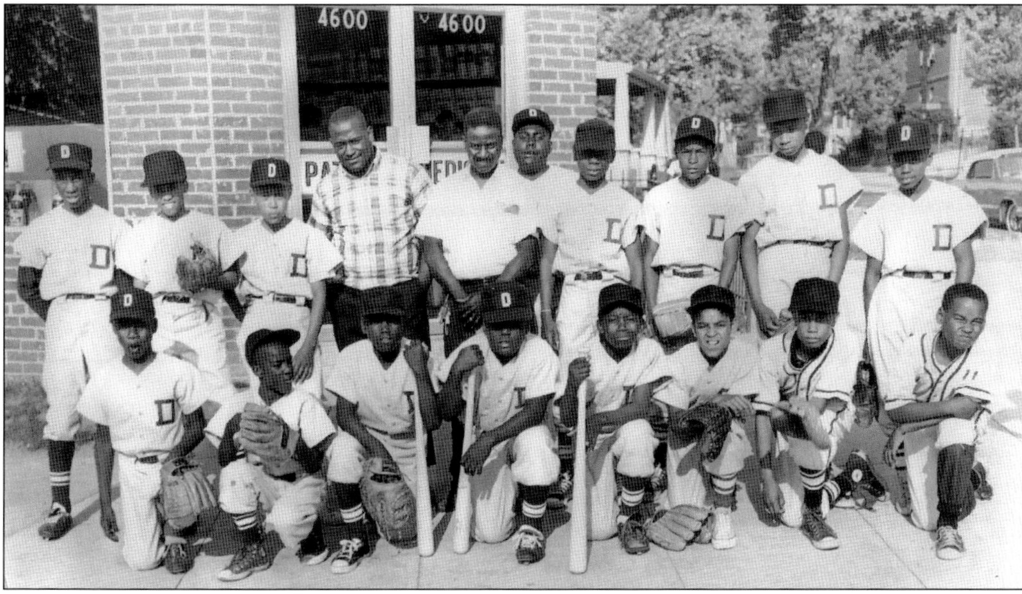

DEANWOOD BASEBALL TEAM, C. 1965. Some business owners helped youth by sponsoring neighborhood teams. Junior high school boys participated in the Roper Recreation Center's baseball team. To support their efforts, Henry Parker purchased their uniforms. Deanwood was the league champion from 1965 to 1967. Here the team poses in front of Parker's store, Suburban Market, with Parker's two adult sons, Irving (left center) and Reginald (right center) at 4600 Sheriff Road. (RP.)

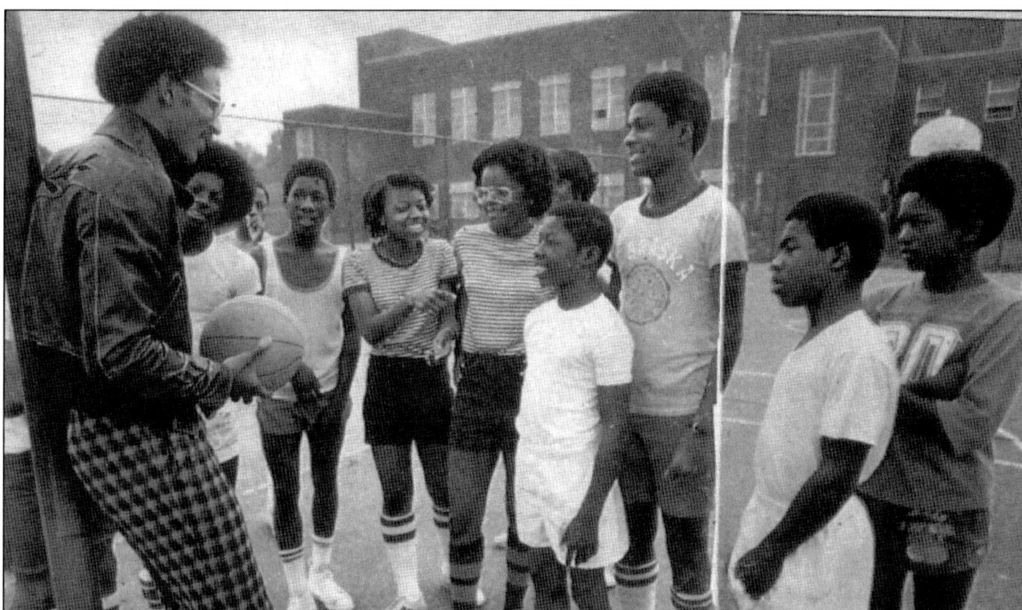

DAVE BING, C. 1969. Dave Bing was one of the athletes mentored by Sleepy Harrison. As his career grew, he stayed connected to the community. Here he visits with students at Kelly Miller Junior High School. Bing was a D.C. public high school graduate, attending Spingarn Senior High School before going on to play professional basketball with the Detroit Pistons, the Washington Bullets, and the Boston Celtics. (Sleepy Harrison.)

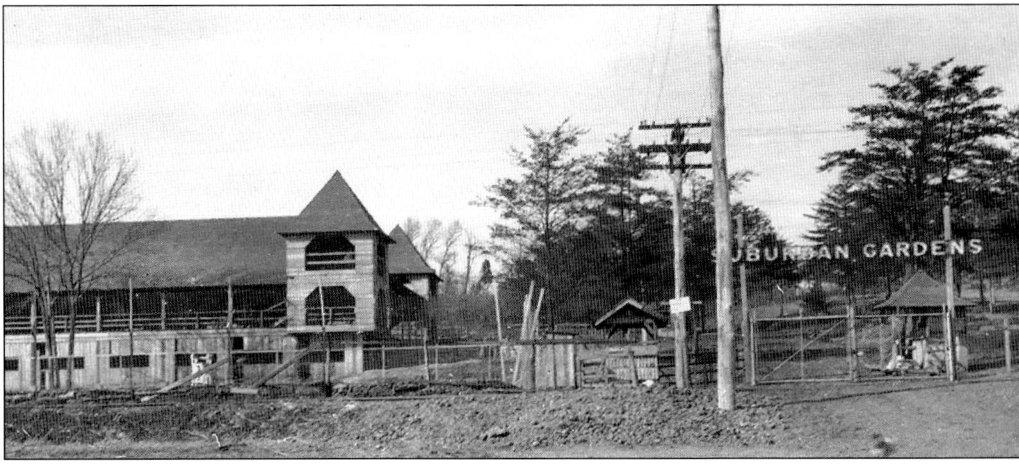

Suburban Gardens, c. 1920s. Suburban Gardens opened in 1921. It was black owned and operated and was the only permanent amusement park ever located in Washington, D.C. Patrons listened to popular performers of the day like Cab Calloway, Ella Fitzgerald, and Dinah Washington at the bandstand on Sundays and used the park's swimming pool to keep cool during the summer. (WF.)

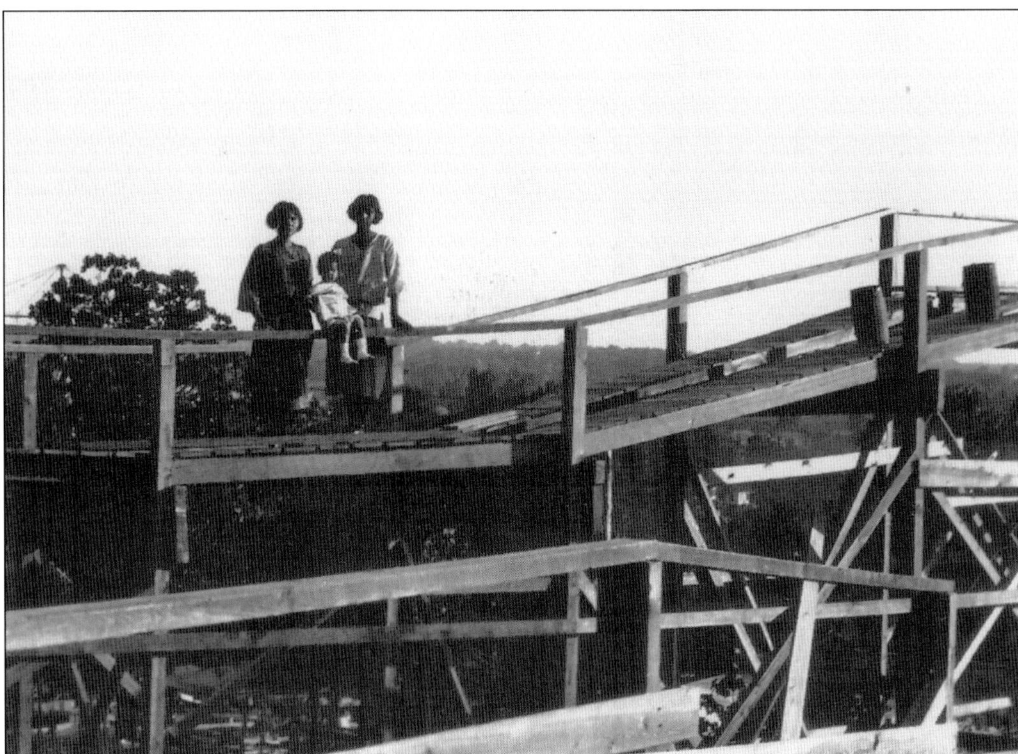

The Deep Dipper, c. 1920s. One of Suburban Garden's favorite attractions was the Deep Dipper, a roller coaster designed and built by John Miller and Harry C. Baker. Riders were treated to a 60-foot rise and three dips during their ride. Here three unidentified patrons wait for their turn on the Deep Dipper. (WF.)

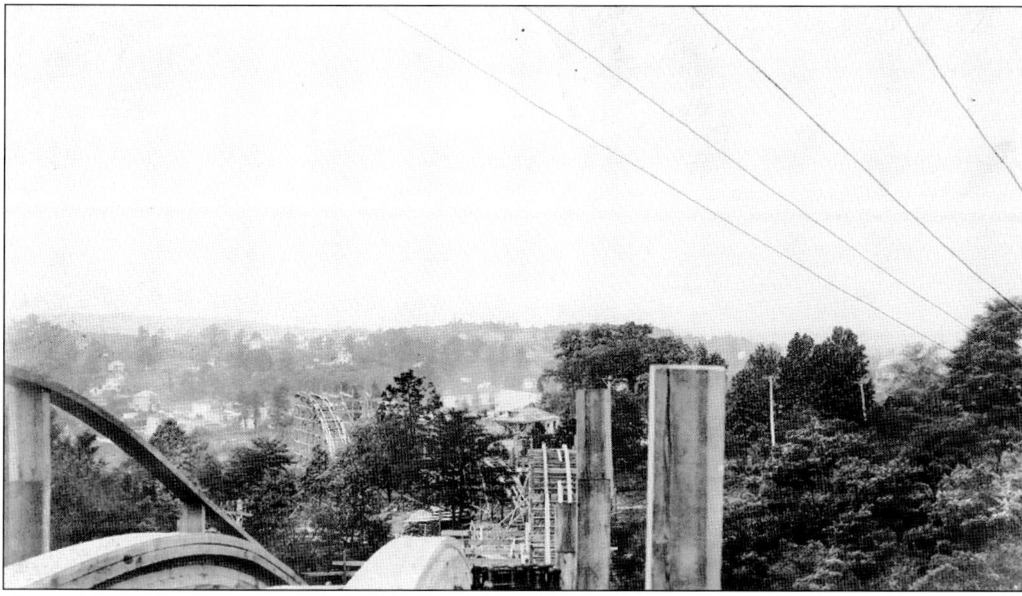

VIEW FROM THE DEEP DIPPER, C. 1920S. A bird's-eye view from the top of the Deep Dipper looks out over the "woods" of Deanwood. Longtime resident Geraldine Carroll recalls childhood memories of sneaking into Suburban Gardens with her friends by walking through the woods in order to try to get a free dip in the Suburban Gardens pool. (WF.)

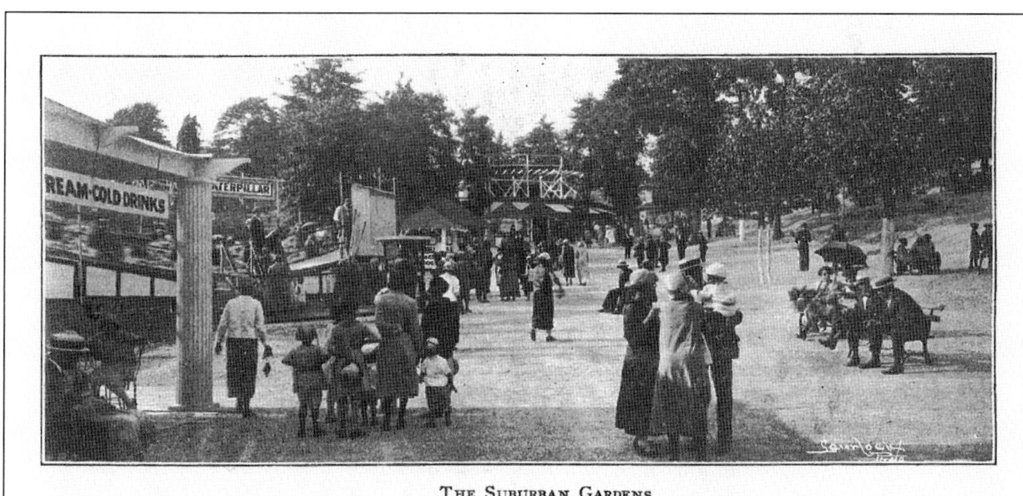

SUBURBAN GARDENS INTERIOR, 1920S. This interior view of Suburban Gardens Amusement Park shows patrons dressed in their finery as some relax, some stroll through the park, and others enjoy the rides. One of the park's popular rides, the Caterpillar, can be seen in the background to the left. Lewis Giles designed the dance pavilion, café, and ticket office. (DCPL, WD.)

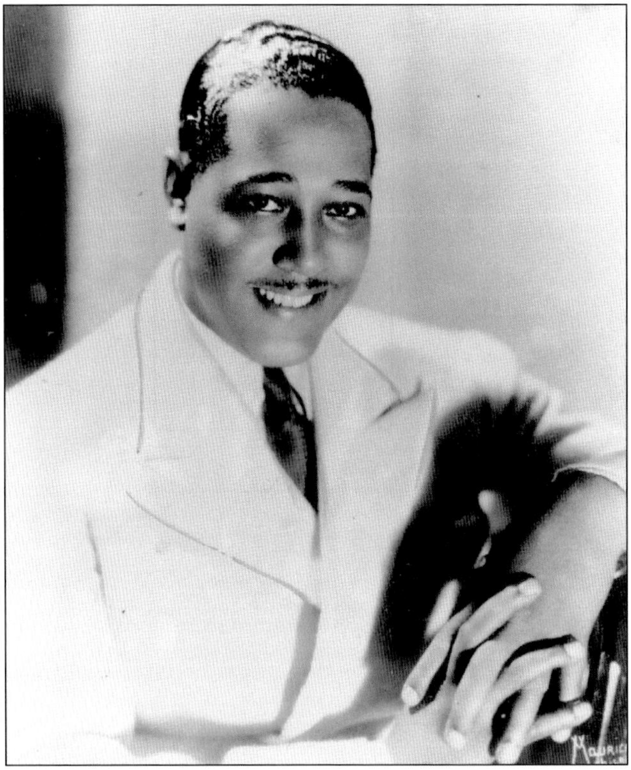

Duke Ellington, c. 1935. Duke Ellington was one of the many big-band performers who made the Suburban Gardens Amusement Park a stop on their trips to Washington, D.C. Deanwood residents would dress up in their finest attire and come out to hear the music at the bandstand. (DCPL, WD, *Washington Star* Collection.)

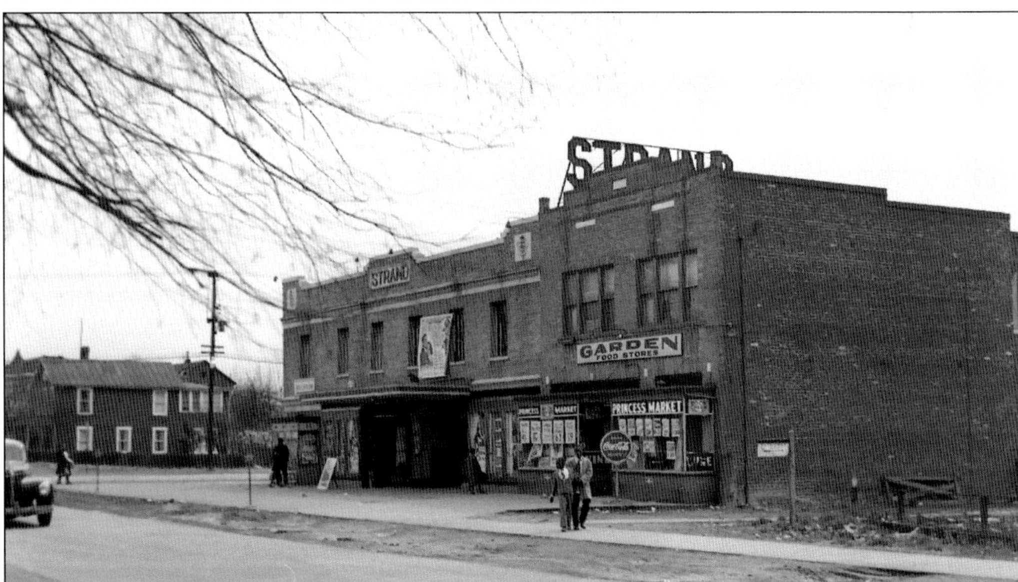

The Strand Theater, 1948. Built in 1928, the Strand played a central role in entertaining Deanwood residents. Each week, children attended the Saturday morning serials. The Strand was also home to community-based businesses such as the Princess Market. The theater building was constructed by Abe Lichtman, a Jewish businessman, to serve African American patrons and employed many Deanwood residents. (JTWC, HSWDC.)

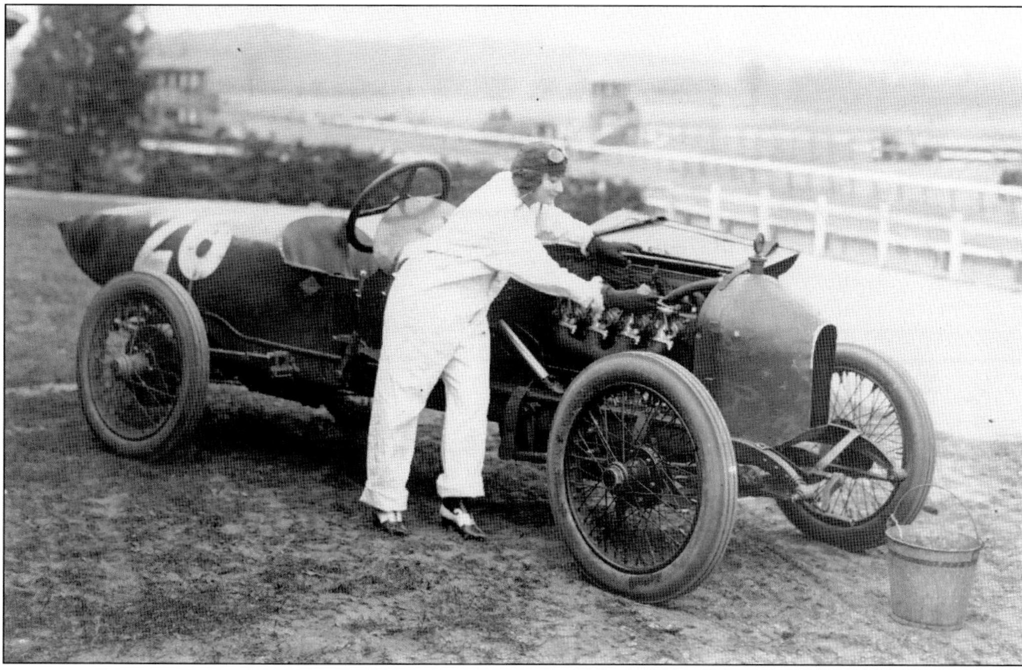

FEMALE MECHANIC, 1916. In addition to being used as a horse racetrack, the Benning Race Track was also used as an automobile racetrack. Here a female mechanic works under the hood of a Stutz Weightman Special No. 26 race car. (Library of Congress, Prints and Photographs Division, LC-USZ62-100194.)

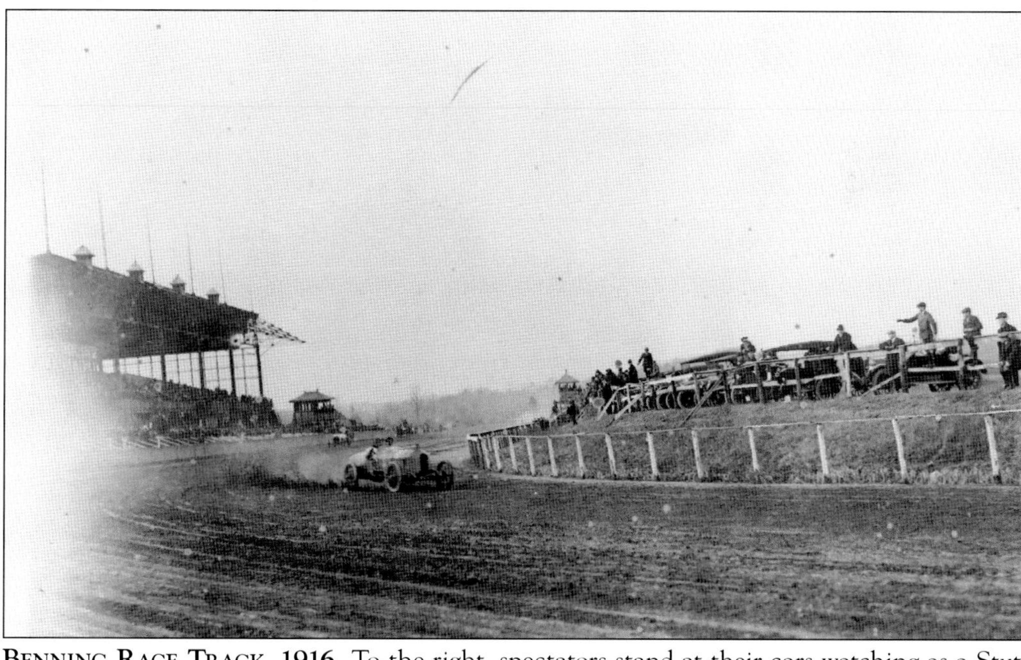

BENNING RACE TRACK, 1916. To the right, spectators stand at their cars watching as a Stutz Weightman Special goes around a turn in a race on the Benning Race Track. To the left is the track's grandstand, where patrons could sit to watch races. (Library of Congress, Prints and Photographs Division, LC-USZ62-100197.)

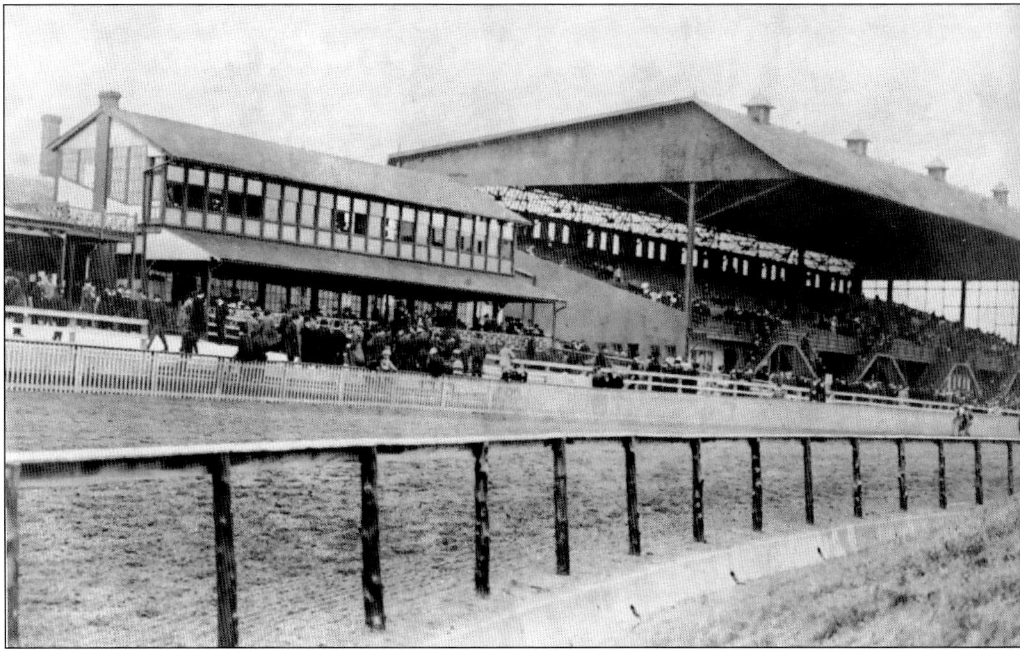

BENNING RACE TRACK, EARLY 1900S. An expanded view of the track reveals the betting hall and the grandstand where spectators sat to view the races. Here spectators make their way to the hall to place their bets, mill along the side of the track, and climb the steps to their seats as they wait for the race to begin. (DCPL, WD.)

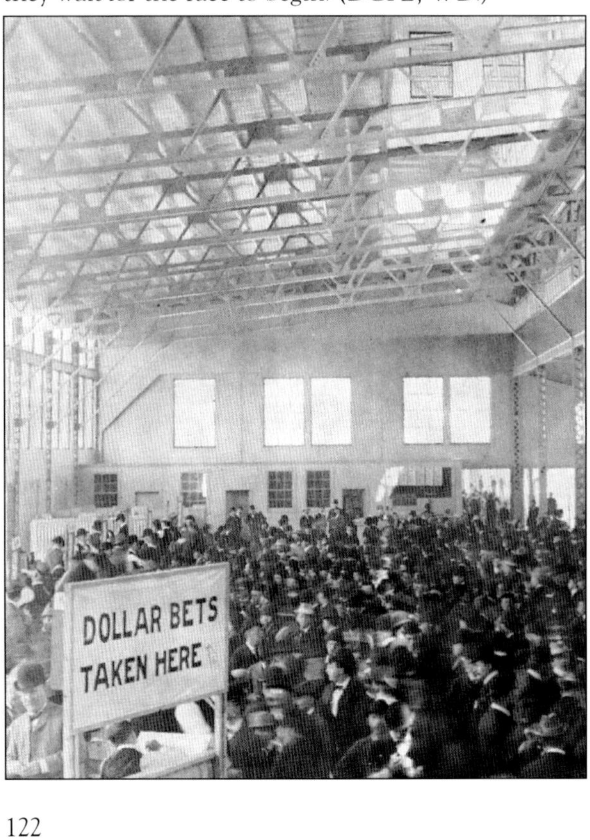

BETTING HALL, EARLY 1900S. Horse racing was not just a popular pastime among residents of far Northeast; it drew Washingtonians from all over the city. The view of the crowded betting hall shows hundreds of patrons making their way to windows to place dollar bets on their favorite horses. (Keeneland Research Library, Cook Collection.)

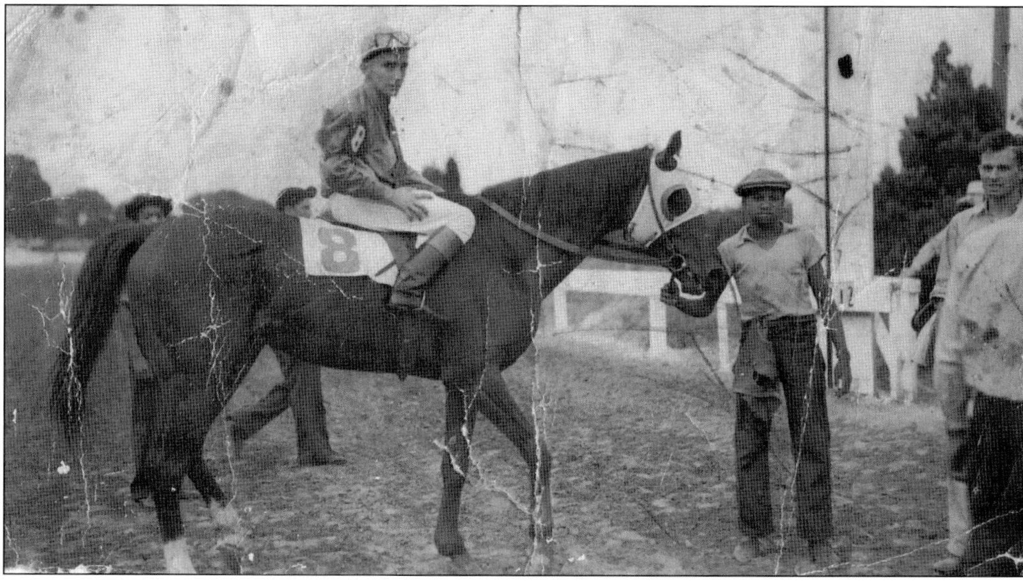

Pierpont Morgan Raymond, c. 1939. Also known as "Scamp," Deanwood resident Pierpont Raymond (center) worked as a stable hand at the Benning Race Track. Working in the equestrian field was a family tradition. His father, William Andrew Raymond, was born in Lexington, Kentucky, and moved to Washington, D.C., in 1914 to work for the owners and trainers of the Benning Race Track. (Luther Raymond.)

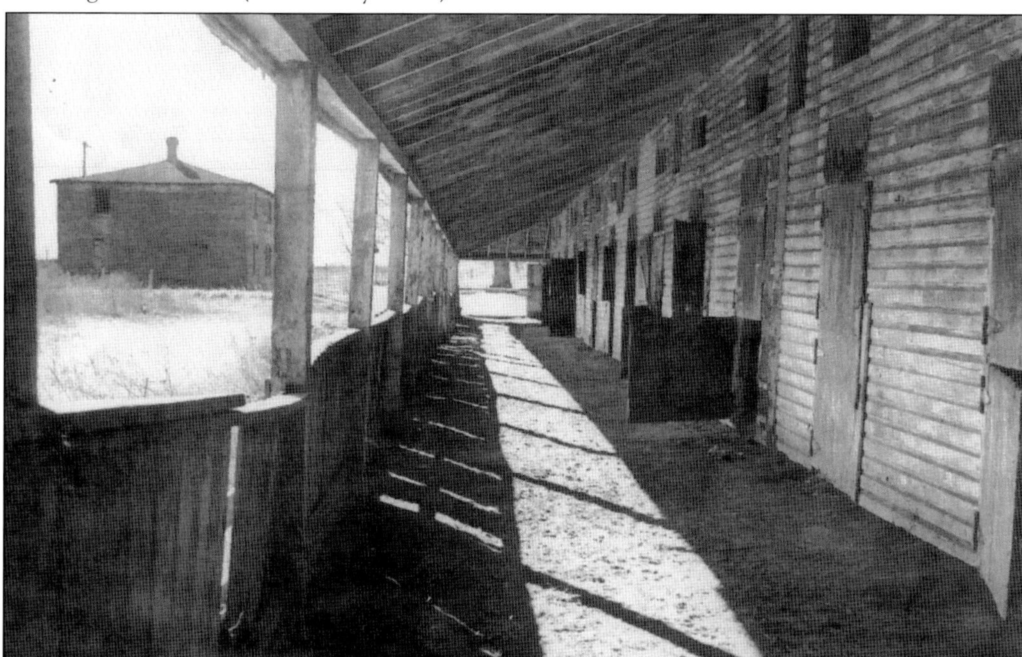

Stables, 1941. In 1908, Congress banned betting at the Benning Race Track and closed its betting hall. However, it was still used to train and exercise horses through the 1940s. When not with their trainers, horses could be found in these wooden stables. They were razed in 1942 for premier housing development Mayfair Mansions, a project of religious leader Elder Lightfoot Michaux designed by prominent architect Albert Cassell. (DCPL, WD.)

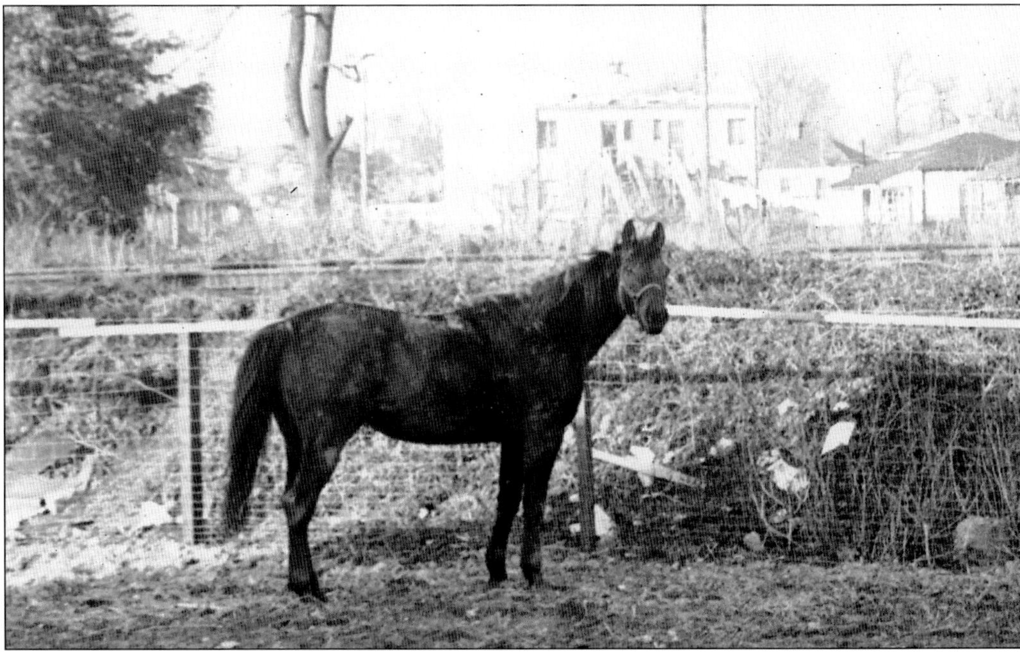

ROSALIND, C. 1949. Rosalind belonged to the Parker family and was housed beside their garage at 1945 Dix Street. While the Parkers purchased her from the Bowie Race Track, people in Deanwood were sometimes given the opportunity to buy old horses from the Benning Race Track. It was not unusual to see someone riding a horse down Deanwood's dirt roads well into the 1950s. (RP.)

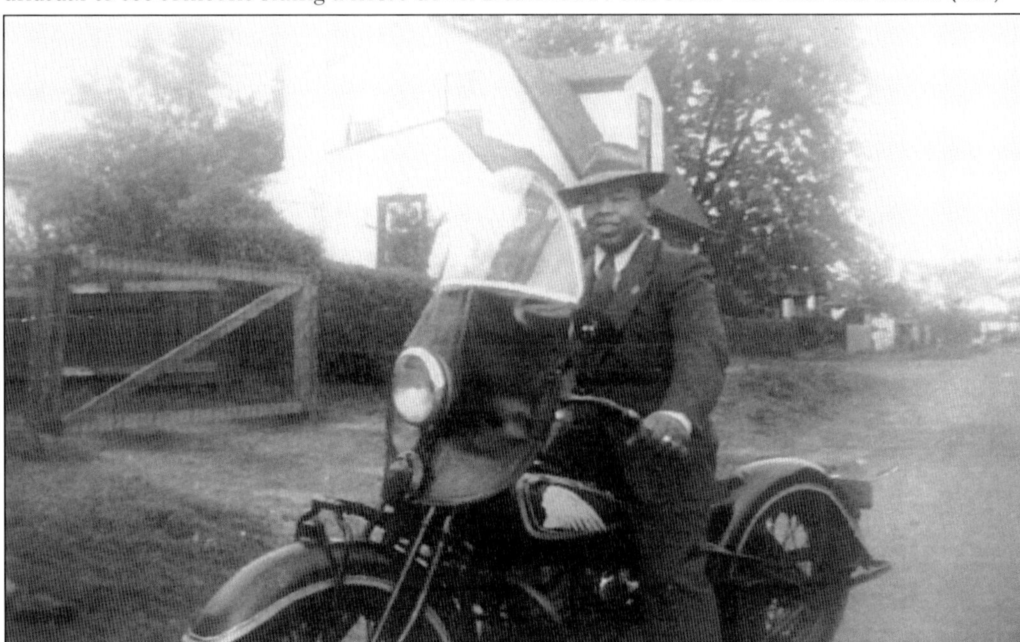

HERBERT TURNER, 1940S. In addition to horses, Deanwood residents used other means of transportation to get around the neighborhood. Herbert Turner enjoyed moving at higher speeds. Here he tries out his Indian Chief motorcycle on the Kane Place dirt road, which ran in front of his house. (AM.)

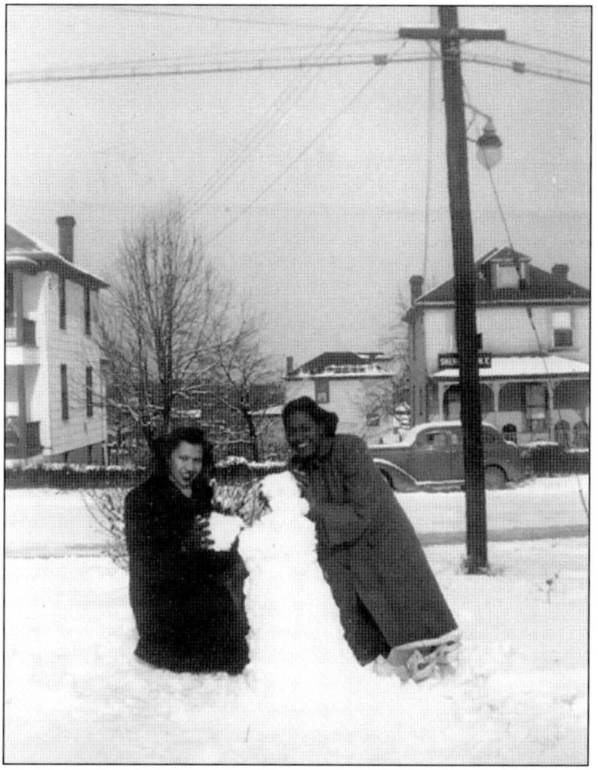

BUILDING A SNOWMAN, C. 1943. Residents of Deanwood did not have to travel far from home to have fun. Charlean Haywood (left) and Naomi Strachen take time out to enjoy a winter day as they work together to build a snowman on the front lawn of Charlean's in-laws' home at 4838 Sheriff Road. (Geraldine Carroll.)

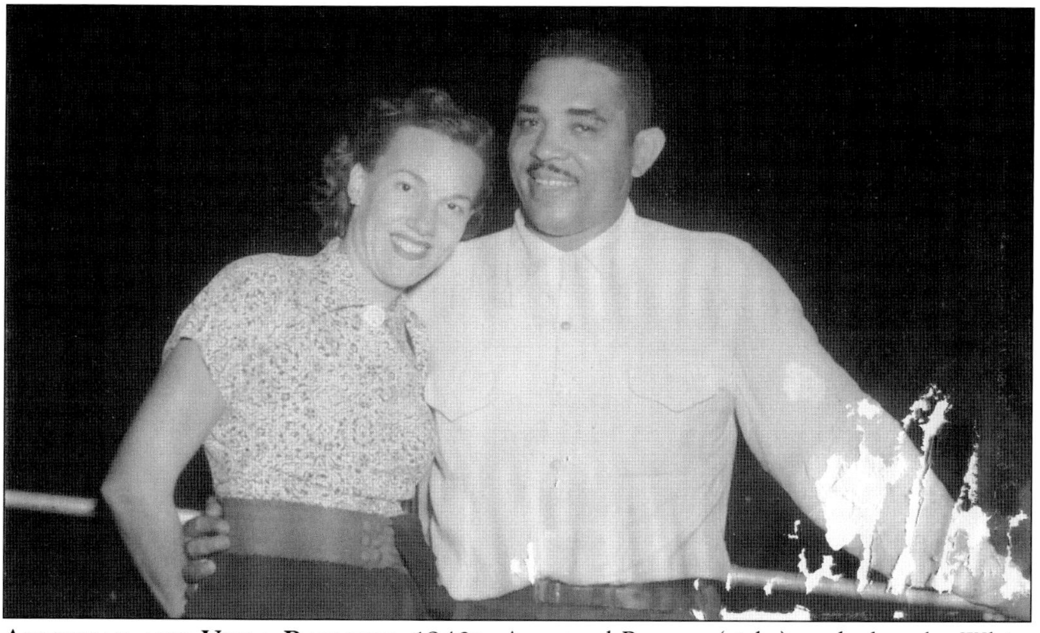

ARMSTEAD AND VIOLA BARNETT, 1940S. Armstead Barnett (right) worked at the White House through the Roosevelt, Truman, and early Eisenhower years before establishing Barnett's Caterers and Barnett's Crystal Room in the 1950s. The Crystal Room, located at 601 Division Avenue across from the Strand Theater, became a popular after-hours spot for locals as well as entertainers of the day. (Yul J. Hill.)

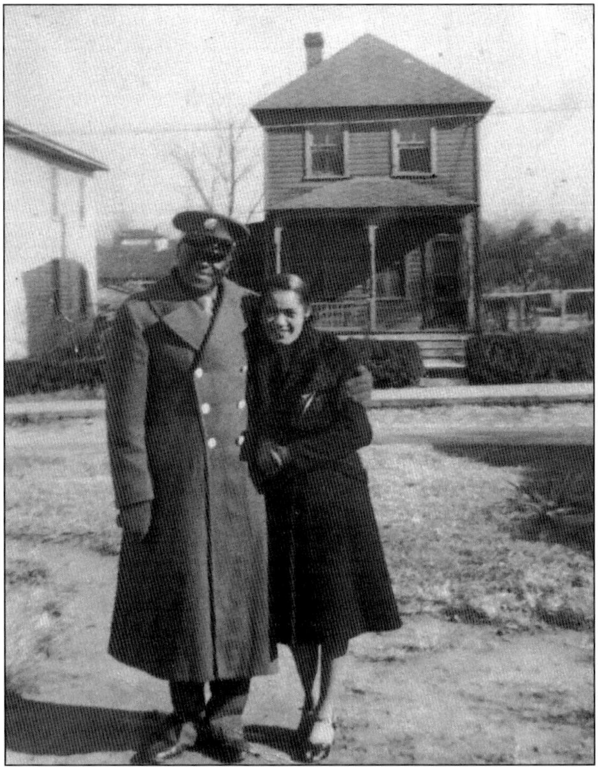

ELVA JACKSON, 1950S. Elva Jackson (right) and her friend pose in front of 1128 Forty-eighth Place before going out for a night on the town. Not only did Deanwood residents believe in having a good time, but they also believed in being stylish. Jackson sports a fox stole, a popular accessory among women of the day. (Sandra Brown.)

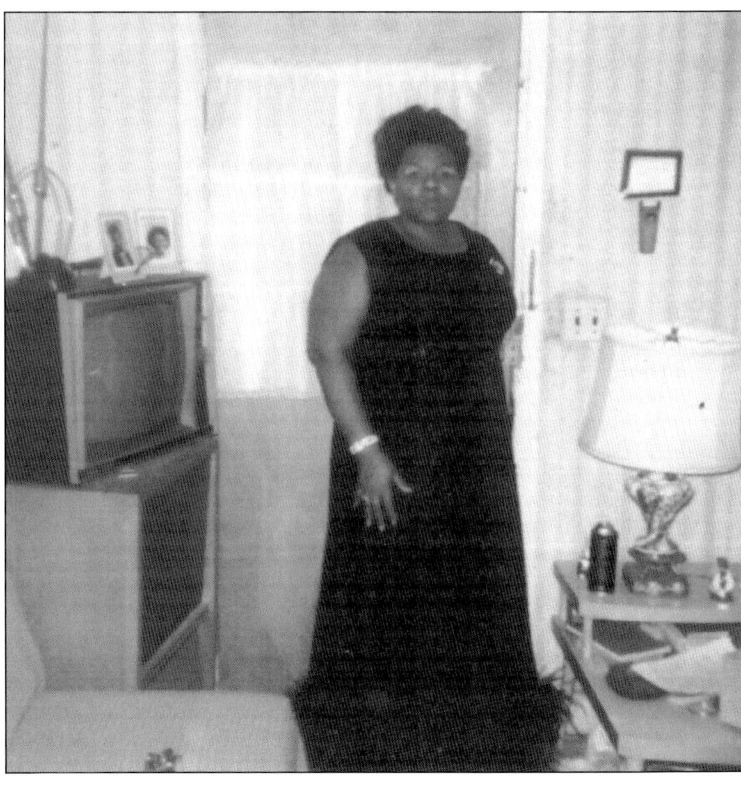

FORMAL NIGHT OUT, JUNE 1972. On her way out to a formal banquet, Barbara J. Moore also shows how Deanwood ladies traveled in style. She takes time out to be photographed in her home at 1028 Forty-sixth Street before beginning her evening with friends. (Barbara J. Moore.)

KENILWORTH DUMP, MARCH 24, 1967. Downtown stores sent their unsold merchandise to the Kenilworth Dump to be destroyed. Deanwood residents knew the schedule for such deliveries and took advantage of the opportunity to "shop" among the treasures before they were burned. Here a group of unidentified men can be seen scavenging among the heaps. (DCPL, WD, *Washington Star* Collection; photograph by Paul M. Schmick.)

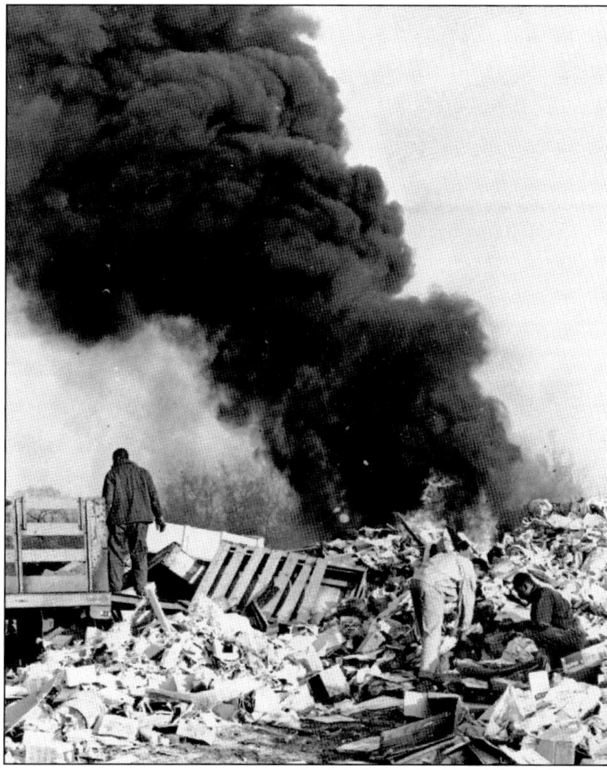

FIRES AT THE DUMP, 1967. While the dump served as a place for residents to find things that enriched their lives, such as toys, furniture, and other unused merchandise from downtown stores, it also had its negative effects. When the fires burned, a thick cloud of black smoke filled the surrounding neighborhoods. (Jack Rottier, NCPE, NPS.)

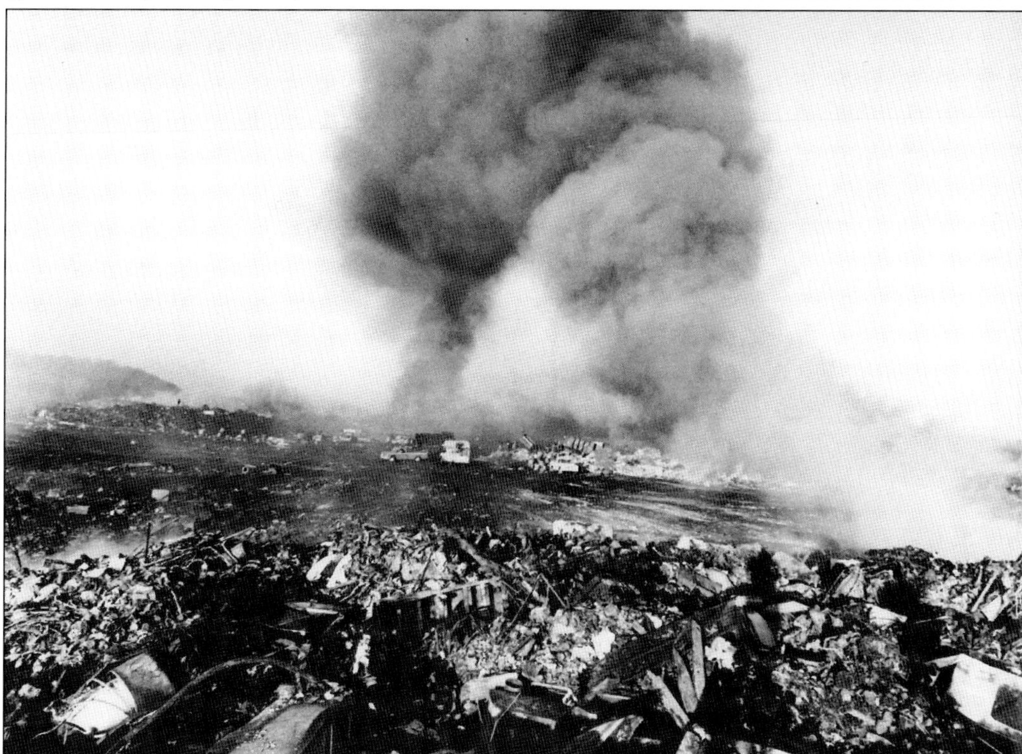

Discover Thousands of Local History Books Featuring Millions of Vintage Images

Arcadia Publishing, the leading local history publisher in the United States, is committed to making history accessible and meaningful through publishing books that celebrate and preserve the heritage of America's people and places.

Find more books like this at
www.arcadiapublishing.com

Search for your hometown history, your old stomping grounds, and even your favorite sports team.

Consistent with our mission to preserve history on a local level, this book was printed in South Carolina on American-made paper and manufactured entirely in the United States. Products carrying the accredited Forest Stewardship Council (FSC) label are printed on 100 percent FSC-certified paper.

MADE IN THE USA